Applying AutoCAD®
A Step-by-Step Approach
(Based on AutoCAD® version 2.1 with ADE 2 and 3)

by
Terry T. Wohlers
Colorado State University
Department of Industrial Sciences
Office of Research, Development and Training

GLENCOE PUBLISHING COMPANY
BENNETT & McKNIGHT DIVISION

Consultants and Reviewers

Eric Dietmeyer, Highland Junior College, Freeport, IL
Paul C. Driscoll, Lincoln Land Community College, Springfield, IL
Dave East, Richwoods High School, Peoria, IL
Jim Fox, Joliet Junior College, Joliet, IL
Jay Manahan, formerly of Wentworth Institute of Technology, Boston, MA
Dr. Michael H. Pleck, Department of General Engineering, University of
  Illinois, Urbana, IL

Thanks are given to Autodesk Inc. for permission to reproduce the artwork on
pages 101, 158, 172, 184, 252, 254, and 255.

Send all inquiries to:
Glencoe Publishing Company
15319 Chatsworth Street
Mission Hills, California 91345

Printed in the United States of America

ISBN 0-02-668070-X (Work-Text)
ISBN 0-02-668080-7 (Instructor's Guide)

3 4 5 6 7 91 90 89 88 87

With the exception of the sketches that accompany "AutoCAD at Work"
articles, all drawings were created with AutoCAD. Unless otherwise stated,
they were developed and plotted by the author using a Houston Instrument
Pen Plotter.

Acknowledgments

The author wishes to thank the staff at Bennett & McKnight in Peoria, Illinois, for their dedication to the development of the book. A special thanks to the editors, Wes Coulter and Trudy Muller, for their insight, talents, and overall contribution to the book.

Thanks to Josef Woodman and Dr. Joseph Oakey of Autodesk Inc. for their support, reviews, and comments and for their software donation of the AutoCAD version 2.1. The author thanks Donald Gimbert, also of Autodesk Inc., for supplying several AutoCAD drawings.

The author wishes to thank Mark Francischetti of Texas Instruments Inc. for his special contributions to the book, including the donation of the TI Model 850 printer for the manuscript preparation, the use of the Texas Instruments Professional Computer for testing the book exercises, and for the contribution of his time.

Thanks to John D. Fisher of Kurta Corporation for the donation of the Kurta Series I digitizer. Also thanks to Gary Nelson of Lab Technologies for his assistance in obtaining the digitizer.

The author wants to thank Kevin Higginbotham and Jim Bell of Houston Instrument for the use of the HIPLOT DMP-52 and DMP-29 pen plotters and for the supply of plotter paper and pens.

Thanks to Marmon Pine and Mehlinae Douglas of Cad Design Systems Inc. for their technical support and the use of the AcadPLUS software and the CALCOMP 2000 digitizer.

The author wishes to thank Rik Jadrnicek of ARCHSOFT Corp. for the use of the AE/CADD Master Template and the Generic Template.

Finally, the author wishes to thank CSU graduate student Bob Weiland and former CSU graduate students Daniel A. Myers and Erich von Stroheim for their review and comments on the manuscript.

Trademarks

AcadPLUS is a registered trademark of Cad Design Systems Inc.

AE/CADD is a registered trademark of ARCHSOFT Corporation.

AutoCAD, AutoCAD 2, ADE, 3D Level 1, CAD/camera, and AutoLISP are trademarks of Autodesk Inc.

AutoLINK is a registered trademark of Interactive Graphics Service Company Inc.

BASIC is a registered trademark of the Trustees of Dartmouth College.

CADAM is a registered trademark of CADAM Inc.

dBASE II and dBASE III are registered trademarks of Ashton-Tate.

HIPLOT is a registered trademark of Houston Instrument.

IBM and PC-DOS are registered trademarks of International Business Machines Corporation.

Kurta is a registered trademark of Kurta Corporation.

Lotus 1-2-3 is a trademark of Lotus Development Corp.

MS-DOS is a trademark of Microsoft Corporation.

NC Programmer is a registered trademark of NC Microproducts.

OMNI 800 is a registered trademark of Texas Instruments Inc.

Volkswriter Deluxe is a registered trademark of Lifetree Software Inc.

WordStar is a registered trademark of MicroPro International Corp.

Table of Contents

Introduction

Applying AutoCAD®: A Step-by-Step Approach is a work-text based on the AutoCAD® computer-aided drafting and design package, version 2.1 with ADE 2 and 3. It is designed primarily for new users of AutoCAD, although experienced users also will find it to be a helpful aid for reference and review. Through step-by-step instruction, the book takes students from the beginning to the advanced level. Along the way, they are encouraged to experiment, to create, and to learn firsthand the power and versatility of AutoCAD.

Applying AutoCAD is not dedicated to one specific drafting or graphic discipline. Rather, it serves all disciplines which require methods of graphic communication. Traditional areas for using the work-text are courses in architecture, civil engineering, mapping, landscaping, mechanical engineering, electrical/electronics design, facilities management, and interior design. Less common but potentially very productive areas include theater set and lighting design, museum display design, graphic arts, archaeology, and perhaps even artificial intelligence.

Format

The book is divided into thirty-five units and fourteen appendices. It covers most AutoCAD commands, features, characteristics, drawing aids, and shortcuts. It is liberally illustrated with AutoCAD-produced drawings; students are encouraged to produce many of these drawings as well as their own on their AutoCAD systems.

The contents are formatted and sequenced in a straightforward, simple-to-use manner so that instructors, regardless of their background, can easily adapt the book to their existing courses. Its structure lends itself to picking and choosing units and problems as instructors see fit. Therefore instructors should by no means feel forced to use the entire work-text to accomplish their course objectives.

For educators beginning a new course using AutoCAD, the book provides an excellent base for developing the course. Since the units are sequenced in the best order for learning AutoCAD, instructors are likely (and encouraged by the author) to use the book's outline as their course outline.

The book contains plenty of exercises to fill an entire semester course. The instructor can adjust the pace and assignments according to the level of the learner group and to the number of hours the students receive on the AutoCAD workstations.

Features

- Thirty-five clearly-defined units guide students in their progress from basic to advanced levels. Progress is easy to see and review is simple.
- In addition to the fundamentals of AutoCAD, the book presents topics of special interest, including: preparation of prototype drawings, creation of symbol libraries, creation of attributes, bill of materials generation, creation of customized screen and tablet menus, digitization of hardcopy drawings, generation of 3D drawings, and production of slide shows.
- Notations in margins correlate every topic to the *AutoCAD User Guide* to easily expand students' instruction through individual reading.
- Hint sections throughout the units help students effectively tap the full power of AutoCAD.
- Questions and problems at the end of each unit ensure mastery of AutoCAD.
- Optional problems section challenges and motivates advanced students.
- Useful appendices on topics such as disk formatting, preparing data/storage diskettes, producing backup copies, and reconfiguring AutoCAD help students manipulate and manage AutoCAD-related files.
- "AutoCAD at Work" articles help students understand how AutoCAD is used in business and industry.
- As a bonus, a full-function tablet menu and overlay have been included in the book (Unit 33). In addition, step-by-step instructions teach students how to create their own.

To the Student

By following the step-by-step exercises in this book, you will learn to use AutoCAD to create, modify, store, retrieve, and manage AutoCAD drawings and related files. For review and practice, questions and problems have been provided at the end of each unit. In addition, there is a section of more challenging problems following Unit 35.

When working through the exercises and problems, don't become discouraged if you need to attempt the exercise or problem more than once—that's normal. The steps in using AutoCAD are presented as simply as possible in this book. However, the sequence of "what to enter" is not always obvious. It takes practice to master the AutoCAD commands.

In order to derive the full benefit of this book, you should be aware of the following:

- *Notational conventions.* Computer keyboards differ. In this book, you will find many references to the RETURN key. On your keyboard, however, this key may be marked ENTER, NEXT, NEW LINE, etc. Likewise, you will find references to the CTRL (control) key. On some keyboards this key is marked ALT.

    In the step-by-step instructions, user input is in boldface type. For example, the instruction "enter the **LINE** command" means that you should either type the word LINE on the keyboard or select it from a screen menu or tablet menu. Note: Although command names are shown in uppercase letters, you can type them in either upper- or lowercase letters.

    On the computer screen, AutoCAD default values are displayed within < > . You can select the default value by simply pressing the RETURN key or the space bar.

- *ACAD.DWG prototype drawing.* As you work with AutoCAD, you will learn of the AutoCAD defaults and how these modes and settings are stored in AutoCAD's default prototype drawing called ACAD.DWG. If/when you want to learn more about these default modes and settings, turn to Appendix B, which contains details on the ACAD.DWG prototype drawing.

- *End-of-unit questions.* The questions at the end of each unit are intended to help you review the material in the unit *and* to expand your knowledge. Therefore, in order to answer some of the questions, you will need to work on the computer or refer to the *AutoCAD User Guide.*

About the Author

Terry Wohlers is currently employed by Colorado State University in the Department of Industrial Sciences' Office of Research, Development and Training. Mr. Wohlers received a Master of Science degree in Industrial Sciences at Colorado State University and a Bachelor of Arts degree in Industrial Technology Education at Kearney State College.

At Colorado State University, Mr. Wohlers developed and taught the first series of semester courses and industry workshops on microcomputer-based computer-aided design and drafting (CAD), and he continues to conduct them. His other university responsibilities involve a variety of research and development activities, such as analysis of CAD software and hardware configurations, and curriculum development.

Mr. Wohlers has published over fifteen articles and technical papers on CAD, most recently in the Computer Graphics Tokyo 86 conference proceedings and the proceedings from the Electronic Production Efficiency Exposition 86 held in London, England. In addition, he has given numerous presentations at regional, national, and international meetings and conferences.

In July 1984, Mr. Wohlers served as the conference director for the First Annual International Forum on Micro-based CAD, and he was Program Director for the Third Annual International Forum on Micro-based CAD.

Unit 1 — En Route We Pass the Main Menu

■ OBJECTIVE:

To understand the purpose of the AutoCAD Main Menu and the components found in the Drawing Editor and to learn the function of the SAVE, END, ENDSV, and QUIT commands

AutoCAD's Main Menu is the starting point through which you will always pass prior to drawing with AutoCAD. Therefore it is important for you to understand it.

1.4.1, 2.4

The AutoCAD Drawing Editor is where you spend 95 percent of your time when using AutoCAD. The Drawing Editor allows you to create, change, view, and plot drawings. It is therefore important that you understand the purpose of each component found in the Drawing Editor.

1.4, 2.5

■ *Taking a Look Around*

1. Load AutoCAD into your computer, and you will find yourself in the Main Menu.

————— NOTE: —————

If you don't know how to load AutoCAD, see Appendix F at the back of this book.

```
Main Menu

    0.  Exit AutoCAD
    1.  Begin a NEW drawing
    2.  Edit an EXISTING drawing
    3.  Plot a drawing
    4.  Printer Plot a drawing

    5.  Configure AutoCAD
    6.  File Utilities
    7.  Compile shape/font description file
    8.  Convert old drawing file

Enter selection:
```

---

2. Select option 1, "Begin a NEW drawing," and press **RETURN**. The computer will ask you to name the drawing. Type **STUFF** and press **RETURN**.

2.4.2

————— CAUTION: —————

When using a floppy diskette-based system, NEVER REMOVE A DISKETTE FROM THE DRIVE WHILE YOU ARE IN THE DRAWING EDITOR. If you do, you will damage your drawing file.

---

*The numbers in this column correspond to sections in the *AutoCAD™ User Guide.* Refer to these sections if you would like additional information about the topics covered in *Applying AutoCAD.* For example, if you would like to learn more about the Main Menu, turn to Sections 1.4.1 and 2.4 of the *User Guide.*

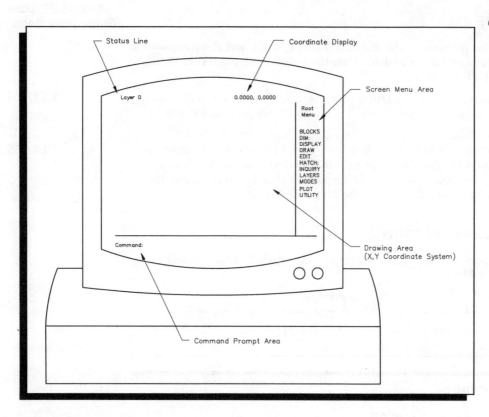

You should now be in the AutoCAD Drawing Editor.

At the right of the screen, you'll find the Root Menu. Note each of the components (words) found in the Root Menu.

Notice the prompt line at the bottom of the screen. Keep your eye on this area. This is where you will receive messages from AutoCAD.

At the top of the screen is the status line. The status line tells you the name of the current layer, the status of various AutoCAD modes, and the coordinates of the screen crosshairs (coordinate display).

The rest of the screen is the drawing area.

Let's see how the screen changes when we enter information.

③ Using your pointing device (mouse or digitizer), select **DRAW** from the Root Menu and watch what happens.

2.7.1

④ Next, select one of the Draw commands, such as **LINE**. Notice that the prompt line has changed:

Command: LINE From point:

AutoCAD is asking you to tell it where you want the line to start. In Unit 2, you'll actually draw some lines. For now, proceed to Step 5.

2

5 Select the **LASTMENU** option. Where does this take you?

6 Next, select the **ROOTMENU** option.

7 Now select another item from the Root Menu and step through the submenus as you did above.

NOTE:

In Appendix N you'll find the entire screen menu structure, including all of the AutoCAD submenus and their commands.

8 Look over Appendix N and then further experiment with moving around in the Root Menu and submenus.

Have fun!

9 Enter the AutoCAD command **END** when you are finished. (Either type it and press RETURN or select END from the Utility Submenu.) The END command will store your drawing contents on the disk and will take you back to the Main Menu. (In this case, all you are storing is the name STUFF.)

3.2.1

10 After the Main Menu appears, you can exit AutoCAD by choosing option **0**.

2.4.1

SAVE, END, ENDSV, and QUIT Commands

There are various ways of storing your drawing to disk and/or exiting the Drawing Editor. They are described below. When drawing with AutoCAD, these commands should be used as appropriate.

SAVE — will save your work but will *not* exit you out of the Drawing Editor.

3.3

END — will save your work and *will* exit you out of the Drawing Editor.

3.2.1

ENDSV — will save your work, exit you out of the Drawing Editor, and will create a vector refresh file. (The vector refresh file will save you drawing regeneration time when bringing up the drawing for editing, but it takes up additional disk space. You'll have opportunities to apply the ENDSV command in later units.)

3.2.3

QUIT — will exit you out of the Drawing Editor but will *not* save your work.

3.2.2

What If I Enter the Wrong Command?

2.9

As you work with AutoCAD, you will be entering commands either by selecting them from the screen menu or typing them at the keyboard. Occasionally you might accidentally select the wrong command or make a typing error. It's easy to correct such mistakes.

(continued)

3

If you catch a typing error *before* you press RETURN . . .	use the back-space key to delete the incorrect character(s). Then continue typing.
If you catch the typing error *after* pressing RETURN or if you select the wrong command from the screen menu . . .	you can usually get back to the "Command:" prompt if you press the space bar once or twice; *OR* select CANCEL from the screen menu; *OR* type CTRL C (press the control and C keys at the same time).

AUTOCAD™ AT WORK

Picture This

A metropolitan police department in the East is using AutoCAD to create composite drawings which are used to identify crime suspects. Using AutoCAD, a police artist draws different noses, ears, faces, and hairstyles and then stores these shapes in a customized "library." With the help of eyewitness descriptions, the police artist begins to "sketch" the suspect on the computer screen by calling up facial features from the library and modifying them as needed. Basically, this is the same process that police artists already use, but AutoCAD sketching is faster and easier to revise. Because the sketches have been stored on disk, they can be sent from one department to another quickly over a telephone hook-up. Because speed is often essential in catching criminals, computer sketching gives police another advantage in their fight against crime.

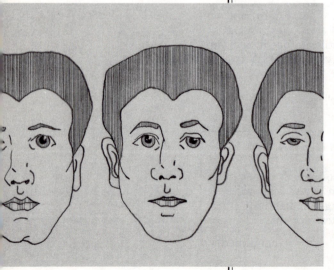

A midwestern police department is using AutoCAD's sketching feature for making scale drawings of crime scenes. Most crime scene investigators go to the scene of the crime, measure and photograph everything, and then produce detailed, hand-drawn sketches. Using AutoCAD, police artists can sketch the scenes faster and more accurately, and those scenes can be stored on disk and printed out as they are needed. But AutoCAD's layering feature is the biggest advantage in crime scene sketches. A police artist can put one category of evidence, such as furniture, on one layer and another kind, such as fingerprints, on a different layer. Investigators can look at the whole crime scene or focus on particular categories of evidence, such as the floor plan of the scene. With AutoCAD's zoom feature, an investigator can note the fingerprints at a crime scene and then zoom in to see those fingerprints larger than lifesize. Not only will this help investigators solve crimes, but printouts of the sketches could also be used as valuable courtroom evidence.

Questions

1. Describe the purpose of the first two Main Menu options:

    0. Exit AutoCAD _____

    _____

    1. Begin a NEW drawing _____

    _____

2. Explain the overall purpose of the Main Menu.

    _____

    _____

3. Briefly describe the function of the following menu options:

    LASTMENU _____

    DRAW _____

    ROOTMENU _____

    LINE _____

4. Briefly explain the basic function of the AutoCAD prompt line "Command:".

    _____

    _____

5. Explain the purpose of the following AutoCAD commands:

    SAVE _____

    END_____

    ENDSV_____

    QUIT _____

Problems

Select the following submenus from the Root Menu. Then select the commands indicated and list the options available under each command. The first problem has been completed as an example.

ROOT MENU ITEM	COMMAND	AVAILABLE OPTIONS
DRAW ⟶	LINE ⟶	continue
		close
		undo
DRAW ⟶	CIRCLE ⟶	_____
		_____
		_____
		_____
EDIT ⟶	CHAMFER ⟶	_____
		_____
		_____
EDIT ⟶	ERASE ⟶	_____
		_____
		_____
		_____
		_____
EDIT ⟶	MOVE ⟶	_____
		_____
		_____
		_____
		_____

Unit 2 — The Line Forms Here

■ **OBJECTIVE:**

AutoCAD™ User Guide Reference

To apply the LINE command and the Undo option

The LINE command is the most often used AutoCAD command simply because almost every drawing contains lines. There are a number of ways to produce these lines. Some ways are simple; others can be a bit confusing. This exercise uses the simplest approach to producing lines and is appropriate if this is your first time with the system.

4.1

Have fun and good luck!

Drawing Lines with a Pointing Device

1 Load AutoCAD and select from the Main Menu option **2**, "Edit an EXISTING drawing."

2 Enter the drawing called **STUFF**.

3 After you find yourself in the Drawing Editor, select the **LINE** command from the screen menu.

4 With your pointing device, draw one of the polygons shown here.

2.8.1.4

HINT:
To automatically close a polygon, type the letter **C** and press **RETURN**, prior to constructing the last line of the polygon.

4.1.2

After you've completed a polygon, you will want to bring up the LINE command again to construct the next polygon. Simply press the **space bar** on the keyboard. This will activate the previously used command — a real shortcut and timesaver. Now draw the remaining polygons.

2.7.5

NOTE:

From time to time, it's necessary to back up or undo what you have done while using the LINE command. Let's say, for example, you have drawn three lines in creating a polygon, and you're about to enter your fourth point when you realize the third line you drew was incorrect. The easiest and fastest way of correcting this is to simply select the **Undo** option from the screen menu or type **U** (short for Undo) and press **RETURN**.

5 After drawing the polygons, enter **END** to save your masterpiece and exit back to the Main Menu.

AUTOCAD™ AT WORK

Dentists Plan Surgery with AutoCAD

Computer-aided design is now being applied to oral surgery and orthodontics, thanks to a customized AutoCAD program developed by a dentist in West Virginia. The program enables dentists to create multicolored representations of their patients' facial structures.

Dentists can do a better job of planning their procedures, and their patients can find out ahead of time how the treatment will affect their looks.

Dentists use AutoCAD mainly for three kinds of procedures: cosmetic surgery, which can alter a patient's looks dramatically; oral surgery, which involves the removal of troublesome teeth (such as wisdom teeth); and orthodontics, which involves straightening teeth with fitted braces.

Here's one example of how AutoCAD can help surgical planning. In oral and jaw surgery the dentist cuts into the soft tissue of the lips and chin in order to remove teeth and sections of jawbone. Because there is little room for misjudging when bone structure is involved, the dentist must make sure the restructured bone will form a pleasing jawline.

The dentist therefore photographs the patient before surgery with a video camera, stores the photograph in the computer's memory, and then manipulates the photograph to produce "before, during, and after" illustrations of the surgery. As a result, the dentist has a better idea of what must be done during surgery, and the patient has a better understanding of the surgical procedure and the results.

The Future. In the future dentists will use AutoCAD to chart and store information about a patient's dental history. They will be able to store a library of tooth shapes and filling locations in AutoCAD, allowing them to eliminate bulky, handwritten paper charts. Also, electronically stored dental charts could be transmitted over telephone lines in case of emergencies or for identification needs.

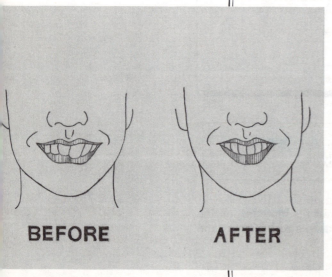

BEFORE   **AFTER**

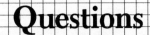 **Questions**

1. Describe the purpose of Main Menu option 2.

   _____

   _____

2. Explain the relationship between your pointing device and the screen crosshairs.

   _____

   _____

3. What is the fastest and simplest method of re-entering the previously entered command?

   _____

4. What is the fastest method of closing a polygon?

   _____

5. Explain the use of the Undo option.

   _____

Problems

Using the LINE command and your pointing device, draw each of the following objects. Don't worry about exact sizes, but do try to make them look as much like the ones below as possible.

How to Save Your Problems _____

Most units of this workbook conclude with some problems for you to do using AutoCAD. You'll probably want to save your problems, so start a new file for each one. Code the file by unit and problem number. For example, for the problems in this unit:

1. Select option **1** from the Main Menu.
2. For the first problem, call the file **PRB2-1**. (Abbreviation is necessary because AutoCAD can't accept any names longer than eight characters.)
3. When you are finished with that problem, enter **END** to save it and return to the Main Menu.

Now you are ready to start PRB2-2. Repeat Steps 1 through 3 for each problem you do.

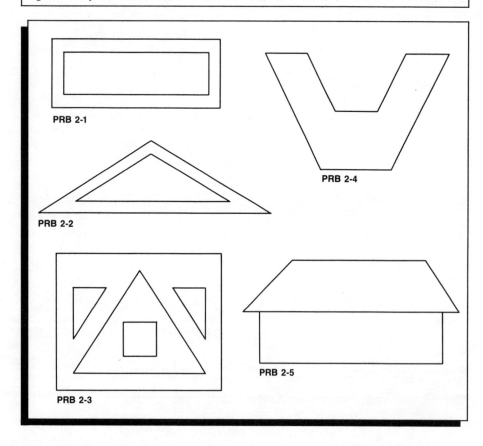

PRB 2-1

PRB 2-4

PRB 2-2

PRB 2-3

PRB 2-5

 **Unit 3** And Around We Go

■ OBJECTIVE:

To apply the CIRCLE, ARC, and DRAGMODE commands and the Ellipse feature

The purpose of this exercise is to experiment with the AutoCAD commands that allow you to produce arcs and circular lines and objects.

The following race car drawing is typical of the extent to which drawings utilize round and curved lines. Note the many curved surfaces in the drawing. Later, you may wish to try drawing this car.

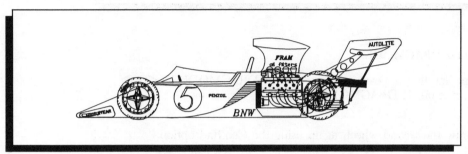

AutoCAD Drawing Courtesy of BNW, Inc.

CIRCLE Command _____ 4.3

AutoCAD makes it easy to draw round and curved lines. For example, to draw simple wheels, follow these steps.

1 Load AutoCAD and proceed into the Drawing Editor by beginning a new drawing. Name it **CAR**.

2 Select the **CIRCLE** command from the Draw Submenu.

3 Select the **CEN,RAD** option. 4.3.1

4 Draw the larger (outer) circle of the wheel first. Use your pointing device to pick the center point and then the radius. AutoCAD will complete the circle. Don't worry about exact location or size at this time.

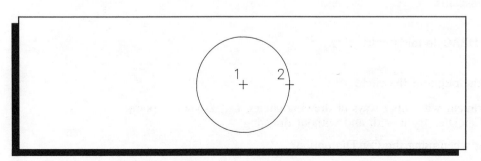

5 Next, draw the smaller circle, again by selecting **CEN,RAD** from the screen menu and picking the center point and the radius.

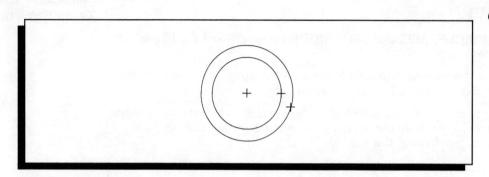

6 Now enter **DRAGMODE**.

6.9

Note the prompt line that appears on the screen. If DRAGMODE is <On>, type **OFF** to turn it off. If DRAGMODE is <Off>, turn it on.

7 Now draw the second wheel, again using the Cen,Rad option.

What is the difference between drawing the circles with DRAGMODE on and drawing them with DRAGMODE off?

NOTE:

When DRAGMODE is on, dragging can be initiated in one of two ways. (1) You can enter the word DRAG at the appropriate times. (2) If the Drag request is imbedded in the menu item — as was the case with the Cen,Rad option you selected from the screen menu — you do not need to type DRAG.

4.3.5

To learn more about how Drag works, try the following.

8 With DRAGMODE on, draw a circle as before.

Now, let's draw another circle, but this time . . .

9 . . . instead of selecting the Cen,Rad option from the screen menu, press the **space bar**.

10 Pick a center point for the circle. Note what happens when you move the crosshairs.

11 Type **DRAG** to initiate dragging.

12 Pick the radius of the circle.

13 Experiment with other ways of drawing circles, *i.e.*, 2-point, 3-point, and Cen,Dia. Try it with and without dragging.

Can you Drag when using the Cen,Dia option?

ARC Command _____ 4.4

Now let's focus on the ARC command. (If you need to clear the screen, see Unit 4 for instructions on how to ERASE.)

1 Select the **ARC** command from the Draw Submenu.

2 Select the **3-Point Arc** option and produce several different arcs.   4.4.1

Let's experiment with other methods of creating arcs.

1 Select the **S,C,E** (start point, center, endpoint) option from the menu.   4.4.2

2 Simply specify three consecutive points: start, center, and end.

Did it work?

3 Select the **S,C,A** (start point, center, included angle) option.   4.4.3

4 Specify a start point and center point.

5 Then enter a number (positive or negative) up to 360. The number specifies the angle in degrees.

What happened?

6 Try the **S,E,R** (start point, endpoint, radius) option.   4.4.5

7 Simply enter three consecutive points. Remember, you can enter a numerical value for the radius.

8 Experiment with the remaining ARC options. What do the following options specify?

S,C,E = _____ Start, Center, End _____

S,C,A = _____

S,C,L = _____

S,E,A = _____

S,E,R = _____

S,E,D = _____

C,S,E = _____

C,S,A = _____

C,S,L = _____

Next, let's produce the following curved line, which is really a series of arcs.

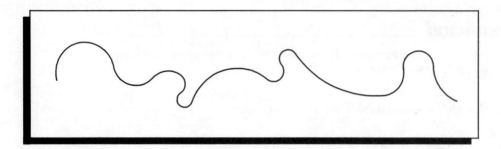

1 Make sure DRAGMODE is on.

2 Enter the **ARC** command and draw the curved line by making a series of arcs.

HINT:
Use the Continue option (CONTIN) found in the Arc Submenu in conjunction with the ARC command.

Ellipse Feature

Now let's work a bit with the Ellipse feature.

1 Make sure DRAGMODE is on.

2 Select **ELLIPSE** from the Circle Submenu and specify a first point.

3 Specify the second point above and to the right of the first point.

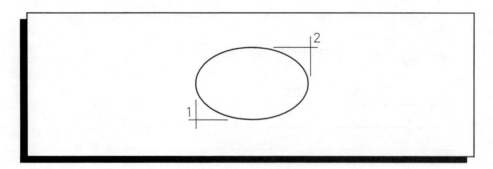

4 If you'd like to rotate the ellipse, enter either a positive or negative number, or Drag it into place (provided DRAGMODE is on), before pressing RETURN.

Did it work?

5 Experiment with Ellipse by constructing additional ellipses of various shapes and sizes.

6 Store your curved objects and exit the Drawing Editor by entering the **END** command.

AUTOCAD™ AT WORK

Customizing Buses with AutoCAD

Executive Coach Corporation of Fox River Grove, Illinois, specializes in the design and conversion of buses into luxury motor homes and business facilities. And some of the results have been astonishing.

Clients range from Saudi Arabian royalty to country music stars. A typical conversion takes several months to complete and can cost up to $400,000. In addition to standard conversions such as dining areas, kitchens, and bathrooms, the corporation's craftsmen have installed such exotic features as solid gold fixtures, saunas, steambaths, and even a revolving clothes rack under a bed.

By using AutoCAD, the designers can involve the clients in the design process. Instead of huddling over a bunch of hand-drawn sketches, the clients can watch the evolution of their design on a large computer screen. If they want to move the kitchen a few feet or double the size of the bathroom, a designer using AutoCAD can make the changes with a few keystrokes while the clients watch.

The layering feature of AutoCAD is helpful during both the design stage and the construction stage. With layering, the designer can position all the appliances on one layer, the furniture on a second, and the wiring, plumbing, and heating features on still other layers.

Once the final design is agreed upon, the designer prints out a multicolored copy for the company craftsmen to use as construction "blueprints." Since the company began using AutoCAD, customers and employees are a lot more satisfied. The accurate drawings make the customizing work easier and faster, the company can make more conversions in less time and for less money, and the savings are passed on to the customer.

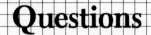 Questions

1. When drawing circles, arcs, and ellipses, what happens when the DRAGMODE command is on?

   _____

   _____

2. What happens when the DRAGMODE command is off?

   _____

   _____

3. Briefly describe the following methods of producing circles.

   2-point _____

   3-point _____

   Cen,Dia _____

4. In what AutoCAD submenu are the ARC and CIRCLE commands found?

   _____

5. In what submenu is Ellipse found?

   _____

6. What function does the Arc Contin option serve?

   _____

   _____

7. When specifying an angle in degrees, what direction does a negative number specify: clockwise or counterclockwise?

   _____

Problems

Using the commands you've just learned, complete the following drawings. Don't worry about text matter or exact shapes, sizes, or locations, but do try to make your drawings look similar to the ones below.

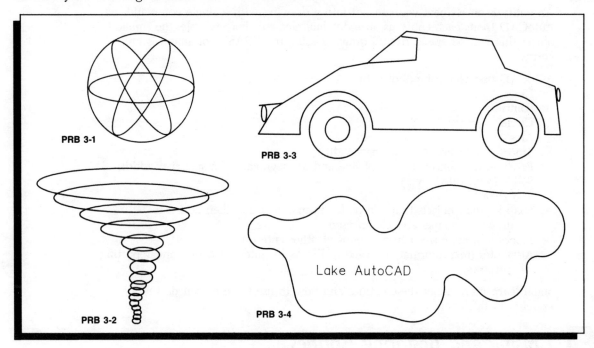

PRB 3-1

PRB 3-2

PRB 3-3

Lake AutoCAD

PRB 3-4

Unit 4 Now You See It . . .

■ **OBJECTIVE:**

AutoCAD™ User
Guide Reference

To apply the ERASE, REDRAW, and OOPS commands

As you use AutoCAD, you will often need to delete all or part of a drawing. This unit will show you how to do these operations.

First, a Word about Entities

1.4.2

An entity is an element you can put into a drawing with a single command. AutoCAD treats each entity as an individual element. For example, the smallest object that can be erased from a drawing using the ERASE command is an entity.

AutoCAD uses eleven types of entities:
  Lines
  Points
  Circles
  Arcs
  Traces (solid lines of a specified width)
  Polylines (a connected series of line and arc segments of a specified width)
  Solids (solid filled areas)
  Text (words)
  Shapes (small objects that can be filed separately and then added to
    drawings; shapes are seldom used)
  Blocks (objects formed from groups of other entities)
  Attributes (text information stored in Blocks for later extraction and reporting
    purposes)

You'll learn more about these entities and how to use them as you do the exercises in this book.

Erasing and Restoring Entities

1 Load AutoCAD and Begin a New Drawing. Call it **MISTAKES**.

2 Using the LINE and CIRCLE commands, draw the following figures.

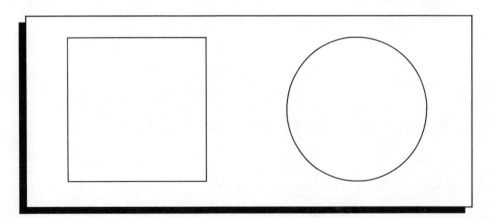

③ Select **ERASE** from the screen menu.

④ AutoCAD will ask you to "Select objects or Window or Last." Select
window from the screen menu (or type **W** and press **RETURN**).

5.1

⑤ Place a window around the square you created. To do this, imagine a
box or rectangle surrounding the entire figure. Move the crosshairs to
one of the corners of the imaginary box and pick that point. Then
move the crosshairs to the opposite corner and pick that point.

Notice what happens. The object to be erased is highlighted with broken lines.

⑥ Press **RETURN** to make it go away.

Now the lines are gone, but the "blips" (construction points) remain.

⑦ To clear the screen of these, type **REDRAW** and press **RETURN**. If
you are using a mouse or a digitizer containing buttons, the REDRAW
command usually can be entered by pressing the third button.

6.4

What if you erased an object by mistake and you want to restore it?

⑧ Enter the **OOPS** command to get it back.

5.2.2

What if you want to select one entity at a time for erasure?

① Enter **ERASE**.

AutoCAD will ask you to "Select objects or Window or Last."

5.1

② Use your pointing device to pick the objects (lines) you want to erase.

③ Press **RETURN** and the objects highlighted will be erased.

Now let's try the Last option.

① Use **OOPS** to restore the original figures.

19

2 Select the **ERASE** command.

3 Select **last** from the screen menu. (Or type **L** and press **RETURN**.)   5.1

What happens?

If you continued to enter ERASE and Last, entities would be erased in the opposite order from which you entered them.

Now let's erase all of the square except for one of its lines.

1 Enter **OOPS** to restore the original figure.

2 Enter the **ERASE** command.

3 Place a window around the square, but do not press RETURN yet.

4 Type **R** and press **RETURN**, or select the **remove** option from the menu.

Notice that the prompt line changes to "Remove objects or Window or Last."   5.1
You can now remove a line or lines from your erase window. The line(s) you remove will *not* be erased.

5 Remove one of the lines by simply picking one with your pointing device.

Note that the line you picked is no longer highlighted.

What if you want to do more erasing? How can you restore the "Select objects or Window or Last" prompt?

6 Simply type **A** for Add and press **RETURN**.   5.1

7 Now use your pointing device to select the circle.

8 Press **RETURN** to make the highlighted lines disappear.

So you see, you can select and remove objects as you wish until you are ready to perform the Erase. The objects selected are indicated by broken lines. These procedures work not only with the ERASE command but also with all commands that require object selection, such as MOVE, COPY, MIRROR, ARRAY, and many others.

9 Enter **OOPS** to get the figures back on the screen.

10 Enter **END** to exit the Drawing Editor and return to the Main Menu.

 **Questions**

1. After you enter the ERASE command, what three options does AutoCAD give you?

   _____

2. What command is used to delete the construction points?

   _____

3. How do you place a window around a figure during object selection?

   _____

   _____

4. If you erased an object by mistake, how can you restore it?

   _____

   Will this method work if you drew something else after erasing the object?

   _____

5. How can you retain part of what has been selected for erasure?

   _____

Problem

To gain skill in using the ERASE command, try the following exercise.

1. Load the drawing called **STUFF**.

2. Enter the **ERASE** command and use the various options to accomplish the following:
   - Place a window around polygon *a*.
   - Pick two of polygon *b*'s lines for erasure.
   - Place a window around polygons *c* and *d* but "remove" two lines from erasure.
   - Pick two lines from polygon *e* for erasure but then "remove" one of the lines so it won't be erased.

3. Now press **RETURN**.

4. Enter **REDRAW**.

What does the drawing look like?

5. Enter **OOPS** to restore your drawing to its original form.

HINT:

If you run into difficulties, type **QUIT** and discard the changes you've made. This will take you back to the Main Menu and you can again load **STUFF**.

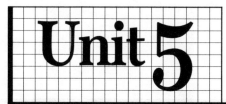

Unit 5 Obtaining Help

■ **OBJECTIVE:**

AutoCAD™ User Guide Reference

To obtain help when using AutoCAD commands

Working with AutoCAD is easy as long as everything goes smoothly, but what if you get stuck on how to use a certain command? Don't worry. Help is available, and this unit will show you how to get it.

3.1

HELP Command _____

1 Load AutoCAD and select option **2** from the Main Menu. Type in **STUFF**.

2 After the drawing is on the screen, enter **HELP** or **?**.

You will get the following prompt:

```
        Command name (RETURN for list):
```

At this point you can type in the name of a command and get instructions on how to use that command. Or you can press RETURN and get a list of AutoCAD commands. Let's try both.

3 Type **MOVE**. (Don't forget to press **RETURN**.) You should get a screen that looks like this:

```
The MOVE command is used to move one or more existing drawing
entities from one location in the drawing to another.

Format:  MOVE  Select objects or Window or Last:  (select)
               Base point or displacement:
               Second point of displacement:  (if base selected above)

If you have the ADE-2 package, you can "drag" the object into position
on the screen.  To do this, designate a reference point on the object in
response to the "Base point..." prompt, and then reply "DRAG" to the
"Second point:" prompt.  The selected objects will follow the movements
of the screen crosshairs.  Move the objects into position and then press
the pointer's "pick" button.

Reference:  Section 5.2 of User Guide.

Command:
```

Note the reference to the *User Guide* in the above screen. This is the same guide that is referred to in the marginal notations throughout *Applying AutoCAD*.

23

4 Turn to Section 5.2 of the *User Guide*. This section describes Edit commands. Note that section 5.2.3, "MOVE Command," includes detailed information that is not provided when using the HELP command on the computer.

5 Press **RETURN**.

You will again get the message "Command name (RETURN for list):".

6 Press **RETURN** to see the list of commands.

```
        Command List    (+1 = ADE-1,   +2 = ADE-2,   +3 = ADE-3)

APERTURE +2   CIRCLE      FILES        LIST        PRPLOT      SKETCH +1
ARC           COPY        FILL         LOAD        PURGE       SNAP
AREA          DBLIST      FILLET +1    LTSCALE     QTEXT       SOLID
ARRAY         DELAY       GRAPHSCR     MENU        QUIT        STATUS
ATTDEF +2     DIM +1      GRID         MIRROR +2   REDRAW      STYLE
ATTDISP +2    DIST        HATCH +1     MOVE        REGEN       TABLET
ATTEDIT +2    DRAGMODE +2 HELP / ?     MSLIDE +2   REGENAUTO   TEXT
ATTEXT +2     DXBIN +3    HIDE +3      OOPS        RENAME      TEXTSCR
AXIS +1       DXFIN       ID           ORTHO       REPEAT      TRACE
BASE          DXFOUT      INSERT       OSNAP +2    RESUME      UNITS +1
BLIPMODE      ELEV +3     ISOPLANE +2  PAN         RSCRIPT     VIEW +2
BLOCK         END         LAYER        PEDIT +3    SAVE        VPOINT +3
BREAK +1      ENDREP      LIMITS       PLINE +3    SCRIPT      VSLIDE
CHAMFER +1    ENDSV       LINE         PLOT        SHAPE       WBLOCK
CHANGE        ERASE       LINETYPE     POINT       SHELL +3    ZOOM

At the "Command:" prompt, you can enter RETURN to repeat the last
command.  Press RETURN for further help.
```

This is useful if you aren't sure how to spell a command.

7 Press **RETURN** again, and you will get tips on entering coordinates and selecting objects.

8 Return to the Drawing Editor by pressing the flip screen function key (typically **F1**).

There is another very useful way of obtaining help. Let's try it.

1 You should have the drawing called STUFF on your screen. Select the **Edit** option from the Root Menu.

A submenu will be produced containing several Edit commands, including MOVE.

2 Select **MOVE** from that screen menu.

Note that one of the options in the Move Submenu is HELP.

3 Select **HELP** from the screen menu.

What happens?

4 Exit the Drawing Editor by entering **QUIT**. (Get HELP if you're unsure how to use QUIT.)

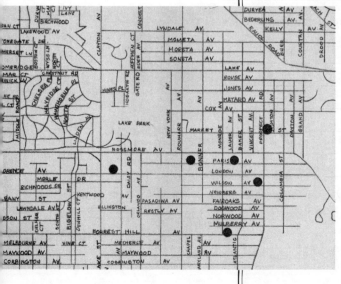

AUTOCAD™ AT WORK

Cracking Down on Crime with AutoCAD

The police in Concord, California, are winning the fight against crime by using CAD to help them stop burglaries before they begin.

In order to prevent burglaries, police look for "crime patterns": What areas of the city are hit most often? What kinds of places are being burglarized? And what property is being stolen? Before AutoCAD, keeping track of all this information was nearly impossible. Recording burglary information on city maps didn't work because they soon became too crowded with information to read. And using "pin maps" didn't work because they couldn't indicate the number or kinds of burglaries that were committed at the same location.

By using AutoCAD, the Concord Police Department can not only record the number and types of burglaries, but it can also display that information on a map of the city. In addition, the department uses AutoCAD's "zoom" feature to make detailed maps of the officers' assigned areas so that they can do a better job of patrolling.

According to Concord's chief of police, AutoCAD is having a big impact on the city's crime rate. "We've found that the presence of police officers in areas where crime is predicted discourages people from committing crimes. Our AutoCAD program shows us graphically where our patrol cars should be and when they should be there." AutoCAD also allows the police department to track the movement of burglaries from one area of the city to another and to chart what effect the arrest of especially active burglars might have on the crime rate in certain areas of the city. **Other Uses.** In addition to the police department, several other city departments in Concord are planning projects involving AutoCAD. Various departments are funding a joint project that would take advantage of AutoCAD's layering feature to make above-ground maps of city streets and addresses and underground maps of water, sewer, and gas lines. The city's traffic department is using AutoCAD to map traffic density and to record traffic accidents.

Questions

1. How do you obtain a listing of all AutoCAD commands if you are in the Drawing Editor?

   _____

   _____

2. Suppose you have the Mirror Submenu on the screen. At this point, what is the fastest way of obtaining AutoCAD screen help on the MIRROR command?

   _____

   _____

3. How do you get back to the graphics screen after obtaining help?

   _____

4. How is the information in the *AutoCAD User Guide* different from the screen help information?

   _____

   _____

5. After you've obtained screen help on one command, how do you get help on the next?

   _____

   _____

Problems

1. Obtain AutoCAD screen help on each of the following commands and state their general purpose.

   REDRAW _____

   QUIT _____

   TRACE_____

   SOLID _____

   FILL _____

   REGEN _____

2. Locate each of the above commands in the *AutoCAD User Guide* and read what it says about each of them.

Unit 6 Becoming a Keyboard Artist

■ OBJECTIVE:

AutoCAD™ User
Guide Reference

To draw polygons of specific lengths and angles from the keyboard

So far, you have used only the pointing device to draw lines. Another method is to use the keyboard to specify coordinates. As you know, CAD drawings are created along X (horizontal) and Y (vertical) axes. Thus, you can create lines by specifying the coordinates of the lines' starting and ending points.

2.8.1

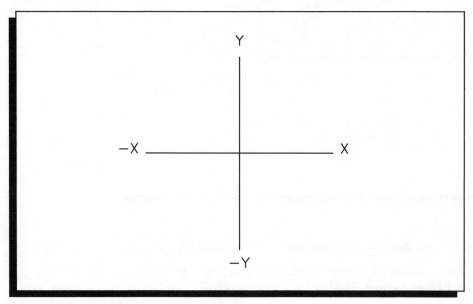

Methods of Entering Lines

There are three ways to specify coordinates.

Absolute Method

2.8.1.1

Example: LINE from point: 2,3
    To point 5,8

This will begin the line at absolute point 2,3 and end it at 5,8.

Relative Method

Example: LINE From point: 2,3
    To point:@2,0

This will draw a line 2 units in the positive X direction and 0 units in the Y direction from point 2,3. In other words, the distances 2,0 are relative to the location of the first point.

2.8.1.2

Polar Method

Example: LINE From point: 2,3
    To point: @4<60

This will produce a line segment 4 units long at a 60-degree angle. The line will begin at point 2,3.

2.8.1.2

The Polar Method is useful for producing lines at a precise angle. Note the drawing on the next page. If you specified an angle of 120 degrees, in which direction would the line slant?

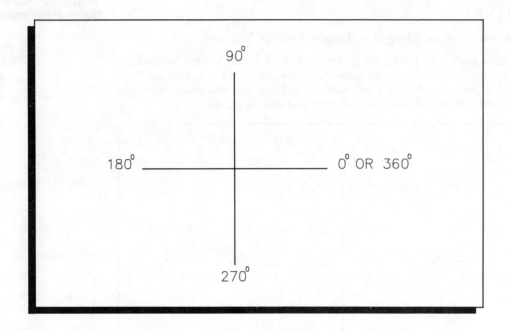

1 Load AutoCAD and Begin a New Drawing. Name it **GASKET**.

2 Enter the **LINE** command and input the following sequence to produce a drawing. Don't forget to press **RETURN** after each entry.

Command: LINE From point: **4,3**

To Point: **@3,0**

To Point: **@2.5<90**

To Point: **C**

What object was produced by entering these coordinates?

Now erase that drawing and let's try something a little more complex.

1 Bring up the **LINE** command again.

2 Using the keyboard, create the following drawing of a gasket. Don't worry about the exact location of the holes. Do not try to place the dimensions on the drawing at this time. However, do make your drawing exactly this size and place it near the bottom of the screen.

HINT:
Use Undo if you need to back up one step but remain in the LINE command sequence.

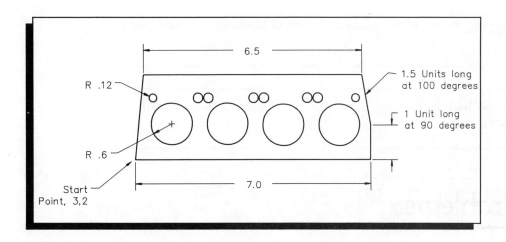

3 Enter **REDRAW** to delete the "blips."

4 Enter **END** to save your drawing and return to the Main Menu.

Questions

1. Briefly describe the differences between the absolute, relative, and polar methods of point specification.

_____

_____

_____

_____

2. What is the advantage of specifying endpoints from the keyboard rather than with the pointing device?

_____

_____

3. What is the advantage of specifying endpoints with the pointing device rather than the keyboard?

_____

_____

4. Why is entering absolute points impractical much of the time when completing drawings?

_____

_____

5. How can you back up one step if you make a mistake in specifying LINE endpoints?

_____

Problems

For each of the following drawings, list exactly what you would enter when using the LINE command to produce the drawings. Try to incorporate all three methods—absolute, relative, and polar—to enter the points. After completing all of the blanks, enter the sequence into your computer.

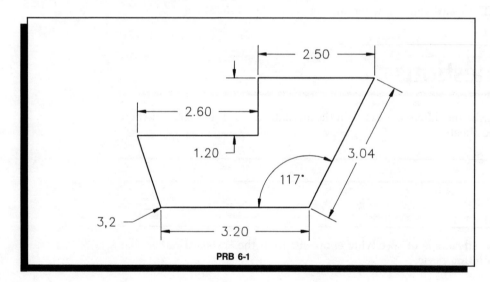

PRB 6-1

1. Command: LINE From point: _____

   To point: _____

   To point: _____

   To point: _____

   To point: _____

   To point: _____

   To point: _____

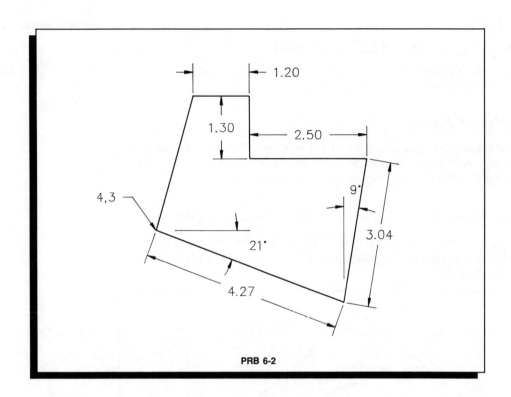

PRB 6-2

2. Command: LINE From Point: _____

   To point: _____

   To point: _____

   To point: _____

   To point: _____

   To point: _____

   To point: _____

 Grabbing Points

■ **OBJECTIVE:**

To apply Object Snap and the APERTURE command

This exercise covers the powerful Object Snap capability and shows how to set the Target Box size for use with Object Snap.

8.6

Using Object Snap

There will be times when you will want to automatically "grab" a specific point in your drawing, such as an endpoint of a line or the center of a circle. With AutoCAD's Object Snap feature, you can do both, and more. Let's try it.

1 First, load AutoCAD and Begin a New Drawing. Name it **OBJSNP.**

2 To get ready for using the Object Snap feature, draw the following object. Omit all numbers and, at this point, ignore the words. Don't worry about exact sizes and locations.

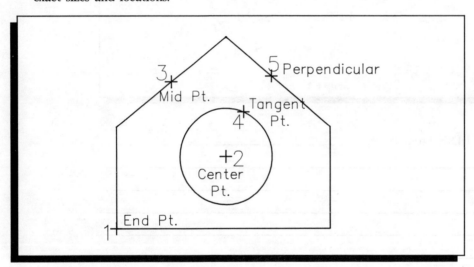

When you are finished with the above drawing, let's practice using the Object Snap feature.

8.6.4

1 Enter the **LINE** command.

2 After the LINE command is entered, type the Object Snap mode called **END** and press **RETURN.**

Did your crosshairs change? They should have; you should now have what AutoCAD calls a target box at the center of the crosshairs.

3 Move your crosshairs/target box so that it touches the horizontal line near point 1, and pick it.

NOTE:

The crosshairs do not have to lie exactly on point 1. The crosshairs can be away from point 1 as long as the target box touches the line and is closer to point 1 than to the other endpoint of the line.

This begins to illustrate the power and accuracy of Object Snap. Let's experiment with another Object Snap mode.

4 In response to the "To point:" prompt on the screen, type **CEN** and press **RETURN.** "Cen," by the way, is short for "center."

5 Move your crosshairs/target box and pick any spot on the circle.

Did your line snap to the center of the circle? It should have.

Instead of typing the Object Snap modes, you can select them from the Osnap Submenu found in the Line Submenu. The LINE command, by the way, will remain entered.

The following is a list of all the Object Snap modes. Note that endpoint and center are included in the list.

8.6.2

Select from
screen menu...   Or type...

quick . . . . .qui
center . . . . .cen
endpoint . . . . .end
insert . . . . .ins
intersec .int
midpoint . . . . .mid
nearest . . . . .nea
node . . . . .nod
perpend .per
quadrant . . . . .qua
tangent .tan
none . . . . .non

LASTMENU

During the following steps, pick the modes from the screen menu.

6 Snap to point 3 by picking **midpoint**.

7 Snap to point 4 by picking **tangent**.

8 Snap to point 5 by picking **perpend**.

Your drawing should now look like the one on the next page. If it doesn't, try it again.

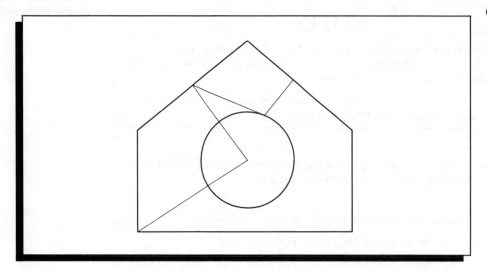

⑨ Experiment with each of the remaining Object Snap modes.

Even though the Osnap Submenu may seem convenient, most of the time you will probably type the modes as you need them. This is because you will usually have another submenu on your screen, and it is faster to type the Snap mode than to call up the Osnap Submenu.

APERTURE Command _____

8.6.5

Now, let's practice changing the size of the target box.

① Enter the APERTURE command.

You can now choose any size from 1 to 50 pixels. A pixel is a picture element on a screen. All the images you see on the computer screen are made up of these tiny dots called pixels.

② Type **15** for the aperture size.

③ Use one of the Object Snap modes to see the new size of the target box.

④ Change the target box size to 5 pixels.

⑤ Again, view the new size by using Object Snap.

⑥ Type **END** to save your drawing and return to the Main Menu.

Questions

1. Explain the purpose of Object Snap.

   _____

   _____

   _____

2. In order to snap a line to the center of a circle, what part does the target box need to touch?

   _____

3. What command do you use to change the size of the target box? Describe a situation in which you would want to change the target box size.

   _____

   _____

   _____

4. Briefly describe the use of each of the following Object Snap modes.

   quick_____

   cen _____

   end _____

   ins_____

   int_____

   mid _____

   nea _____

   nod _____

   per _____

   qua _____

   tan _____

   non _____

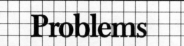 **Problems**

1. Draw this square.

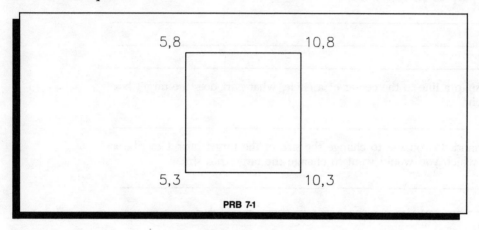

5,8   10,8

5,3   10,3

PRB 7-1

Use Object Snap to make these additions.

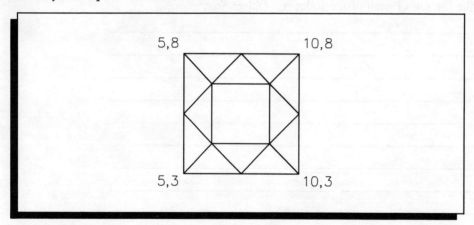

5,8   10,8

5,3   10,3

2. Using Object Snap, construct the following object. Don't worry about exact sizes and locations.

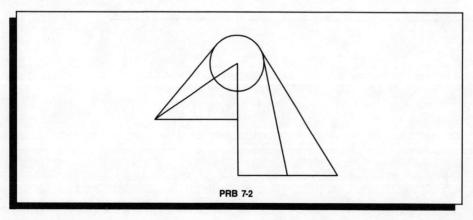

PRB 7-2

 # Three Special Features

■ **OBJECTIVE:**

To control certain AutoCAD features including Printer Echoing, Coordinate Display, and Ortho

This unit describes several AutoCAD features. The intent of this unit is to apply these features by using the proper keys on the keyboard.

Printer Echoing

Simultaneously pressing CTRL (control) and Q on your keyboard will cause AutoCAD to print everything you type. The printing actually occurs after you have typed your text and pressed RETURN. That is why it is referred to as echoing to the printer.

2.10

Let's try it.

NOTE:

Before you begin, make sure a printer is properly connected to your computer, is turned on, and is loaded with paper.

1 Bring up the Drawing Editor by entering option 1 or 2 from the Main Menu.

2 Press **CTRL** and **Q** at the same time.

3 Now simply enter an AutoCAD command of your choice and complete the entire command.

Did the text echo to the printer?

4 Practice by echoing other information to the printer.

5 Press **CTRL Q** to turn off the printer echo.

NOTE:

As you've just seen, CTRL Q serves to turn the printer echo both on and off. Thus it acts like a toggle switch. Using keys in this manner is referred to as toggling.

Coordinate Display

Another useful feature is the display of coordinate status. This information, displayed in digital form, is found in the upper portion of your Drawing Editor and is part of what AutoCAD calls the *status line*. The coordinate display, found in the right-hand portion of the status line, shows the current position (or coordinate position) of your crosshairs as you move your pointing device.

8.7

Let's take a look at the coordinate display feature.

8.8

1 Turn on the coordinate display by pressing **CTRL D**.

2 Move the crosshairs on your screen by moving your pointing device.

Note how the coordinate display changes with the movement of the crosshairs.

3 With the coordinate display still on, select the LINE command and draw a simple polygon.

Note exactly what comes up on the coordinate display at each step of the polygon development. Is this information similar to specifying line endpoints using the polar method of point specification?

4 You can turn (toggle) off the coordinate display by again pressing **CTRL D.**

The Ortho Mode

Now let's focus on an AutoCAD feature called Ortho. Ortho is a very useful feature which allows you to quickly and easily draw lines either horizontally or vertically. Let's work with it a bit.

8.4

1 Enter the **ORTHO** command (found in the Modes Submenu) and specify **on.** Or, simply type **CTRL O,** and you can toggle Ortho on or off.

8.8

Ortho is on if the word "Ortho" is displayed on the status line at the top of the screen.

2 Experiment by drawing lines with Ortho turned on and then with Ortho off. Note the difference.

HINT:

Ortho can be toggled on and off at any time, even while you're in the middle of a command such as LINE. Simply press CRTL O, or press the function key that toggles Ortho on and off.

3 Attempt drawing an angular line with Ortho on. What happens?

4 Now, draw the following object, first with the Ortho off and then with Ortho on. Don't worry about exact sizes and locations.

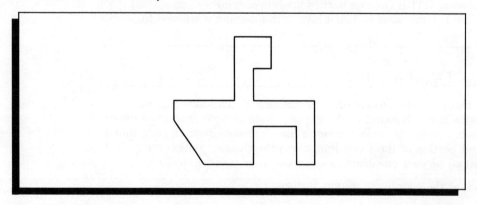

Was it faster with Ortho on?

5 Enter **END** if you want to save the drawing you just made. Enter **QUIT** if you don't want to save it.

AUTOCAD™ AT WORK

AutoCAD Is into Rock

The lighting for a typical 1950s rock and roll concert consisted of a few dim stage lights and four or five spotlights aimed at Elvis Presley or Chuck Berry. But as the performers and their music gained sophistication, so did the lighting. Four or five spotlights gave way to thousands of multicolored lights arranged in precise designs.

In 1983 a theatrical lighting company in Atlanta, Georgia, decided that lighting design had become too complicated and time-consuming to do by hand, so they turned to AutoCAD for help. After switching to AutoCAD, the firm won contracts to design two extravagant concert lighting projects — the Jacksons' Victory Tour in 1984 and Madonna's Virgin Tour in 1985. The Atlanta-based firm has also designed the lighting for artists as varied as Hank Williams, Jr., and Kool and the Gang.

One of the biggest advantages of AutoCAD for lighting designers is its speed. Instead of drawing each lamp in a design by hand, for example, the designers can call up an array of lamps from the AutoCAD "library." Also, by using AutoCAD's "zoom" feature, designers can magnify areas that need detail work.

AutoCAD also allows the designer to make changes more easily. This easy-revision feature came in especially handy while the firm was working on the Madonna tour. After the lighting for the tour had been designed, Madonna attended a Prince concert and decided she wanted a set to accompany the lighting for her concerts. Within three days the firm had designed a set and redesigned the lighting to fit.

Theatrical designers using AutoCAD can make more professional presentations to musicians and producers looking for creative concert lighting. A designer using AutoCAD can print a multicolored drawing of the proposed lighting system to show clients what the lighted stage will look like during a performance.

The Future. The entertainment industry is just beginning to explore the uses of AutoCAD. Besides lighting design, AutoCAD could be used in live theater (as well as television and moviemaking) for blocking, choreography, special effects, and costume design.

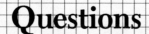

Questions

1. What two keys activate the printer echoing process?

   _____

2. Why would you want to echo your text to the printer while entering and responding to AutoCAD commands?

   _____

   _____

   _____

3. How do you turn off the printer echo?

   _____

   _____

4. What key, in conjunction with CTRL, allows you to turn on the coordinate display feature?

   _____

5. How do you turn off the coordinate display?

   _____

   _____

6. Of what value is the coordinate display?

   _____

   _____

7. What's the name of the feature that forces all lines to be drawn only vertically or horizontally?

   _____

8. What key, used with CTRL, controls this feature?

   _____

Problems

Practice using Ortho by drawing the following shapes. Utilize Ortho when appropriate. Don't worry about exact sizes and locations. Turn on the coordinate display, and note the display as you construct each of the shapes. Lastly, when you construct one (just pick one) of the objects, echo everything you enter on the keyboard to the printer.

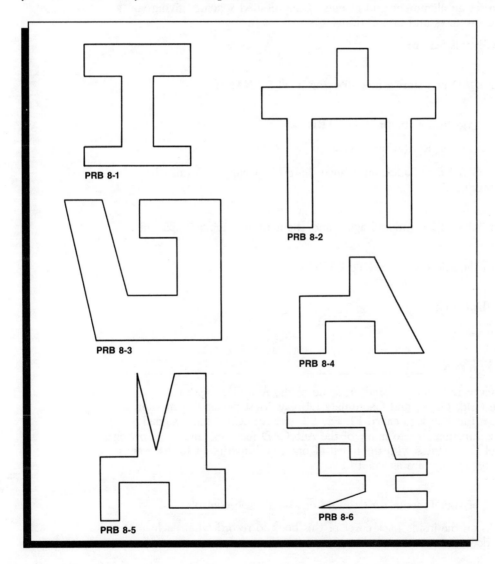

PRB 8-1

PRB 8-2

PRB 8-3

PRB 8-4

PRB 8-5

PRB 8-6

Unit 9   Helpful Drawing Aids

■ **OBJECTIVE:**

AutoCAD™ User
Guide Reference

To apply the GRID, AXIS, and SNAP commands

This exercise focuses on three very helpful drawing aids. They are related to one another in that they assist the AutoCAD user during the layout and/or placement of objects within drawings.

GRID Command

The Drawing Editor Grid is simply a visual drawing aid. The GRID command allows you to set an alignment grid of dots of any desired spacing, giving you a better feel for distances and overall drawing size.

8.2

Let's work with this feature.

1 Load AutoCAD and start a new drawing. Call it **SNAPPY**.

2 Toggle the grid feature by pressing **CTRL G**.

Is there now a grid of dots on the screen? (If not, continue anyway.)

3 Enter the **GRID** command and change the grid spacing to .5 units by simply entering **.5**.

4 Bring up the **GRID** command again and change the spacing to **.25** units.

5 Next, turn the grid off by pressing **CTRL G**...

6 ... and then back on.

It's easy, huh?

Function Keys

There's a quick way to turn on and off some of the AutoCAD features, including the Grid, Ortho, and Coordinate Display. Most personal computer keyboards have function keys called F1, F2, F3, etc. AutoCAD has assigned many of these function keys to many of the AutoCAD features, thereby allowing you to control the features with the touch of one key. Experiment to discover what your function keys are assigned to.

1 Press each of your function keys to find out what each controls.

Use the blanks on the inside back cover of this book to record what each function key does.

NOTE:

All function keys may not be assigned to a specific function or feature.

AXIS Command

The Axis feature is similar to the Grid feature because it, too, provides a visual means of referencing distance. The AutoCAD Grid could be viewed as an electronic alignment grid, whereas the AutoCAD Axis could be viewed as an electronic ruler. Again, both are used for visual reference only; they do not become part of the drawing.

8.3

Let's work with the AXIS command.

1 Enter the **AXIS** command. Turn it on by entering **on**.

2 Enter **AXIS** again and change the unit spacing to .25 by typing **.25**.

And that's all there is to it. You have just experienced the use of the AXIS command.

SNAP Command

Now let's work with an AutoCAD feature called Snap, which most AutoCAD users agree is extremely useful. The AutoCAD Snap feature is similar to the Grid feature in that it is a grid, but it is an imaginary one. In other words, you cannot see the Snap feature, but you can realize the effects of Snap as you move the crosshairs across the screen. At first, it may be difficult to visualize. Therefore, let's work with it a bit.

8.1

1 Press **CTRL B** to turn on the Snap feature. The word Snap should appear on the status line when Snap is on.

8.8

2 Slowly move your pointing device and watch closely the movement of the crosshairs.

Is it different than before?

3 Enter the **SNAP** command.

4 Now type in **.25** to specify the snap resolution.

5 Move your pointing device and note the crosshair movement.

HINT:

Turn the Grid on to better see the movement of the crosshairs. Can you place the crosshairs between dots on the grid?

There will be times when you want the crosshairs to snap one distance vertically and a different distance horizontally. Here's how to do it:

1 Enter the **SNAP** command.

2 Enter the **aspect** option.

The prompt line will ask for Horizontal spacing.

3 For this exercise, type in **.5**.

Next you will be asked for Vertical spacing.

4 For now, type in **1**.

5 Use your pointing device to move the crosshairs on the screen. Note the difference between the amounts of vertical and horizontal movement.

Now, let's try drawing an object.

1 Draw the following object with the Snap set at .5 units each way. Use only your pointing device to specify all points.

HINT:
Turn on Ortho to speed up the drawing of the horizontal and vertical lines.

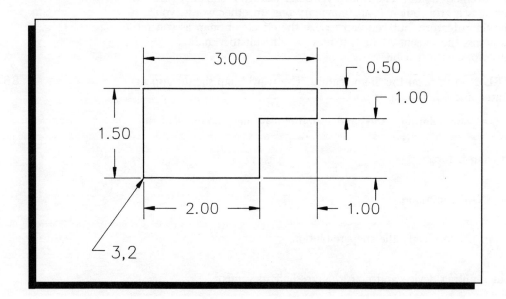

2 When you are finished, enter **END** to save your drawing and return to the Main Menu.

Questions

1. What is the purpose of the GRID command?

_____

_____

2. How is the Axis feature similar to the Grid feature?

_____

_____

3. How do the Axis ruler lines change as you change the spacing?

_____

_____

4. When would you use the Snap feature?

_____

_____

5. How can you set the Snap feature so that the crosshairs move a different distance horizontally than vertically?

_____

_____

Problems

Draw the following objects using the Grid, Axis, and Snap settings provided beside each object.

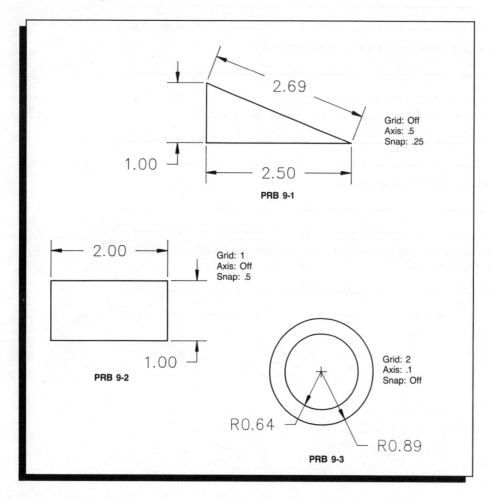

PRB 9-1

Grid: Off
Axis: .5
Snap: .25

PRB 9-2

Grid: 1
Axis: Off
Snap: .5

PRB 9-3

Grid: 2
Axis: .1
Snap: Off

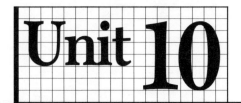

Unit 10 Altering Entities

■ OBJECTIVE:

To practice using the CHAMFER, BREAK, and FILLET commands

These commands allow you to make chamfered or rounded corners and to break a line.

CHAMFER Command

The CHAMFER command allows you to place a chamfer at the corner formed by two lines.

5.2.9

1 Load AutoCAD and select option **2** from the Main Menu. Specify the drawing called **GASKET**.

2 Enter the **CHAMFER** command.

You will receive a prompt line like this:

```
Command: CHAMFER Polyline/Distances/<Select first line>:
```

3 Type **D** for Distance or pick it from the submenu.

4 Specify a chamfer distance of **.25** units for both the first and second distances.

5 Enter the **CHAMFER** command again and place a chamfer at each of the corners of the gasket by picking the two lines which make up each corner. (You will have to enter **CHAMFER** or hit the **space bar** before selecting each pair of lines.)

When you're finished, your drawing should look similar to the one below.

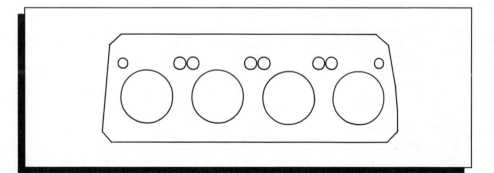

BREAK Command

Now let's remove or break out sections of the gasket so that it looks like the drawing on the next page.

5.2.7

As you know, the bottom edge of the gasket was drawn as a single, continuous line. Therefore, if we were to attempt to use the ERASE command to break the line, it would erase the entire line since the line is an entity. The BREAK command, however, allows us to "break" certain entities such as lines, arcs, and circles. Let's try it.

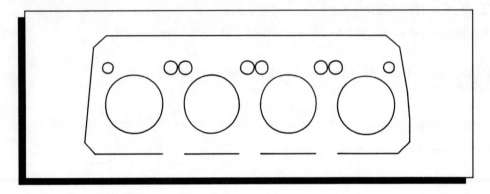

1 Enter the **BREAK** command.

2 Pick a point where you'd like the break to begin. Since the locations of the above breaks are not dimensioned, approximate the location of the start point.

3 Pick the point where you'd like the break to end.

Did a piece disappear?

4 Break out two more sections of approximately equal size as shown in the above gasket drawing.

When you're finished breaking out the small sections, let's place arcs in the broken sections as shown below.

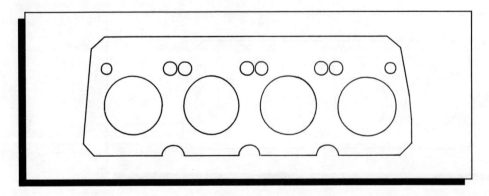

5 Using the **ARC** command, insert arc-shaped ribs along the broken edge of the gasket.

Now, for practice, let's break out a section of one of the holes in the gasket.

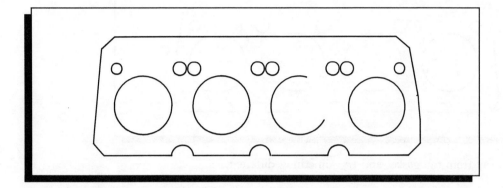

1 Enter the **BREAK** command.

2 Pick the first break point on the circle.

3 Working counterclockwise, pick the second point. Did it work?

4 Enter **OOPS**.

Did the broken piece of the circle return? Why not? Is it, perhaps, because OOPS works only in conjunction with the ERASE command and not BREAK?

FILLET Command _____

5.2.8

Now let's change the chamfered corners on the gasket to rounded corners, or fillets.

1 First, **ERASE** each of the chamfered corners.

2 Enter the FILLET command and set the radius at .3 units. The fastest way to do this is to enter **FILLET**, then **R**, and then **.3**. Be sure to press **RETURN** after each entry.

3 Reenter the **FILLET** command and produce fillets at each of the four corners of the gasket by picking each pair of lines.

Your gasket drawing should now look similar to the drawing on the next page.

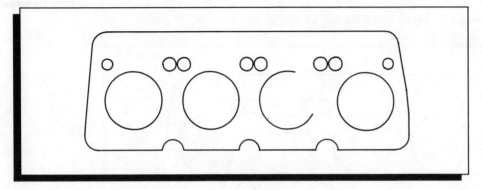

Let's move away from the gasket and try something different.

1 Draw lines on your screen similar to the ones below. Omit the numbers.

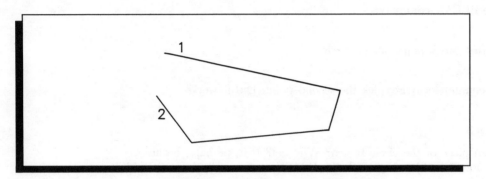

2 Set your **FILLET Radius** at **0**.

3 Reenter the **FILLET** command and select lines 1 and 2.

What happened to the two lines?

Clever, huh?

It works using the CHAMFER command as well.

4 Erase the polygon you just drew.

5 Enter **END** to save the rest of the drawing.

Questions

1. What is the function of the CHAMFER command?

   _____

   _____

2. How do you get from the Root Menu to CHAMFER?

   _____

   _____

3. How is using the BREAK command different from using the ERASE command?

   _____

   _____

4. If you want to break a circle or arc, in which direction do you move when specifying points: clockwise or counterclockwise?

   _____

5. In what submenu is the FILLET command found?

   _____

6. How do you set the FILLET radius?

   _____

   _____

7. Will the FILLET radius change or stay the same after you END and exit back to the Main Menu?

   _____

Problems

1. Using the pointing device, create the first drawing shown below. Don't worry about exact sizes and locations, but do utilize SNAP and ORTHO. Then use FILLET to change it to the second drawing. Set the fillet radius at .2 units.

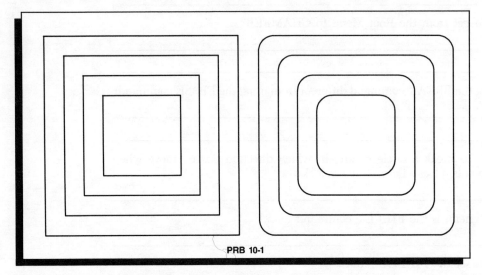

PRB 10-1

2. Create the triangle shown below. Then use CHAMFER to change it into a hexagon. Set the chamfer distance at .66 units.

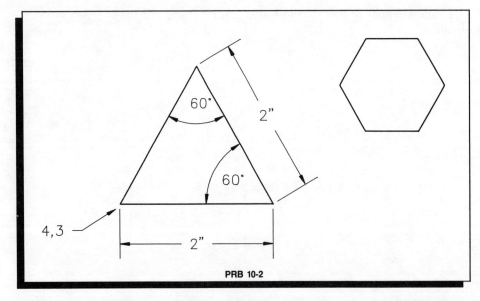

PRB 10-2

3. Draw the following object; don't worry about specific sizes. Use the FILLET command to place fillets in the corners as indicated.

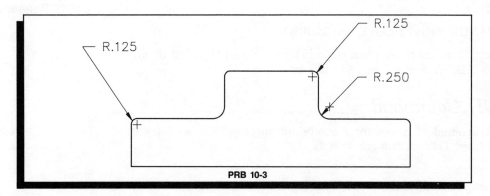

PRB 10-3

4. Draw the following object, but don't worry about specific sizes. Use the CHAMFER command to place a chamfer at each corner.

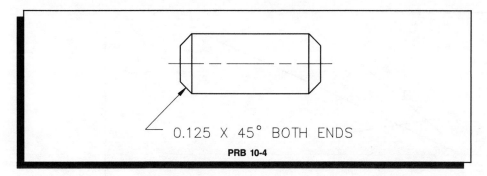

0.125 X 45° BOTH ENDS

PRB 10-4

5. Using the ARC and CHAMFER commands, construct the following object.

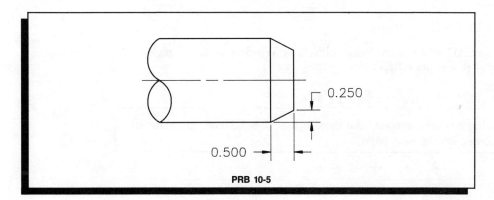

0.250

0.500

PRB 10-5

Unit 11 Moving and Duplicating Objects

■ **OBJECTIVE:**

**AutoCAD™ User
Guide Reference**

To apply CHANGE, MOVE, COPY, and MIRROR

When drawing, there are times when you'd like to move an object or duplicate it. With AutoCAD, it's a simple and fun process.

CHANGE Command

The CHANGE command is used for a number of purposes, such as fixing the placement of lines. Let's experiment with it.

5.2.6

1 Load AutoCAD and bring up your drawing called **GASKET**.

2 Above the gasket, draw three intersecting lines like the ones below. Omit the letters.

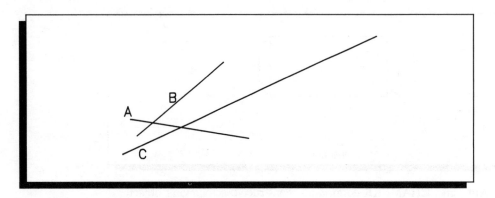

3 Enter the **CHANGE** command.

4 When AutoCAD asks you to "Select objects or Window or Last," pick lines A and B and press **RETURN**.

NOTE:

We're working toward correcting the lines so that they connect to create an arrow as shown on the next page.

54

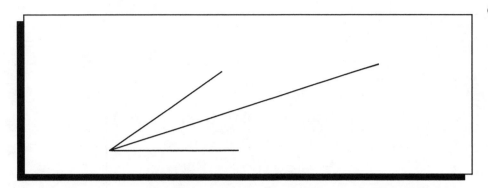

5 To finish the process, pick the leftmost endpoint of line C for the change point.

Did the lines change into the shape of an arrow? If not, try it again.

HINT:

AutoCAD provides HELP on each of its commands, including the CHANGE command. Use it if you need additional information.

We'll explore other ways of using the CHANGE command at a later time.

6 For now, **ERASE** the arrow so that you'll have room on the computer screen for the next drawing.

MOVE Command _____

Let's move the entire gasket to the top of the screen using the MOVE command.   5.2.3

1 Enter the command called **MOVE**.

AutoCAD should now be asking you to "Select objects or Window or Last."

2 Using the **Window** option, place a window around the entire gasket drawing and press **RETURN**.

3 Respond to the next prompt by simply placing a reference (base) point somewhere on or near the gasket drawing.

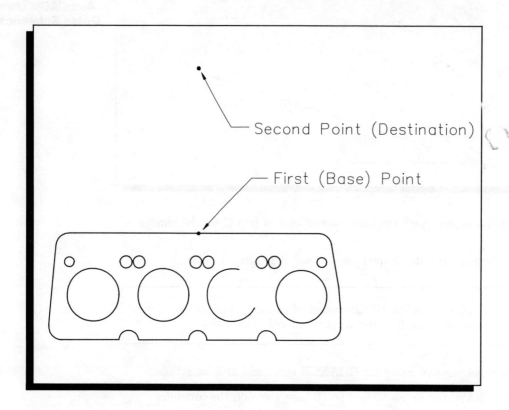

4 Respond to the next prompt by giving a second point, or destination point, as shown above.

Did the drawing move as illustrated below?

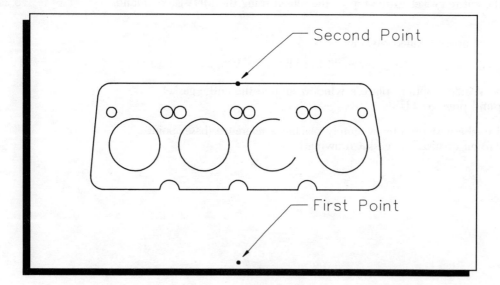

5 Practice using the MOVE command by moving the drawing down to the bottom of your screen.

Now let's drag two of the holes in the gasket to a new location. To use the Drag option in AutoCAD, the Drag mode must be on. This is accomplished by using the command called DRAGMODE.

1 Enter **DRAGMODE**.

2 Enter **ON**. (Or select **on** from the screen menu.)

Now the Drag feature will work until you turn DRAGMODE off.

3 Enter the **MOVE** command as you did before.

4 In response to the prompt "Select objects or Window or Last," pick two of the four holes (circles) and press **RETURN**.

5 Specify the first point (reference/base point). Place the point anywhere on or near either of the two circles.

6 For the second point, type **DRAG** or pick it off the screen menu, and move your pointing device.

What happened?

7 After you decide on a location for the circles, pick that spot with your pointing device.

Neat, huh?

COPY Command

The COPY command works almost identically to the MOVE command.   5.2.4

The only difference is that the COPY command does not move the object; it copies it.

Let's try it.

1 **ERASE** all of the large holes in the gasket except for one.

2 Using the **COPY** command, duplicate the hole three times to complete the gasket drawing. Again, the process is the same as with the MOVE command.

3 Practice using the COPY command by using it in conjunction with the Drag option, as you did before with MOVE.

MIRROR Command

There are times when it is necessary to produce a mirror image of a drawing,   5.2.5
detail, or part. However, a simple COPY of the object is not quite correct
because the object being copied must be reversed, as was done with the butterfly
on the next page. One side of the butterfly was produced and then mirrored to
produce the other side.

The same is true if the engine head gasket we developed is to be reproduced to represent the opposite side of the engine; that is, if the gasket we are producing is for an eight-cylinder engine.

Let's do it.

1 **MOVE** the gasket either to the top or bottom of your screen to allow space for another gasket of the same size.

2 Enter the **MIRROR** command, select the gasket by placing a **Window** around it, and press **RETURN**.

3 Provide a horizontal Mirror Line near the gasket by selecting two points on a horizontal plane as shown below.

4 The prompt line will ask if you want to delete old objects. Enter **N** for "no."

The gasket should have mirrored as shown below.

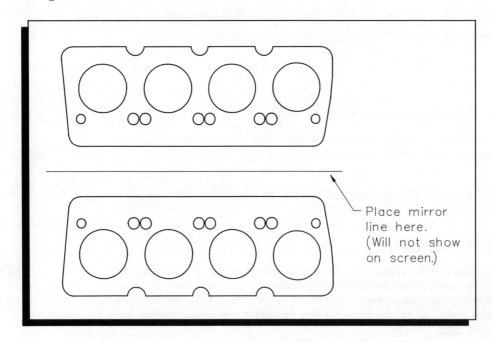

Place mirror line here. (Will not show on screen.)

NOTE:

Mirrors can be performed only around a horizontal or vertical axis.

⑤ Enter **END** to save your drawing and return to the Main Menu.

Questions

1. In what submenu is the CHANGE command found?

   _____

2. Describe a situation where CHANGE would be used for changing endpoints of lines.

   _____

   _____

3. In what submenu is MOVE located?

   _____

4. Explain how the MOVE command is different from the COPY command.

   _____

   _____

   _____

5. At what point do you enter Drag when wanting to dynamically drag during a MOVE or COPY?

   _____

   _____

6. How does DRAGMODE affect the MOVE and COPY commands?

   _____

   _____

7. Describe a situation in which a MIRROR command would be helpful.

   _____

   _____

8. During a MIRROR operation, can the Mirror Line be specified at any angle? Explain.

   _____

   _____

Problems

In problems 1 and 2, follow each step to create the objects. Use the MIRROR and COPY commands to complete Steps 3 and 4.

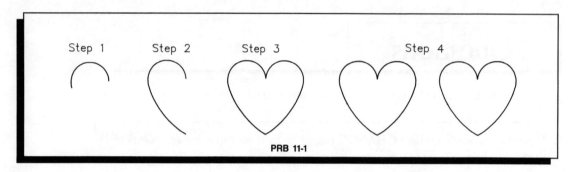

PRB 11-1

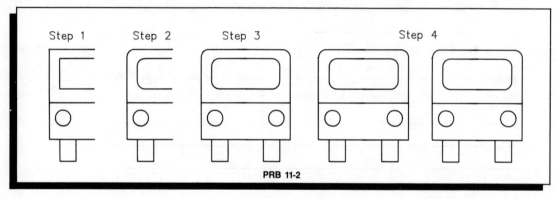

PRB 11-2

In problem 3, draw the objects and room as shown. Then use the MOVE and COPY commands to move the office furniture into the room. Omit the lettering on the drawings.

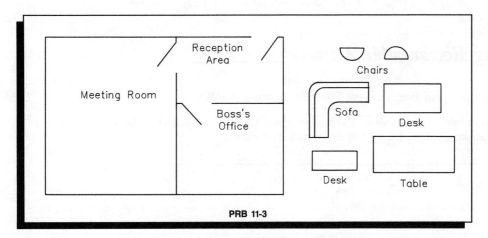

PRB 11-3

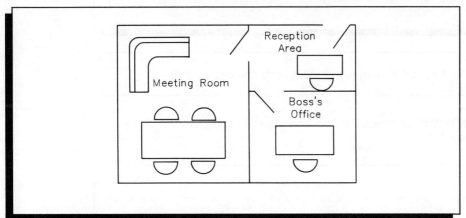

HINT: MOVE and COPY may work better with the Ortho and Snap modes off.

61

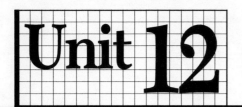
Unit 12 The Powerful ARRAY Command

AutoCAD™ User Guide Reference

■ OBJECTIVE:

To create rectangular and circular arrays

The following exercise utilizes the ARRAY command to complete two different types of drawings: (1) a schematic of computer chip sockets and (2) a bicycle wheel with spokes.

5.2.10

■ *Producing Rectangular Arrays* ─────────────

1 Load AutoCAD and Begin a New Drawing. Name it **CHIPS**.

5.2.10.1

2 In the lower left-hand corner of the screen, draw the following and make it small (approximately 1/2 unit wide by 2/3 unit tall).

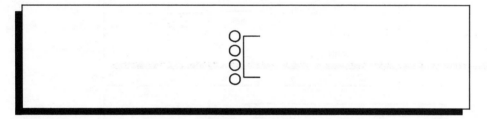

HINT: Use the COPY command to duplicate the small circle.

3 Using the **MIRROR** command, mirror the object to complete the opposite side as shown below.

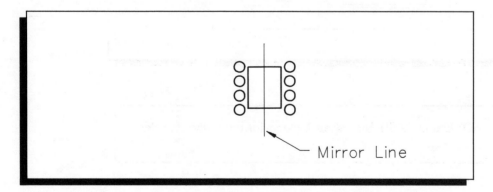

Mirror Line

The object you have just drawn represents a computer chip socket. It looks similar to a schematic of the sockets found inside your computer. The sockets, by the way, house the RAM chips that are currently holding the information you see on your screen.

4 Enter the **ARRAY** command.

5 In reply to the prompt, select the chip socket by placing a window around it, and press **RETURN**.

6 Enter the Rectangular Array option by typing **R** and pressing **RETURN**, or by selecting it from the screen menu.

7 Specify **3** rows and **5** columns.

8 Also specify that you want **1.5** units between the rows and **1.75** units between the columns.

You should now have 15 chip sockets on your screen, arranged in a 3 x 5 array. Does your screen look similar to the illustration below?

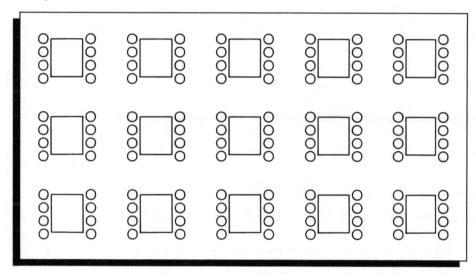

If your array does not look like the above, ERASE everything except for the chip socket in the lower left corner of your screen and try again.

If it does look like the figure above, GOOD JOB!

9 Save your array by entering **END**.

Producing Circular Arrays

Next, we're going to produce a bicycle wheel using the Circular Array option.

5.2.10.2

1 Begin a New Drawing and name it **WHEEL**.

2 After you arrive at the Drawing Editor, draw a tire/wheel similar to the one on the next page. Don't worry about the exact sizes of the circles, but do make the wheel large enough to fill most of your screen.

HINT:

Use Object Snap to make the circles concentric.

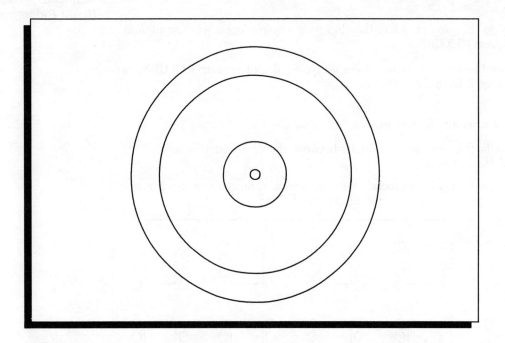

3️⃣ Using the **LINE** command, draw two crossing lines similar to the ones below.

HINT: Use the Object Snap mode "nearest" to begin and end the lines on the appropriate circles.

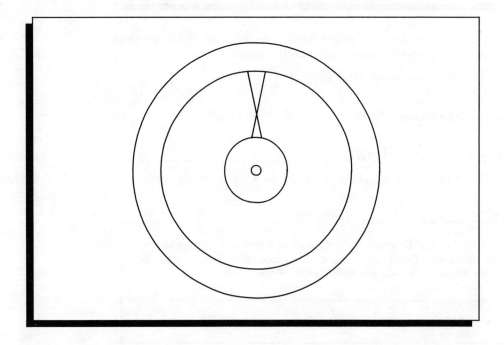

4 Enter the **ARRAY** command and use the following information when responding to each step.

(a) Select each of the two crossing lines for the Array.
(b) Choose the Circular Array (**C**) option.
(c) The center point of the Array is the center of the wheel. (Use Object Snap to locate the center point precisely.)
(d) Make the angle between items 20 degrees.
(e) Specify 18 times.
(f) ... and yes, you want to rotate the spokes as they are copied.

Did it work? If you were not successful, try again. The wheel should now like like the following.

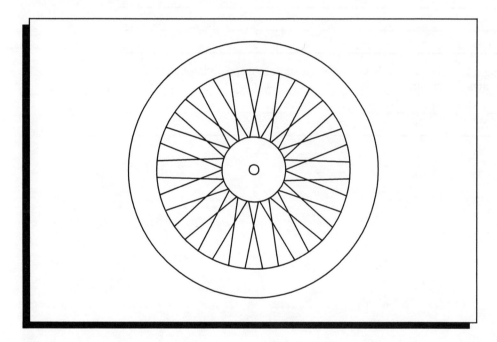

5 Enter **END** to save your drawing and return to the Main Menu.

Questions

1. In what submenu is the ARRAY command found?

   _____

2. Name the two types of Arrays.

   _____

3. State one practical application for each type of Array.

   _____

   _____

   _____

4. When using a Circular Array, do you have the option of specifying less than 360 degrees of array? Explain.

   _____

   _____

Problems

1. Using the ARRAY command, draw the following figure. Use the Circular Array option and make the angle between items 90 degrees.

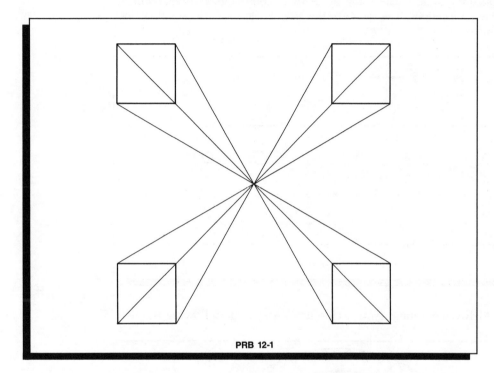

PRB 12-1

2. Use the Circular ARRAY option again to create the following figure. (Start by drawing an ellipse and then ARRAY it.) Experiment to see how changing the shape of the ellipse, the angle between ellipses, and the number of ellipses changes the figure.

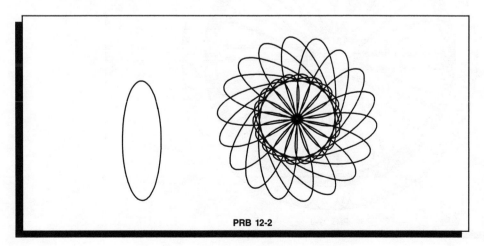

PRB 12-2

3. Develop an auditorium with rows and columns of seats using the ARRAY command. Design the room any way you'd like.
4. Identify another practical application for using an Array. Draw the first object and then ARRAY it.
5. Load your drawing called GASKET. Erase each of the circles. Replace the large ones according to the locations shown below, this time using the ARRAY command. Also reproduce the small circles using the ARRAY command, but don't worry about their exact locations. The radius of the large circles is .6; the small circles have a radius of .12.

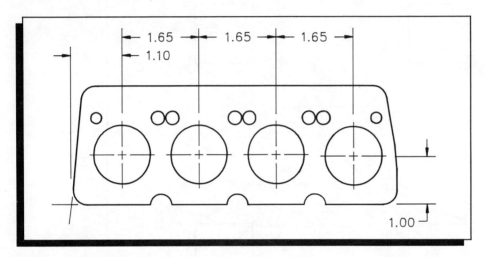

6. Using the ARRAY command (you decide how), draw the following figure.

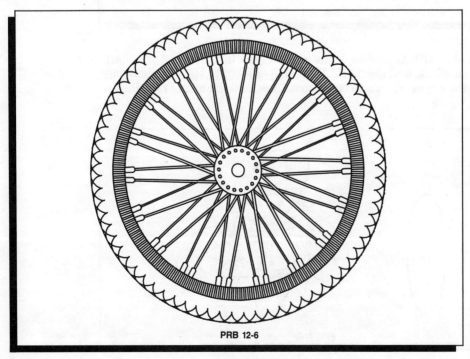

PRB 12-6

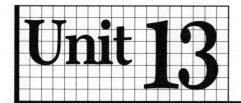

Unit 13 AutoCAD's Magnifying Glass

■ OBJECTIVE:

To practice the ZOOM and REGEN commands

The ZOOM command allows you to magnify or reduce portions of drawings on the screen. ZOOM can magnify objects by a factor of ten trillion! This exercise utilizes the ZOOM command to practice this process, and it covers screen regenerations caused by ZOOM.

6.1.1

■ *ZOOM Command* _____

Let's work with the ZOOM command.

1 Load AutoCAD and Begin a New Drawing. Name it **ZOOM**.

2 Draw the following room, including the table and chair representations. Don't worry about exact sizes and locations of the objects, but do fill most of your screen.

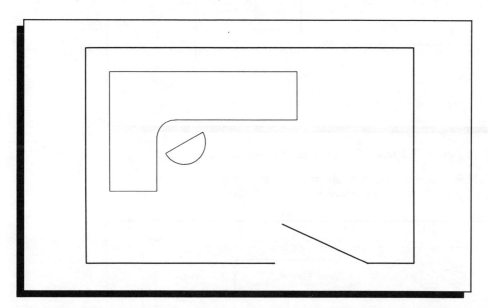

3 Enter the **ZOOM** command. Note each of the ZOOM options, as shown below.

```
Command:  ZOOM Magnification or type (ACELPW):
```

4 Select the **W** (Window) option and place a window around the table as shown on the next page.

6.1.4

69

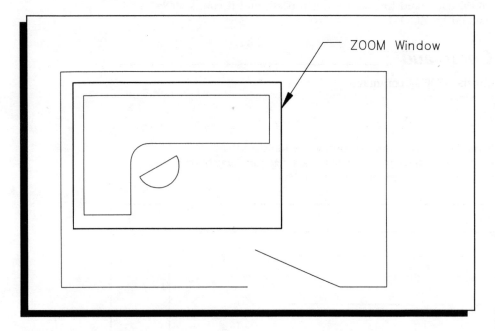

Did the table magnify to fill most of your screen? It should have.

5 Next, draw schematic representations of several components which make up a CAD system as shown below. Omit the text information.

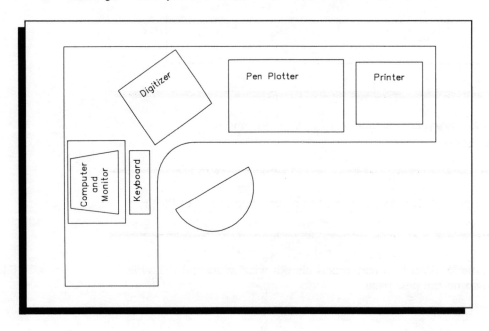

Now let's ZOOM in on the keyboard. This can be done using ZOOM L.

6 Enter **ZOOM** and then enter the **L** (Left) option.　　　　　　　6.1.6

The prompt line will ask for a lower left corner point.

7 With your pointing device, pick a point in the lower left corner of the *screen.* (If you pick a point within the keyboard drawing, you will lose the borders of the keyboard when the computer zooms.)

The prompt line will now ask for magnification or height.

8 Use the pointing device to pick a point at the height you want.

You may have to ZOOM again so that the keyboard fills most of your screen.

9 In the upper left corner of the keyboard (which is actually the lower left corner of the screen), draw a small square to represent a key.

10 ZOOM in on the key, this time using **ZOOM C** (Center). Pick a center　　6.1.5
point of your ZOOM and then specify the height.

11 Draw a small trademark on the key as shown below.

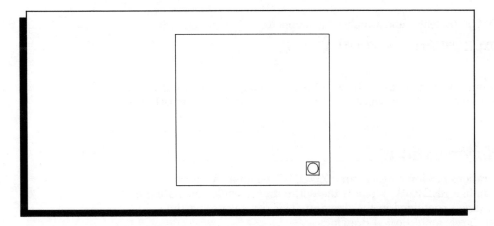

12 Next, **ZOOM P** (Previous) and watch what happens.　　　　　　　6.1.7

You should now be at your previous ZOOM factor. What does the trademark now look like?

13 Using the **ARRAY** command, array the key to create two rows and five columns as shown on the next page. These ten keys, by the way, represent the function keys on a computer keyboard.

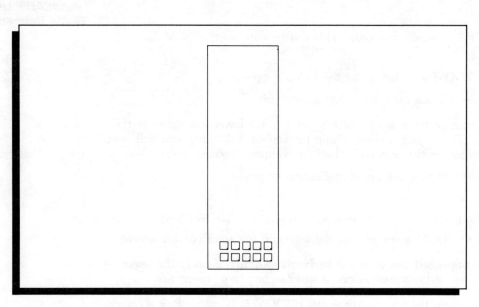

14 Next, **ZOOM A** (All).

Is your original drawing now on the screen?

6.1.2

15 **ZOOM E** (Extents) and watch what happens.

6.1.3

How is ZOOM E different from ZOOM A?

16 Continue to practice using the ZOOM command by ZOOMing in on the different CAD components of the drawing and including detail on each.

Screen Regenerations _____

Screen regenerations are forced each time ZOOM is entered. A screen regeneration, unlike REDRAW, repaints the entire screen while calculating each of the vectors (lines) contained in the drawing. This can take some time, especially with large, sophisticated drawings.

6.5

Let's force another screen regeneration with the ZOOM command.

1 Enter **ZOOM A**.

Since your current drawing is not large and complex, it did not take long to regenerate.

Screen regenerations can also be forced using other AutoCAD commands, including the REGEN command. Let's do it.

2 Enter **REGEN**.

Did your screen REGENerate as it did when you ZOOMed All? As you work with AutoCAD commands such as QTEXT and FILL, you will identify applications for using REGEN. But most of the time a simple REDRAW will suffice because REDRAW takes much less time and cleans up your drawing.

③ When you are finished working with REGEN and ZOOM, enter **END** to save your work and to exit the Drawing Editor.

Questions

1. Explain why the ZOOM command is useful.

   _____

   _____

2. Cite one example of when it would be necessary to use the ZOOM command for completing a technical drawing and explain why.

   _____

   _____

   _____

3. In what submenu is the ZOOM command found?

   _____

4. State what each of the following ZOOM options stands for.

   A _____   L _____

   C _____   P _____

   E _____   W _____

5. Explain a screen regeneration.

   _____

   _____

6. How is REGEN different from REDRAW?

   _____

   _____

Problem

Create a drawing such as an elevation plan of a building, a site plan of a land development, or a view of a mechanical part. Using the ZOOM command, ZOOM in on your drawing and include detail. ZOOM in and out on your drawing as necessary using the different ZOOM options (ACELPW). Be as creative as possible and have fun.

Unit 14 — Getting from Here to There

■ OBJECTIVE:

To apply the PAN and VIEW commands

How can you use a small monitor to develop large, complex drawings? Like most CAD systems, AutoCAD provides a means for moving around on large drawings so that you can add details. This unit illustrates and applies this method.

Note the degree of detail in the following architectural floor plan.

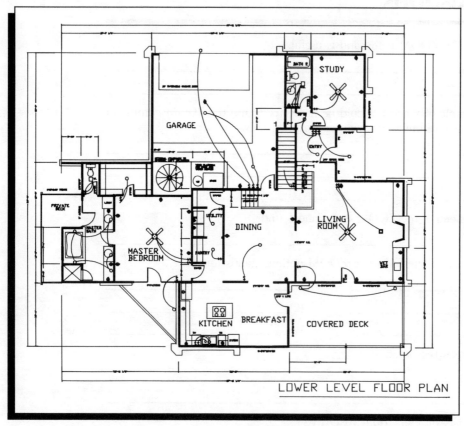

LOWER LEVEL FLOOR PLAN

AutoCAD Drawing Courtesy of Lansing Pugh, Architect

The drafter who completed this CAD drawing ZOOMed in on portions of the floor plan in order to put in details. For example, he ZOOMed in on the kitchen to draw details such as the kitchen cabinets and appliances.

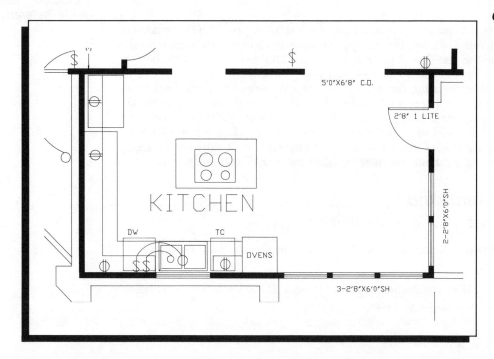

Now let's say the drafter wants to include details in an adjacent room but wants to keep the present ZOOM Factor (magnification). In other words, the drafter wants to simply "move over" to the adjacent room but retain the current display magnification. Is there an AutoCAD command that allows for this? Yes, and it's called PAN.

PAN Command _____

1 Load the drawing called **ZOOM**.

2 **ZOOM** in on the right third of the drawing. (Use the **Window** option.)

Let's PAN (move) to the left side of the drawing.

3 Enter the **PAN** command.   6.2

4 For Displacement, specify two points: the first point in the left portion of your screen, the second point in the right portion of your screen.

Did the drawing move to the right the distance you specified?

If not, try it again.

5 Experiment with the PAN command until you feel comfortable with it.

Now, wouldn't it be nice if you could somehow store or save ZOOM windows for later retrieval? Let's say, for example, you are working on an architectural floor plan like the one shown previously. You've ZOOMed in on the kitchen to include details such as the appliances, and now you're ready to PAN over to the utility room. Before leaving the kitchen, you foresee a need to come back to the kitchen later for final touches or revision. But, by the time you're ready to do this final work on the kitchen, you may be at a different ZOOM magnification and/or at the other end of your drawing. Is there a way of saving the kitchen view and a quick way of getting back to the kitchen from a different location and ZOOM magnification? Yes there is, using the VIEW command.

VIEW Command

Let's use the VIEW command with the ZOOM drawing.

6.3

1 **ZOOM** in on a portion of your ZOOM drawing, if you have not done so already.

2 Using the **VIEW** command, save your present ZOOM window by entering **S** (or **save**) and giving it a one-word name.

3 Now **PAN** to a new location.

4 Enter the **VIEW** command, and this time restore your previously named view by entering **R** (or **restore**) and the name of the view.

Did it work? If not, try again.

5 Practice using the VIEW command by ZOOMing and PANning to different locations on your drawing and saving views. Then restore those named views.

After storing several views, it is possible you may forget their names. Therefore, there must be a way of listing all named views. Let's do it.

1 Enter the **VIEW** command and then simply type a question mark (?) or select **listing** from the screen menu.

Did you receive a listing of all views? You should have. What other information was produced?

2 Return to the drawing by pressing the flip screen function key (usually **F1**).

3 **ZOOM A** to restore your drawing to its original size.

4 Enter **END** to save your named VIEWS and exit the Drawing Editor.

Questions

1. Explain why the PAN command is useful.

   _____

   _____

   _____

2. Explain why the VIEW command is useful.

   _____

   _____

   _____

3. How do you go about listing all of your named views?

   _____

   _____

4. What other information does the listing provide?

   _____

   _____

Draw each of the following shapes on your screen. Don't worry about their exact sizes and locations. ZOOM in on one of the shapes and store it as a View. Then PAN to each of the other shapes and store each as a View. Restore each named View and alter each shape by adding or erasing lines. Be as creative as you wish, and enjoy.

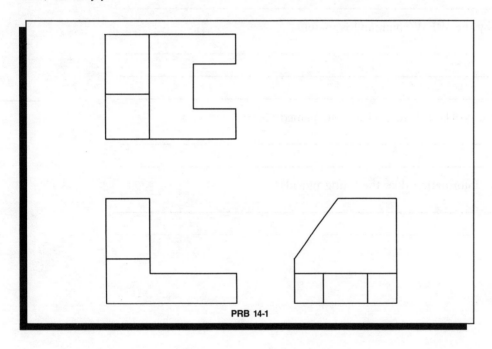

PRB 14-1

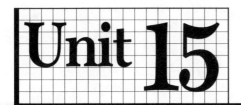

Unit 15

A Look at DOS Functions Inside AutoCAD

■ OBJECTIVE:

To use the File Utility Menu and the FILES and SHELL commands

When working in AutoCAD, there are times when you'd like to use certain DOS (Disk Operating System) functions such as DIRectory, REName, or COPY. This exercise gives you practice in using these functions.

The File Utility Menu _____

Unit 1 showed you how to start a file for a new drawing. By now, you have filed quite a number of drawings. Suppose you want to delete files, rename them, or simply see a list of what you've got. AutoCAD has a File Utility Menu which allows you to do these operations, and others too.

Let's work with it.

1 Load AutoCAD and bring up the Main Menu.

2 Select option 6, "File Utilities."

2.4.7

You should now have a new menu on your screen.

3.7

```
File Utility Menu

    0.   Exit File Utility Menu
    1.   List Drawing files
    2.   List user specified files
    3.   Delete files
    4.   Rename files
    5.   Copy file

Enter selection:
```

3 Select option 1, "List Drawing files," and press **RETURN**.

3.7.1

You will get a message like the following:

```
Enter drive or directory:
```

4 Press **RETURN** again.

You should get a listing of all the drawings stored on the default drive or directory. If your drawings reside on a drive or directory other than the default, select option 1 again, but this time specify the correct drive or directory. An example of a drive specification is shown on the next page.

B.1

```
Enter drive or directory: b:
```

Now let's produce a list of all files located on one of your drives or directories.

1 Press **RETURN** to bring back the File Utility Menu.

3.7.2

2 Select option **2**, "List user specified files."

3 Type *.* (the wild-card or global specification) and press **RETURN**.

NOTE:

See Appendix D for more information on the wild-card specification.

Did you get a list of all files located on the default drive? If not, try again.

Note that different types of files are listed. The type of file is indicated by the three-letter file extension following the period. For example, for a file named GASKET.DWG, "DWG" is the file type. Appendix D provides additional information on file extensions.

4 Experiment with each of the menu options, except for #3, "Delete files." Also, save option 0, "Exit File Utility Menu," until last. Option 0 will take you back to the Main Menu.

3.7.3
3.7.4
3.7.5

NOTE:

If you'd like to select each of the options, but don't want to actually perform each of them, simply cancel the operation by pressing **CTRL C**.

◼ *FILES Command* _____

Next, we're going to take a look at getting into the File Utility Menu while in the Drawing Editor.

3.7

1 Bring up the Drawing Editor by choosing option 1 or 2 from the Main Menu.

80

② Enter the **FILES** command.

Did you receive the same File Utility Menu as before?

③ Select **0**, "Exit File Utility Menu."

Where does this take you?

SHELL Command

There is another way of performing DOS functions while using AutoCAD. The command SHELL allows you to access DOS commands in addition to executing utility programs while remaining in AutoCAD. With SHELL, you can call up, for example, a word processor and create or edit a text file. Later, you may find this very useful when creating and editing screen and tablet menus and script files.

3.8

Let's use the SHELL command.

① First, obtain Help on the SHELL command.

HINT:

See Unit 5 if you are unsure how to obtain Help.

② Then, enter the **SHELL** command.

NOTE:

If you received an error message, then your computer does not contain sufficient free memory to run SHELL.

③ If you were successful in entering SHELL, then try the DOS **DIR**ectory command.

④ If you have access to another program such as a word processor like VOLKSWRITER® or a spreadsheet like LOTUS 1-2-3™ on your hard drive, then try bringing it up.

⑤ Return to the Drawing Editor by using **F1** (the flip screen function key).

⑥ Enter **QUIT** to exit the Drawing Editor.

Questions

1. What is the purpose of the File Utility Menu?

_____

_____

2. What is the purpose of the FILES command?

_____

_____

3. In what submenu is the FILES command found?

_____

4. Explain the purpose of the SHELL command.

_____

_____

5. Identify a practical application for using the SHELL command.

_____

_____

Problems

Using the above commands, complete the following.

1. Generate a list of all drawing files from each of your drives or directories.

2. Generate a list of all menu files found on each of your drives or directories.

HINT:
AutoCAD menu files have an extension of .MNU. Therefore enter *.MNU.

3. Generate a list of all AutoCAD drawing backup files.

HINT:
AutoCAD backup files have an extension of .BAK. Therefore enter *.BAK.

4. Rename one of your drawing files to a different name. Then change it back to its original name.

5. Delete the .BAK file from one of your drawing files.

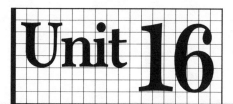

■ OBJECTIVE:

To apply the use of TEXT, STYLE, and QTEXT

This unit focuses on the placement of text using the TEXT command and on the creation of new Text styles using the STYLE command. The QTEXT command is practiced as a time-saving device during screen regenerations due to ZOOMs and PANs.

The following drawing shows the number of notes and specifications typical in many drawings. Some drawings, of course, contain many more.

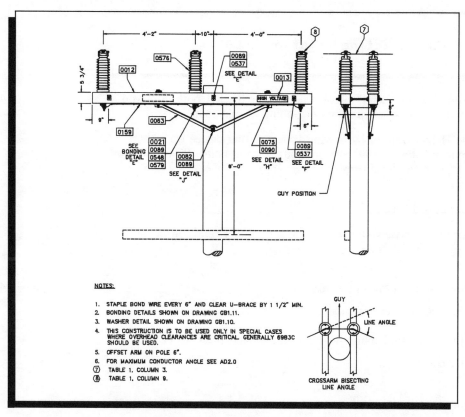

AutoCAD Drawing Courtesy of Russ Burns, Sacramento Municipal Utility District

As you can see, the text information is an important component in describing the drawing. With traditional drafting, the text would be placed by hand, consuming numerous hours of tedious work. With CAD, the words are placed on the screen almost as fast as you can type them.

NOTE:

If you are unable to carry out the following activities, the reason could be that the fonts have not yet been *compiled*. Before the standard text fonts available on AutoCAD can be used, they must be compiled using Main Menu task 7, "Compile shape/font description file." This process changes .SHP files to .SHX files which can be used in the Drawing Editor.

TEXT Command _____

1 Load AutoCAD and Begin a New Drawing. Name it **TEXT**.

2 Enter the **TEXT** command.   4.8

You should now have the following information on your screen.

```
TEXT Starting point or (ACRS):
```

---

3 In response to "Starting point" place a point near the left portion of your   4.8.1
screen. Your text will be left justified beginning at this point.

4 Reply to the Height prompt by moving your pointing device up a short
distance (approximately .25 units) from your starting point. Pick that point.
(You could type in the height instead.)

5 Rotate your text 0 degrees.

6 At the Text prompt, type your name using both upper- and lowercase
letters and press **RETURN**.

7 After entering the above, press the **space bar**.   4.8.5

You should again have the Text prompt.

8 Type your P.O. Box, rural route, or street address and press **RETURN**.

Where was it placed?

9 Press the **space bar** again and type your city, state, and zip code.

Now let's enter the same information you entered above, but this time in a
different format.

1 Repeat each of the above steps, but this time select the **C** (Center) option   4.8.2
from the list of TEXT options. Place the center point near the center of
your screen and set your Text height at .2 units. Do not rotate the text.

When you're finished, your text should have a format like the one on the next
page. If it doesn't, try again.

```
Mr. John Doe
601 West 29th Street
Caddsville, CA   09876
```

AutoCAD provides five Text fonts: TXT, SIMPLEX, COMPLEX, ITALIC, and VERTICAL. For samples of these fonts, see Appendix I. (Additional fonts can be created as described in Appendix B of the *AutoCAD User Guide*.)

4.9

You can vary the style of these fonts. AutoCAD lets you expand, condense, slant, and even draw them upside down or backwards. New Text styles are created using the STYLE command. Let's try it.

STYLE Command ———————————————

1 Enter the **STYLE** command and reply to each of the prompts using the following information.

4.9.1

Text style name:	**COMP**
Font file:	**COMPLEX**
Height:	**0** (not fixed; height can be varied)
Width factor:	**1**
Obliquing angle:	**0**
Backwards:	**N**
Upside-down:	**N**

When you're finished, you are ready to use the newly created COMP Text style with the TEXT command. Let's do it.

1 Enter the **TEXT** command and select the **S** (Style) option.

4.8.6

2 Type **COMP** for the Style name.

3 Right-justify the text by selecting **R** (Right) from the list of options. Place the endpoint near the right side of your screen.

4.8.3

4 Set the Height at **.3** units.

5 Set the Rotation angle at **0**.

6 For the Text, type the following three lines. Be sure to press the space bar after each.

```
┌─────────────────────────────────────┐
│                                      │
│      Computer-aided                  │
│   Design and Drafting                │
│           Saves Time                 │
│                                      │
└─────────────────────────────────────┘
```

Does yours look like the Text style above? It should.

HINT:

If you've made a spelling error, ERASE the entity (line of text) which contains the error and enter the correct text. You also can change the text or the Text style by using the CHANGE command.

Try creating other styles of your own design. With the STYLE command, you can develop an infinite number of Text styles. You can give them any name, up to thirty-one characters.

The Text styles you create remain within your current drawing file. They cannot be transported into other drawings unless the *entire* drawing containing the styles is inserted into the other drawings.

As you create more and more Text styles within your current drawing file, you may occasionally want to check their names. Let's try that now.

1 Enter the **STYLE** command.

2 In response to "Text style name (or ?):" enter **?**.   4.9.1

Did you receive a listing of all the Text styles available for your current drawing? What information is included about each style?

QTEXT Command

Now let's work with the QTEXT command.   6.7

1 Enter **QTEXT** and specify **On**.

2 Enter **ZOOM** and Zoom **All** or **Extents**.

What happened to your text?

3 Place more text on your screen.

Does it appear on your screen?

4 Force another regeneration of your screen by executing REGEN, ZOOM, or PAN.

What happened?

As you can see, QTEXT (short for Quick Text) replaces text with lines which form rectangles where your text once was. The purpose of this is to speed up screen regenerations when ZOOMing and PANning. As you may know, each text character is made up of many short lines. The greater the number of lines on your screen, the longer it takes to regenerate the screen. QTEXT reduces the total number of lines and consequently saves time, especially with heavy use of text.

5 Enter **QTEXT** again and specify **Off**.

6 Force another regeneration of your screen.

Neat, huh?

7 Lastly, enter **END** to save your work and exit the Drawing Editor.

AUTOCAD™ AT WORK

Drawing Cable TV Maps with AutoCAD

Recently Viacom Cablevision in San Francisco began using AutoCAD to redraw more than 180 maps showing the locations of the company's cables and subscribers. In addition, Viacom is using AutoCAD to inventory equipment and to update installment information.

Viacom saw several advantages in switching from hand-drawn maps to AutoCAD maps. First, AutoCAD allows the company to revise easily and often, and keeping accurate records on 95,000 viewers in the San Francisco area requires a versatile system.

Second, Viacom needed a system with layering capability so that streets and street names could be placed on one layer, while locations of utility poles and the distances between them were placed on another.

Finally, the company needed AutoCAD's text handling capabilities in order to insert text as well as lines and shapes on the company's maps. In this way the company can find out, for example, how many amplifiers are on a given street while looking at a drawing of the street.

Viacom's construction manager, Robert Gehring, is especially impressed with AutoCAD's usefulness in the cable TV industry: "If we were redrafting the maps by hand, we wouldn't be able to include nearly the level of detail that we need, nor would we be able to go back and revise the new maps with the ease we have now."

Equally impressive to Gehring is the quality of AutoCAD maps. "The lines are crisp, lettering and equipment symbols are consistent, and the customized maps are easily reproduced," says Gehring.

The changeover to AutoCAD hasn't been easy, for some of the maps are crazy quilts of assorted scales, lettering, and equipment designation systems. Gehring notes that it isn't uncommon to find a single piece of equipment represented by two or three different symbols on the old maps.

Although the transfer to AutoCAD is an enormous undertaking for Viacom, Gehring gives AutoCAD a glowing endorsement: "It's the best thing to hit drafting since the eraser."

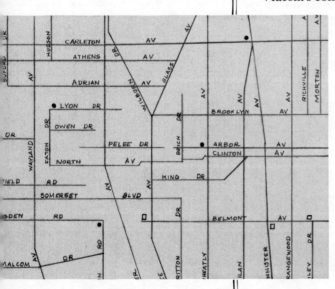

Questions

1. In connection with the TEXT command, what do the letters ACRS stand for?

   A _____   C _____

   R _____   S_____

2. Explain how the A option is used and when you would use it.

   _____

   _____

3. Explain how the S option is used.

   _____

   _____

4. Name the five different Text fonts provided by AutoCAD.

   _____

5. What command is used to create a new Text style?

   _____

6. How does turning on QTEXT speed up screen regenerations?

   _____

   _____

7. Briefly describe how you would create a tall and thin Text style.

   _____

   _____

Problems

In problems 1 and 2, create new Text styles using the information provided.

1. Style name: **SIMP**
   Font file: **SIMPLEX**
   Height: **.25** (fixed)
   Width factor: **1**
   Obliquing angle: **15**
   Backwards: **N**
   Upside-down: **N**

2. Style name: **ITAL**
   Font file: **ITALIC**
   Height: **0** (not fixed)
   Width factor: **.75**
   Obliquing angle: **0**
   Backwards: **N**
   Upside-down: **N**

In problems 3 and 4, place text on your screen using the information provided.

3. Use the SIMP Text style.
   Right-justify the text.
   Do not rotate the text.
   The text should read:

> Someday,
> perhaps in the near future,
> drafting boards
> will be obsolete.

PRB16-1

4. Use the ITAL Text style.
   Center the text.
   Set the text height at .3 units.
   Rotate the text 90 degrees.
   The text should read:

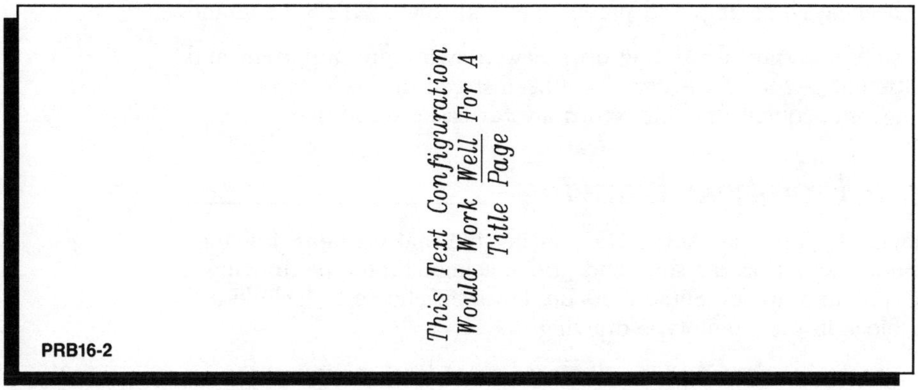

*This Text Configuration
Would Work Well For A
Title Page*

PRB16-2

HINT:
Check the *AutoCAD User Guide*, Section 4.8.7, for information about underscoring words.

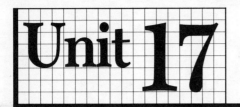

Unit 17   Preparing for a New Drawing

■ OBJECTIVE:

AutoCAD™ User Guide Reference

To apply and practice the use of UNITS, LIMITS, STATUS, and prototype drawings

The purpose of this exercise is to place a special focus on the process of setting up for new drawings. Considerations include: identifying the drawing, the scale, and the paper size; the drawing units and limits; setting the grid and snap resolution; and checking all settings and parameters with the STATUS command.

The first several steps necessary for setting up a new drawing are important and deserve special attention. Once these steps have been stored in the form of prototype drawings, subsequent drawing setups are far easier and faster.

■ *Setting Up a Prototype Drawing*——————

A prototype drawing is simply an AutoCAD drawing file that contains drawing settings and parameters such as the snap and grid spacings. Prototype drawings do not typically contain graphics. Some users do, however, choose to include a border and title block in their prototype drawing.

1.4.2
2.4.2
A.1

The purpose of a prototype drawing is to eliminate, or at least minimize, the need to establish new drawing settings each time you begin a new drawing.

Prototype drawing development includes the following steps. Note that the first three steps are common to traditional means of planning and setting up drawings.

- Determine what you are going to draw (e.g. mechanical detail, house elevation, etc.)
- Determine the drawing scale.
- Determine the paper size. (Steps 2 and 3 normally are done simultaneously.)
- Set the drawing units.
- Set the drawing limits.
- ZOOM All. This will zoom your entire limits.
- Set the snap resolution.
- Enter STATUS to review your settings.
- Establish several new layers with colors, linetypes, etc.
- Set linetype scale (LTSCALE).
- Create new Text styles.
- Set DIMSCALE, dimension text size, arrowhead size, etc.
- Store as a prototype drawing and/or proceed with drawing.

This unit and the next two will provide an opportunity to practice these steps in detail.

Let's get started.

1   Load AutoCAD and Begin a New Drawing. Name it PROTO1.

NOTE: ——————

> PROTO1 will be our first prototype drawing. Prototype drawings can have *any* name up to eight characters and are stored with a .DWG file extension. They can be used the same as any AutoCAD drawing file.

Now, let's decide on a specific drawing on which to base our prototype drawing development. How about a stair detail for a house or commercial building?

Next, we should determine the drawing scale. This information will give us a basis for setting our limits, linetype scale, and DIMSCALE later. Let's use a scale of 1/2″ = 1′.

We also need to decide on the paper size for our drawing. Let's use 17″ × 11″ paper.

Now, it's time to enter information into the computer.

2 Enter the **UNITS** command (contained in the Utility Submenu) and select choice 4, "Architectural."   3.6

3 Specify the following for each of the architectural unit options.

Denominator of smallest fraction to display: 8
Systems of angle measurement: choice 1
Number of fractional places for display of angles: 1

NOTE:

To see how the units specified affect the coordinate display, press the flip screen function key and then turn on the coordinate display. Move the pointing device and note how the status line changes.

Now it's time to set the drawing limits. The limits are a sized area or boundary for constructing your drawing, and they should correspond to both your drawing scale and paper size. (See Appendix K for a chart showing the relationships among paper size, drawing scale, and drawing limits.)

Please note that the scaling does not actually occur until you *plot* your drawing, but you have to plan for it. The limits and paper size can be adjusted up to the time that you plot the drawing.

4 Enter the **LIMITS** command.   3.5

5 Leave the lower left limit at 0,0. (To do this, simply press **RETURN**.)

The upper right limit should be based on the drawing scale and paper size.

Examples: if the paper size is 17″ x 11″, your active drawing and plotting area is approximately 15″ x 10″. If your drawing scale is 1″ = 1′, then the upper right limit should be set at 15′,10′. Why? Because 15″ horizontally on your paper will occupy 15′, and 10″ vertically on your paper will occupy 10′.

Let's try another one. If your drawing scale is 1/4″ = 1′, what would your upper right limit be? Since each plotted inch on your paper will occupy 4 scaled feet, it's a simple multiplication problem. Your upper right limit should be set at 60′,40′ because each plotted inch will represent 4′.

6 Since our scale is 1/2″ = 1′, set the upper right limit at 30′,20′.

NOTE:

When entering 30',20' type it exactly as you see it here; use an apostrophe for the foot mark. If you do not use a foot mark, the numbers default to inches.

7 **ZOOM All**. This zooms your entire limits to fill most of your display. The screen will then reflect your paper size, which corresponds to your limits.

8 Enter **GRID**, and set it at 1'.

NOTE:

The main purpose of setting your grid at this point is to give you a visual sense of size of your units and limits. The distance between each grid dot will represent 1'.

9 Move your crosshairs to the upper right corner of the grid.

Does the coordinate display read 30',20'?

10 Enter **SNAP**, and set it at 6".

Use the quote key for the inch mark if you wish. As stated earlier, if no mark is used, the number defaults to inches.

NOTE:

SNAP will provide for a 6" modular layout of your drawing components.

11 To review all of your settings, enter the **STATUS** command.   3.4

You should receive a screen similar to the following. Note each of the components found in STATUS.

```
                                         ┌──────────────────────┐      ┌──────────────────────────┐
                                         │ THIS COLUMN IS FOR   │      │ THIS COLUMN IS FOR UPPER │
                                         │ LOWER LEFT CORNER.   │      │ RIGHT CORNER.            │
                                         └──────────────────────┘      └──────────────────────────┘
Command:  STATUS         0  entities  in  PROTO1
Limits are              X:          0'-0"           30'-0"        (Off)
                        Y:          0'-0"           20'-0"

Drawing uses            X:          0'-0"            0'-0"
                        Y:          0'-0"            0'-0"

Display shows           X:          0'-0"       31'-7 5/8".   ┌──────────────────────────────┐
                        Y:          0'-0"           20'-0"    │ THESE NUMBERS MAY DIFFER     │
                                                              │ BECAUSE OF THE SIZE OF       │
                                                              │ YOUR MONITOR.                │
                                                              └──────────────────────────────┘

Insertion base is       X:          0'-0"    Y:    0'-0"    Z:     0'-0"
Snap resolution is      X:          0'-6"    Y:    0'-6"
Grid spacing is         X:          1'-0"    Y:    1'-0"

Current layer: 0
          Color: 7 (white)        Linetype: CONTINUOUS
Current elevation:      0'-0"      thickness:     0'-0"
Axis off  Fill on  Grid on  Ortho off  Qtext off  Snap on  Tablet off
Object snap modes: None
Free RAM: 28739 bytes   Free disk: 107520 bytes
I/O page space: 56K bytes
                                       ┌────────────────────────────┐
                                       │ THESE NUMBERS MAY DIFFER.  │
                                       └────────────────────────────┘
```

Our prototype drawing, PROTO1, now contains several settings and parameters specific to creating architectural drawings at a scale of 1/2" = 1' and is appropriate for use when beginning our stair detail drawing.

The next steps in preparing for a new drawing (or a prototype drawing) deal with establishing layers. Use of the the LAYER command will be practiced in the next unit.

12 For now, enter **END** to save all you have entered to this point and to exit to the Main Menu.

13 Produce a backup copy of your prototype drawing named PROTO1.DWG.

For details on producing copies of files, see Appendix D, "Commonly Used DOS Commands."

Backup copies are important because if you accidentally lose your original (and you will, sooner or later), you will have a backup. A backup can be produced in just a few seconds, and it can save you hours of lost work. An entire day's work can be lost in a few seconds—be prepared!

Questions

1. What is the purpose of prototype drawings?

_____

_____

2. What is the purpose of the UNITS command?

_____

_____

3. Explain the purpose of the LIMITS command.

_____

_____

4. Explain the importance of the STATUS command and describe the information displayed as a result of entering this command.

_____

_____

_____

_____

Problems

In problems PRB17-1 and PRB17-2, establish the settings for a new drawing based on the information provided. Set each of the commands as indicated.

PRB17-1. Drawing type: Mechanical drawing of a machine part

Scale: 1″ = 2″

Paper size: 17″ × 11″

UNITS: Engineering (You choose the appropriate options)

LIMITS: Lower left corner 0,0
Upper right corner 30″,20″

(Reminder: Be sure to ZOOM All)

GRID value: .5″

SNAP resolution: .25″

PRB17-2. Drawing type: Architectural drawing of a house and its lot (plotplan)

Scale: 1/8″ = 1′

Paper size: 24″ × 18″

UNITS: Architectural (You choose the appropriate options)

LIMITS: Lower left corner 0,0
          Upper right corner 184′,136′

(Reminder: Be sure to ZOOM All)

GRID value: 4′

SNAP resolution: 2′

In PRB 17-3 and PRB 17-4, fill in the missing data, based on the information provided.

PRB17-3. Drawing type: Architectural drawing of a detached garage

Approximate dimensions of garage: 32′ × 20′

Other considerations: Space around the garage for dimensions, notes, specs., border, and title block

Scale? _____

Paper size? _____

UNITS? _____

LIMITS? _____

GRID value? _____

SNAP resolution? _____

PRB17-4. Drawing type: Mechanical drawing of a bicycle pedal

Approximate dimensions of pedal: 4″ × 2.75″

Other considerations: Space around pedal for dimensions, notes, specs., border, and title block

Scale? _____

Paper size? _____

UNITS? _____

LIMITS? _____

GRID value? _____

SNAP resolution? _____

Unit 18 Layering Your Drawings

■ OBJECTIVE:

AutoCAD™ User Guide Reference

To apply the LAYER options of Color, Linetype, Freeze, and Thaw and to practice setting linetype scale

This unit focuses on AutoCAD's layering capability. It covers the following layer-related topics: creating layers; setting the current layer; assigning colors and linetypes to layers; turning layers on and off; freezing and thawing layers; and setting the linetype scale.

7.1

_____ NOTE: _____

Be sure to make a backup copy of PROTO1.DWG if you have not already done so. Instructions for making backup copies are in Appendix D.

This unit will let you practice creating the following layers:

Layer name	State	Color	Linetype
Ø	On	7 (white)	CONTINUOUS
OBJ	On	1 (red)	CONTINUOUS
HID	On	2 (yellow)	HIDDEN
DIM	On	3 (green)	CONTINUOUS
CEN	On	2 (yellow)	CENTER
PHANT	On	5 (blue)	PHANTOM
BORD	On	4 (cyan)	CONTINUOUS

■ *Creating New Layers* _____

1 Load AutoCAD and bring up the drawing called **PROTO1**.

2 Select **LAYERS** from the Root Menu.

3 Then enter the **LAYER** command.

7.7

You should now have the following information after the "Command:" prompt.

```
Command: LAYER ?/Set/New/On/Off/Color/Ltype/Freeze/Thaw:
```

First, let's create the layer called OBJ.

4 After the list of layer options, type **N** and press **RETURN** (or select **new** from the screen menu).

7.7.4

AutoCAD will ask you for the new layer name(s).

5 Type the name **OBJ** (short for object), and press **RETURN**.

The layer options should again be in the prompt line.

6 Do a layer listing by typing **?** or selecting **listing** from the screen menu. Press **RETURN** to do a listing of all layers.

7.7.2

Your listing should look similar to the following.

Layer name	State	Color	Linetype
0	On	7 (white)	CONTINUOUS
OBJ	On	7 (white)	CONTINUOUS

A fast way to create the other five layers is to do it in one step. Let's try it.

7 Enter the **New** option again.

8 This time, type each of the layer names separated by a comma as shown below.

```
New layer name(s): HID,DIM,CEN,PHANT,BORD
```

9 Do another layer listing to see if the layers were created.

Changing the Current Layer

Let's change your current layer from layer 0 to layer OBJ.

1 Enter the LAYER **Set** option and type the layer name **OBJ**. Press **RETURN** twice.

7.7.3

Did the change occur? Look at the beginning of the status line in the Drawing Editor. It should read: Layer OBJ. If it doesn't, try making the change again.

Assigning Colors

Now, let's assign colors to our new layers. We'll begin by assigning color 1 (red) to layer OBJ.

7.1.2

1 Enter the LAYER Color option by typing **C** and pressing **RETURN** or by picking it from the screen menu. Specify color **1** (and **RETURN**) and layer **OBJ** (and **RETURN**).

7.7.7

2 Did the change occur? Do a listing of layers to check whether color 1 is now assigned to layer OBJ.

NOTE:

> Even though you may be using a computer with a monochrome monitor, it is important to practice assigning colors to layers. Colors are directly associated with plotter pens. The colors, therefore, control the layer and pen color/thickness relationship.

---

3 Assign colors to the other layers as indicated in the layer listing at the beginning of this unit.

Drawing on Layers

Now let's draw simple objects on our newly created layers.

1 Draw a circle (at any size) on your current layer OBJ.

2 Set layer HID.

3 Draw a relatively large triangle on layer HID.

Turning Layers On and Off

1 Now turn off layer OBJ by entering **LAYER**, then **Off**, and typing **OBJ**. Press **RETURN** twice.

                    7.7.5

What happened?

2 Do a layer listing.

What changed?

3 Turn on layer OBJ by entering **LAYER**, then **On**, and typing **OBJ**. Press **RETURN** twice.

                    7.7.6

What happened?

Neat huh?

Assigning Linetypes and Setting Linetype Scale

Next, let's take a look at the different linetypes AutoCAD makes available to us.

1 To obtain a listing of linetypes, enter the **LINETYPE** command and then enter the **?** option. Press **RETURN** in reply to "File to list <ACAD>:".

                    7.8

You should get the following on your screen.

NAME	SAMPLE
Dashed	— — — — — — — — —
Hidden	————————————
Center	—— — —— — —— — ——
Phantom	—— — — —— — — ——
Dot	··································
Dashdot	—·—·—·—·—·—·—·
Border	—— —·—— —·—— —·
Divide	—· —· —· —· —·

Courtesy of Autodesk Inc.

2 Press the flip screen function key to return to the previous screen. Enter the **LAYER** command.

3 Enter the **Ltype** option.   7.7.8

4 Enter the linetype called **hidden** and assign it to layer **HID**. Press **RETURN** twice.

Did the triangle on layer HID change from a continuous line to a hidden line? It should, but don't be surprised if it didn't.

5 Do a layer listing to see if the linetype change did in fact occur.

If the linetype change did occur, but the triangle appears as though it did not change, the linetype scale (LTSCALE) needs to be set. Regardless, LTSCALE should be set according to the following steps.   7.9

6 Enter the **LTSCALE** command.

Now let's scale your linetypes to correspond to your drawing scale.

7 Set the linetype scale at 1/2 the reciprocal of the plot scale. By doing this, your broken lines, such as hidden and center lines, will be plotted similar to ANSI standards.

HINT:

Since our drawing scale is 1/2″ = 1′, the plot scale is 1″ = 2′, or 1″ = 24″. The reciprocal of 1/24 is 24, and 1/2 of 24 is 12. Therefore, in this particular case, you would set the LTSCALE at 12.

8 Now view the triangle. Is it made up of hidden lines?

9 If you're not sure, **ZOOM** in on it.

10 Next, assign the center linetype to layer CEN and the phantom linetype to layer PHANT.

11 Do a layer listing to view the changes.

Freezing and Thawing Layers _____

1 Select the **LAYER** command once again.

2 Choose the freeze option by typing **F**, or select **freeze** from the screen menu.   7.7.9

3 Freeze layer **OBJ** and press **RETURN** twice.

What happens?

4 Do a layer listing and note the change.

5 Thaw layer OBJ by entering **Thaw** and typing **OBJ**. Press **RETURN** twice.   7.7.1

Did the circle return? As you can see, freezing and thawing layers is similar to turning them off and on. The difference is that AutoCAD will regenerate a drawing faster if the unneeded layers are frozen rather than turned off. Please note: You cannot freeze the current layer.

6 Lastly, **ERASE** both the circle and the triangle. Set layer OBJ.

7 Enter **END** to save your work in PROTO1 and exit from the Drawing Editor.

The prototype drawing preparation is nearly complete. The last few steps typically involve creation of new Text styles and setting the dimensioning variables and DIMSCALE. Each will be covered in a subsequent unit.

The prototype drawing concept may lack meaning to you until you have actually applied it. Therefore let's begin a new drawing using our prototype drawing PROTO1.

1 While in the Main Menu, begin a new drawing and name it STAIRD=PROTO1.

2 After you arrive at the Drawing Editor, enter **STATUS** and note each of the drawing settings, parameters, layers, etc.

Do they look familiar? They should.

3 Enter **END** to save and exit the new drawing called STAIRD.

NOTE:

Since the contents of PROTO1 were loaded into STAIRD at the beginning, there is no need to specify PROTO1 when editing STAIRD. In other words, prototype drawings are used only when you begin a new drawing.

PROTO1 is also available for the creation of other new drawings, saving you lots of time when beginning new drawings.

AUTOCAD™ AT WORK

Illustrating Books with AutoCAD

Before George Omura began using AutoCAD, he made book illustrations with India ink or colored drawing pens. The work was time-consuming, and sometimes Omura had to throw away a drawing after hours of painstaking work because of an error or spilled ink.

Since Omura began using AutoCAD, however, he doesn't have to worry about such things. Any errors he makes can be corrected quickly and easily.

Easy revision is only one of the AutoCAD features that George finds useful. Other features Omura relies on are his library of frequently used shapes and objects, the zoom feature, and the layering feature, which he uses to experiment with color.

Currently Omura works mostly as an illustrator for technical manuals and textbooks. But because AutoCAD is so efficient and flexible, Omura is interested in taking on more graphic design projects, such as letterheads, logos, and brochures for individuals and small businesses. "AutoCAD takes the dreariness out of drafting work, allowing me to concentrate on the creative part," he says happily.

Questions

1. Explain the purpose of layers.

   _____

   _____

2. Briefly describe the meaning of each of the following layer options.

   ? _____

   Set _____

   New _____

   On _____

   Off _____

   Color _____

   Ltype _____

   Freeze _____

   Thaw _____

3. How do you change the current layer?

   _____

   _____

4. Describe the purpose of the LTSCALE command and explain how it is set.

   _____

   _____

   _____

5. Why/when would you want to freeze a layer?

   _____

   _____

6. Name each of the linetype options available.

   _____

   _____

Problems

Create the following sets of layers with corresponding settings.

Layer name	State	Color	Linetype
Ø	Off	7 (white)	CONTINUOUS
OBJ	On	1 (red)	CONTINUOUS
HID	On	2 (yellow)	HIDDEN
DIM	On	3 (green)	CONTINUOUS
CEN	On	2 (yellow)	CENTER
PHANT	On	5 (blue)	PHANTOM
BORD	On	4 (cyan)	CONTINUOUS
TEXT	Frozen	8	CONTINUOUS

Current layer: OBJ

PRB18-1

Layer name	State	Color	Linetype
Ø	On	7 (white)	CONTINUOUS
FOUND	On	6 (magenta)	DASHED
WALLS	On	1 (red)	CONTINUOUS
ELECT	On	4 (cyan)	CONTINUOUS
PLUMB	Frozen	7 (white)	CONTINUOUS
DIM	On	2 (yellow)	CONTINUOUS
TITLE	Frozen	3 (green)	CONTINUOUS
HID	On	5 (blue)	HIDDEN
CEN	Off	5 (blue)	CENTER
NOTES	On	2 (yellow)	CONTINUOUS

Current layer: ELECT

PRB18-2

Unit 19 Dimensioning

■ **OBJECTIVE:**

AutoCAD™ User Guide Reference

To apply AutoCAD's dimensioning capabilities

One of AutoCAD's powerful features is its capability to do semiautomatic dimensioning. This unit covers the different types of dimensioning, including linear, angular, diameter, and radius dimensioning. Attention is also given to the dimensioning variables and dimensioning utilities.

10.1.1

AutoCAD's dimensioning capability uses numerous subcommands, utility commands, dimensioning variables, and dimensioning terms. Even though all of this may seem quite complex, it isn't. It's really very simple, and it's fun, too!

Let's begin.

Checking the Status of the Dimensioning Variables

1 Load AutoCAD and Begin a New Drawing. Name it **DIMEN**.

Before we begin dimensioning, let's preview the *dimensioning variables*.

10.1.8

2 Select **DIM** from the Root Menu.

You should now have the Dimensioning Submenu on the screen, and the "Dim:" prompt at the bottom rather than the usual "Command:" prompt.

NOTE:

> You must always have the "Dim:" prompt at the bottom of your screen instead of the "Command:" prompt when dimensioning.

3 Select **STATUS** from the Dimensioning Submenu to obtain the current status of the dimensioning variables.

You should receive a list similar to the one on the next page.

```
Dim: status

DIMSCALE     1.0000          Overall scale factor
DIMASZ       0.1800          Arrow size
DIMCEN       0.0900          Center mark size
DIMEXO       0.0625          Extension line origin offset
DIMDLI       0.3800          Dimension line increment for continuation
DIMEXE       0.1800          Extension above dimension line
DIMTP        0.0000          Plus tolerance
DIMTM        0.0000          Minus tolerance
DIMTXT       0.1800          Text height
DIMTSZ       0.0000          Tick size
DIMTOL       Off             Generate dimension tolerances
DIMLIM       Off             Generate dimension limits
DIMTIH       On              Text inside extensions is horizontal
DIMTOH       On              Text outside extensions is horizontal
DIMSE1       Off             Suppress the first extension line
DIMSE2       Off             Suppress the second extension line
DIMTAD       Off             Place text above the dimension line
```

Note each of the dimensioning variables, their current settings, and their brief definitions.

We will work with a few of these variables shortly. But first, let's dimension the object below.

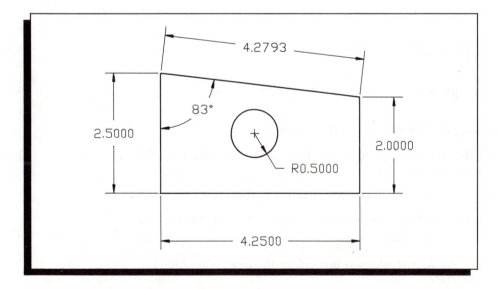

Preparing to Dimension _____

Before we can dimension this object, we need to prepare a few drawing settings and parameters and then draw the object.

1   If you still have the "Dim:" prompt, restore the "Command:" prompt by entering **EXIT.**

2   Create two new layers using the LAYER command. Call one of them **OBJ** and the other **DIM.**

3   Set layer OBJ.

NOTE: _____

> You should place the object lines on layer OBJ and your dimensions on layer DIM.

4   Set your Snap at **.25** units.

5   Draw the object, omitting dimensions at this point. Don't worry about the exact location of the circle.

After your have drawn the object, let's dimension it.

Dimensioning Horizontal Lines _____

1   Set layer DIM.

2   Select **DIM** from the Root Menu.   10.1.2

3   Select the **Linear** option from the screen menu.   10.1.3

4   Then select the **Horizontal** (HORIZ) option.

5   Specify the first extension line origin by picking one of the endpoints of the object's horizontal line.   10.1.3.1

HINT: _____

> The Object Snap feature is sometimes useful when dimensioning.

6   Then pick the second extension line origin (the other end of the horizontal line).

7   Use your pointing device to locate the dimension line approximately 1 unit away from the object.   10.1.3.3

8 For the dimension text, simply press **RETURN**.

Did the dimension come up correctly? If not, use the Undo option found in the Dimensioning Submenu to erase your last dimension, and try it again.

9 Enter **REDRAW** to clean up your construction points.

10 **ZOOM** in on the dimension to examine its detail, and then **ZOOM All**.

Dimensioning Vertical Lines _____

Now, let's dimension the vertical lines in the object. Start with either line.

1 Enter **DIM** to receive the "Dim:" prompt.

2 Select the **Linear** option, and then select the **Vertical** option from the submenu.

3 Select the first and second extension line origins as you did before.

4 Specify the placement of your dimension line as you did before, and press **RETURN** at the dimension text prompt.

Did it come up correctly on your screen?

Let's dimension the other vertical line, but this time let's do it a faster and easier way.

1 Select the **Vertical** option again.

2 This time when the prompt line asks for the first extension line origin, press **RETURN**.

10.1.3.2

3 Now simply touch the vertical line by picking any point on the line.

What happened?

4 Proceed with the next two steps as you did before until the dimension appears on the screen.

Neat, huh?

Dimensioning Inclined Lines _____

Lastly, let's dimension the inclined line by "aligning" the dimension to the line.

1 Again use the **Linear** option, but this time choose **Aligned** from the submenu.

2 Proceed exactly as you did with the last dimension until the aligned dimension appears on the screen.

If it appears to be correct on your screen, then you did it right. GOOD JOB!

Dimensioning Circles _____

Now let's dimension the circle.

1 Select the **Radius** option.   10.1.6

2 Next, pick the circle at the point where the arrow touches it in the drawing on page 107.

3 Press **RETURN** for the dimension text.

4 Specify a short leader length, and locate it down and to the right as shown in the drawing.

Did the dimension appear?

Dimensioning Angles _____

Lastly, let's dimension the angle as shown in the drawing.

1 Choose **Angular** from the screen menu.   10.1.4

2 Pick both lines which make up the angle.

3 Pick any convenient location for the dimension arc.

4 Press **RETURN** for the dimension text.

5 Specify where you'd like the text to appear.

Did it appear? It should have.

Additional Practice

Now let's draw and dimension something a bit more sophisticated—the drawing below.

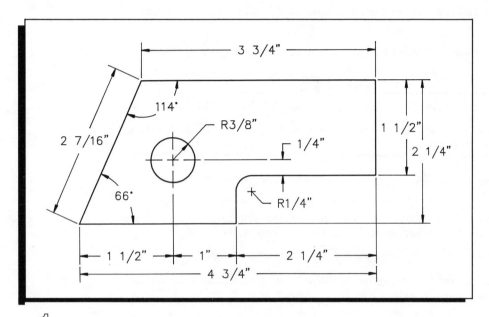

1. First, erase your screen using **ERASE Window**.

2. Establish the following drawing settings and parameters so that the drawing will be more meaningful.

   UNITS: Architectural or Engineering (your choice)
   Scale: 1″ = 1″
   Paper Size: 11″ x 8 1/2″
   LIMITS: Lower left corner 0,0
            Upper right corner 10″,7″
   GRID: 1″
   (Reminder: Be sure to ZOOM All)
   SNAP resolution: .25″
   LAYERs: Name   Color
              OBJ   1
              DIM   2

After setting all of the above, it is necessary to scale the dimensions, using DIMSCALE, to properly fit the dimensions to the drawing. In addition, if you need to make changes to other dimensioning variables, such as the text height, it is important you do it prior to dimensioning.

Let's again review all dimensioning variables by obtaining a DIM STATUS listing.

1. Select **STATUS** from the **DIM** Submenu to get the listing.

Let's set both the dimension text and arrowhead size to 1/8″ (.125″).

2 Select **DIM VARS** and then **DIMASZ** (short for Dimension Arrow Size) from the screen menu. Change it to 1/8″ or .125″.

3 Select **DIMTXT** (short for Dimension Text), and enter 1/8″ or .125″.

4 Next, select **DIMSCALE**. Set it at the reciprocal of your plot scale.

NOTE:

What's your plot scale? 1″=1″. You're lucky; you get to leave DIMSCALE at 1.

What if your plot scale were 1″=120″? What would your DIMSCALE setting be . . . 120, perhaps?

Now let's focus on the Text style to be used in the dimensions.

The Text style used most recently in your drawing will be the one used for the dimensioning text. Therefore, if you have not created and used a new Text style, you will get the default Text style, STANDARD, when dimensioning.

Let's create and use a new Text style for the dimensioning text.

1 Create a Text style using the SIMPLEX text font. Name it SIMP, and do not make the style height fixed; leave it at 0.

2 After creating it, use it at least once. Then erase the text (or leave it as a title for the drawing).

Now the SIMP Text style will be the default style when dimensioning the drawing.

3 Create and dimension the drawing shown on page 111. Be sure to place the object lines on layer OBJ and the dimensions on layer DIM.

NOTE:

For best results, begin at the lower left corner of the object and draw the object in a counterclockwise direction.

Also, when creating the horizontal string of dimensions in the drawing, use the DIM Continue (CONTINU) option found in the DIM Submenu. First, enter either the left- or rightmost dimension by selecting the first and second extension line origins and completing the dimension. Then select the Continue option. At this point, you can simply select the next extension line origin to produce an adjacent dimension. Select the Continue option again to finish the continuous string of dimensions.

HAVE FUN AND GOOD LUCK!

4 If you know how to operate your plotter, plot the drawing using a thick pen (*e.g.*, .7 mm) for color 1 and a thin pen (*e.g.*, .3 mm) for color 2.

5 Be sure to **END** to save your work and exit the Drawing Editor.

AUTOCAD™ AT WORK

Designing Circuit Boards

Before a new computer or printer reaches the market, it must undergo strenuous tests to make sure it is reliable and durable. One way that companies test key computer components, such as transistors and integrated circuits, is with printed circuit boards.

Until recently designers of printed circuit boards had to design each board by hand, a time-consuming task that often created a backlog of overdue deliveries. By using AutoCAD, some designers have reduced the time it takes to design a circuit board from ten days to one.

Requirements for each project vary, and circuit boards must be individually designed and built to exacting specifications. However, because most of the custom boards begin with one of seven or eight basic designs, these basic designs can be stored in AutoCAD and called up whenever a new board is needed.

Another crucial requirement for circuit board design is pinpoint accuracy. AutoCAD promotes accuracy in two ways: It eliminates the human error that can result from people doing repetitive tasks; and it uses master drawings stored in AutoCAD for basic designs that can be modified easily.

By using AutoCAD, circuit board designers increase productivity, improve on accuracy, and save time. According to the president of one circuit board design firm, AutoCAD's time-saving ability impresses clients as well as designers. "We had a hot client who wanted ten boards in two weeks, and he didn't believe we could do it. We had them in his hands in eight days."

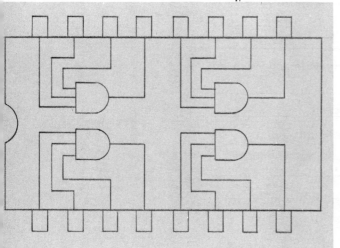

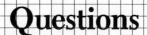

Questions

1. Describe the alternative to specifying both endpoints of a line when dimensioning a line.

   _____

   _____

2. Why is it important to place dimensions on one layer and object lines on another layer?

   _____

   _____

3. Explain how to specify a Text style to be used when dimensioning.

   _____

   _____

4. What is the purpose of the DIM VARS (Dimensioning Variables)?

   _____

   _____

5. How do you determine the DIMSCALE setting?

   _____

6. Explain the difference between AutoCAD's center marks and center lines, and describe how to generate each. Hint: Refer to the *User Guide*, Section 10.1.1.

   _____

   _____

   _____

7. Explain the use of the Continue option found in the Dimensioning Submenu.

   _____

   _____

8. Describe the purpose of the UNDO Utility command found in the Dimensioning Submenu.

   _____

   _____

Problems

Begin a New Drawing and establish the following drawing settings and parameters. Store as a prototype drawing. (You could name it PROTO2.) Then do each of the following dimensioning problems using the prototype drawing.

UNITS: Engineering

Scale: 1"=10' (or 1"=120")

Paper Size: 17"×11"

LIMITS: Lower left corner 0,0
           Upper right corner 150',100'

GRID: 10'

(Reminder: Be sure to ZOOM All)

SNAP resolution: 2'

LAYERs:
Name	Color
Thick	1
Thin	2

Text: Create a new Text style using the **SIMPLEX** font. Do not make the style height fixed; leave it at 0. Use the new style once prior to dimensioning the drawing so that it will become the default style.

DIMASZ: .125

DIMTXT: .125

DIMSCALE: 120

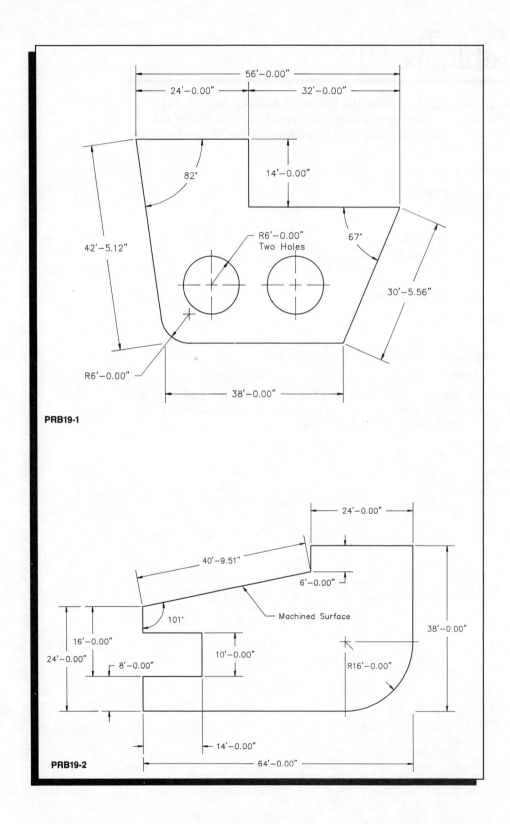

PRB19-1

PRB19-2

Unit 20 Drawing Thick Lines and Solid Objects

■ **OBJECTIVE:**

To apply TRACE, SOLID, and FILL

This exercise focuses on how thick lines and solid objects are produced in drawings such as house elevations.

Note the thick lines and solid polygons in the following drawing.

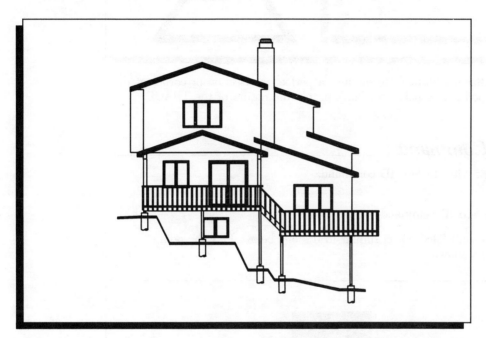

AutoCAD Drawing Courtesy of Hyland Design, Tim Smith

The AutoCAD SOLID and TRACE commands were used to create the thick lines and solid filled areas. Let's draw similar lines and solid objects.

*TRACE Command*_____

1 Load AutoCAD and Begin a New Drawing. Call it **TRACE**.

2 Enter the **TRACE** command.

4.5

The TRACE command is used very much like the LINE command, except TRACE requires you to enter a trace width in units.

3 Specify a TRACE width of **.1** and draw the figures on the next page. Don't worry about exact sizes.

117

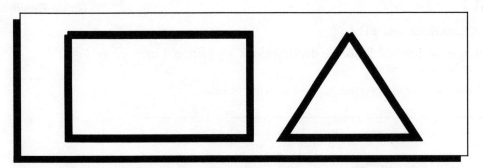

You'll notice that it is difficult to produce a perfect intersection or corner at the first and last points of a polygon. That's simply the nature of the TRACE command.

SOLID Command

Now let's work with the SOLID command.

1 Enter the **SOLID** command.

4.7

2 Produce a solid filled object similar to the one below. Pick the points in the order shown.

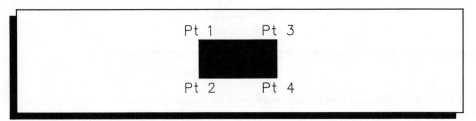

3 Experiment with the SOLID command. What happens if you pick the points in a different order? Try picking five points, six points, etc.

4 Leave your drawings on the screen so that you can practice the FILL command.

FILL Command

The FILL command works in conjunction with the TRACE, SOLID, and PLINE commands. FILL is either turned on or off. When FILL is off, only the outline of a Trace, Solid, or Polyline is represented. This saves time whenever the screen is regenerated. Let's actually see the difference between FILL On and FILL Off.

6.6

1 Enter the **FILL** command, and then turn it off simply by typing **OFF**. Or, select **FILL OFF** from the screen menu.

NOTE:

Each time after turning the FILL on or off, a regeneration of the screen must occur before the change will take place...

2 ... therefore enter the **REGEN** command.

What happened?

3 Reenter the **FILL** command and turn it on...

4 ...and again enter the **REGEN** command to force a screen regeneration.

NOTE:

Remember, REGEN, unlike REDRAW, repaints the screen while calculating each of the lines (vectors) contained in the drawing. This can take some time, especially with large, sophisticated drawings. The REDRAW command does not calculate each of the points in the drawing and that is why a REDRAW takes less time than a REGEN.

5 Enter END to save your drawing and exit to the Main Menu.

Questions

1. In what screen submenu are both the TRACE and SOLID commands found?

2. The FILL command is used in conjunction with both TRACE and SOLID. What is its purpose and how is it used?

3. What might be a limitation of using the TRACE command?

4. How would you draw a triangle using the SOLID command?

5. Can you draw curved objects using the SOLID command?

Problems

1. Construct PRB20-1 using the TRACE and SOLID commands. Specify a TRACE width of .05 units. Don't worry about the exact size and shape of the roof.

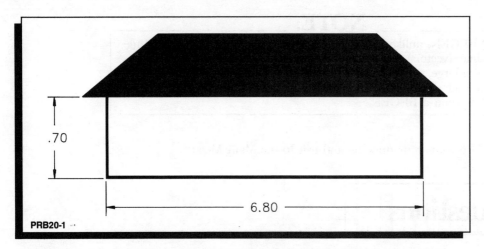

.70

6.80

PRB20-1

2. After you have completed PRB20-1, place the solid shapes as indicated below. Don't worry about their exact sizes and locations.

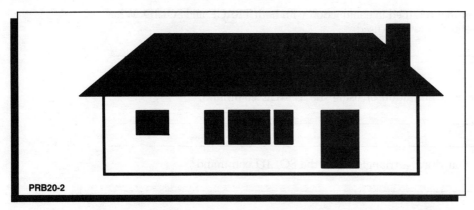

PRB20-2

3. Are the TRACE and SOLID commands entities like the LINE, CIRCLE, and ARC commands? To find out, try erasing a small piece of the roof in PRB20-1. What is your conclusion?

_____

_____

Unit 21 — Combining Straight, Curved, and Solid Objects

■ OBJECTIVE:

To apply Polylines using PLINE and PEDIT

The following unit deals with Polylines and the use of the PLINE and PEDIT commands. Each of these commands contains numerous options, which also are covered in this unit.

A Polyline is a connected sequence of line and arc segments. It is treated by AutoCAD as a single entity. Polylines are often used in lieu of conventional lines and arcs because they are more versatile during creation and editing. The examples below illustrate some uses of Polylines.

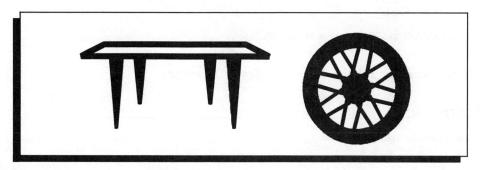

PLINE Command

Let's try creating a simple Polyline, such as the one below, using the PLINE command.

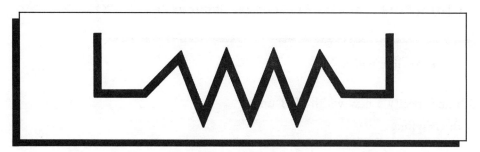

1. Load AutoCAD and Begin a New Drawing. Name it **POLY**.

2. Enter the **PLINE** command and specify a starting point. At this time, simply place it at any convenient spot on your screen. 4.6

You should now have the following PLINE options on your screen. 4.6.1

```
Arc/Close/Halfwidth/Length/Undo/Width/<Endpoint of line>:
```

3. Enter **Width** and give a starting and ending width of **.15** units.

4 Now simply draw the object by specifying endpoints. Don't worry about exact sizes and placement of the endpoints. Press **RETURN** when you're finished.

HINT:
If you make a mistake, use the Undo option.

5 When you are finished, enter the **ERASE** command and pick any point on the Polyline or enter **Last**.

Note that the entire object is treated as a single entity.

6 Enter **OOPS** to restore the Polyline if you completed the erasure.

PEDIT Command

Now let's edit the Polyline using PEDIT.

1 Enter the **PEDIT** command and select the Polyline you just drew.

5.2.12

You should now have the following PEDIT command options on your screen.

```
Close/Join/Width/Edit vertex/Fit curve/Uncurve/eXit <X>:
```

First, let's change the Polyline width.

2 Enter **Width** and specify a new width of **.1** unit.

Now, let's close the Polyline.

3 Enter **Close**.

Let's now do a simple curve fitting operation.

4 Enter the **Fit curve** option.

How did the drawing change?

5 Enter **Uncurve** to bring it back to its previous form.

Next, let's move one of the object's vertices as shown on the next page.

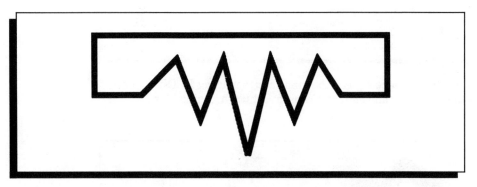

1 Enter the **Edit vertex** option and move the "X" to the vertex you want to change by pressing **RETURN** several times.

5.2.12.1

2 Select **Move** from the list of options and specify a new vertex location.

Did it work? If not, try it again.

Note that there are many more features contained within PEDIT and PLINE. Experiment with each of these on your own.

Questions

1. Briefly define a Polyline.

   _____

2. Briefly describe each of the following PLINE options.

   Arc _____

   Close _____

   Halfwidth _____

   Length _____

   Undo _____

   Width _____

3. Briefly describe each of the PEDIT command options.

   Close _____

   Join _____

   Width _____

   Edit vertex _____

   Fit curve _____

   Uncurve _____

   eXit _____

Problems

1. Create the approximate shape of the following racetrack using PLINE. Specify .4 units for both the starting and ending widths. Select the Arc option for drawing the figure.

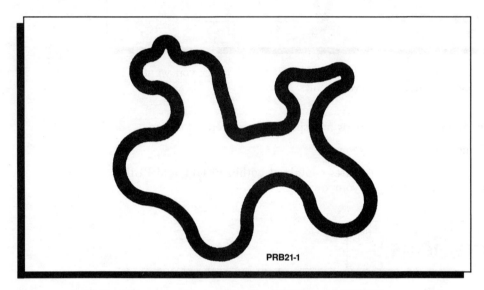

PRB21-1

Draw each of the following objects using the PLINE and PEDIT commands.

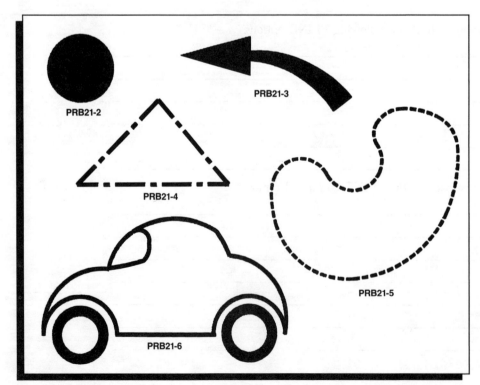

PRB21-2

PRB21-3

PRB21-4

PRB21-5

PRB21-6

Unit 22 — A Calculating Strategy

■ OBJECTIVE:

To apply the ID, DIST, AREA, LIST, and DBLIST commands

This unit focuses on AutoCAD commands that allow you to perform a variety of calculations on your drawings. In addition, it covers the AutoCAD commands that display hidden (but important) data about specific components within your drawing.

The drawing below is an apartment complex with surroundings, including parking lots, streets, and trees. When constructing a drawing such as this, you may want to perform certain calculations on the drawing, such as determining the square footage of the parking lot or the distance between the parking stalls.

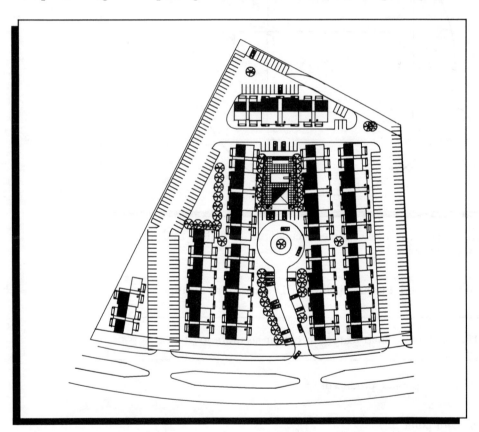

AutoCAD Drawing Courtesy of Buday-Wells, Architects

Let's bring up AutoCAD and practice these functions.

ID, DIST, and AREA Commands _____

1 Load AutoCAD and Begin a New Drawing called **CALC.**

② Draw a rectangle with a circle around it at the sizes shown below. Omit the numbers and dimensions; don't worry about the exact placement of the circle in relation to the rectangle.

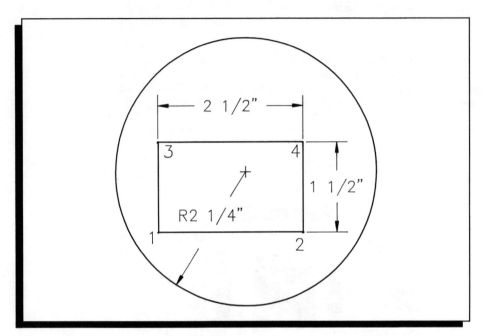

Now we're ready to perform a few simple calculations. First, let's find the absolute coordinates of point 1.

③ Enter the **ID** command and pick point 1. (ID stands for "identify.")

5.3.4

HINT:

Use the Object Snap feature to obtain accurate locations.

Were the coordinates of point 1 produced?

④ Try it again with point 2.

⑤ Enter the **DIST** command and obtain the distance between points 1 and 2 by simply picking point 1 and point 2. Again, use Object Snap to obtain accurate locations.

5.3.3

What is the distance between points 1 and 2?

⑥ Enter the **AREA** command and calculate the area of the rectangle by picking each of its corners. Be sure to end where you started. Press **RETURN** or the **space bar** when you've picked all the points.

5.3.5

What is the area of the rectangle? What is its perimeter?

LIST and DBLIST Commands _____

Now let's find the area of the circle. Will the AREA command work? No,
AREA works only with polygons.

1 Enter the **LIST** command and pick any point on the circle.
Press **RETURN**.

5.3.1

What is the area of the circle? What other information did you receive?

2 Enter **LIST** again, but this time pick the line between points 1 and 2.

What information did you receive?

3 Lastly, enter **DBLIST** and watch what you get.

5.3.2

_____ NOTE: _____

Use **CTRL S** to stop the scrolling; hit any key to resume scrolling.

Questions

1. What AutoCAD command is used to find coordinate points while in the Drawing
   Editor?

   _____

2. With what command do you calculate the area of circles?

   _____

3. What information is produced with the AREA command?

   _____

4. What information is produced with the LIST command?

   _____

   _____

5. Describe the difference between LIST and DBLIST.

   _____

   _____

6. How do you stop the scrolling of information when executing DBLIST?

   _____

7. How do you calculate the perimeter of a polygon?

   _____

8. How do you find the circumference of a circle?

   _____

Problems

Draw the objects found in each of the following problems at any convenient size, omitting all letters. Then perform each of the inquiry commands found next to the objects. Write their values in the blanks provided.

1. ID of point A?_____

   DIST between points A and B? _____

   AREA of the polygon? _____

   Perimeter of the polygon? _____

PRB22-1

2. DIST between A and B? _____

   DIST between B and C? _____

   AREA of circle? _____

   Circumference of circle?_____

   AREA of polygon? _____

   Perimeter of polygon?_____

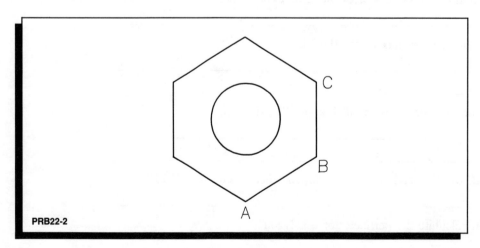

PRB22-2

3. LIST information on arc A?

_____

_____

_____

_____

LIST information on line B?

_____

_____

_____

_____

DBLIST information for entire screen?

_____

_____

_____

_____

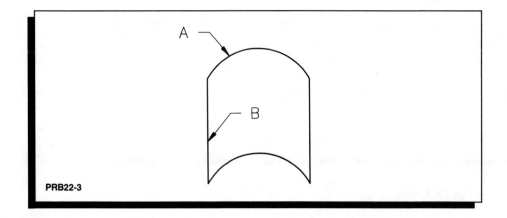

PRB22-3

 **Unit 23** Building Blocks

■ OBJECTIVE:

To apply the BLOCK, INSERT, and WBLOCK commands

If CAD systems are managed properly, their users should never have to draw the same objects twice. This, by the way, is a primary reason why CAD is so beneficial. Success, however, depends on the techniques by which the drawings are created, stored, documented, and retrieved.

This unit focuses on the commands that enable you to create, store, and reuse the symbols, shapes, drawings, and details that you use over and over again.

■ *BLOCK Command* _____

The BLOCK command allows you to combine several entities into one, store it, and retrieve it at a later time. Let's work with the BLOCK command.

1 Load AutoCAD and Begin a New Drawing. Name it **LIVROOM**.

2 Obtain **HELP** on the **BLOCK** command and read it over.

Now that you know what a Block is, let's create one.   9.1

3 On layer 0, draw the following object. Be sure to make it small.

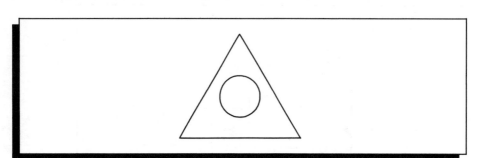

4 Enter the **BLOCK** command.   9.2

5 Create the Block based on the following information.

— Name the Block "MENTAL."
— Specify the lower left corner of the object as the Insertion base point.
— Place a window around the object to select it.
— And press RETURN.

After completing the above, the object should disappear. If it did, then you have successfully created a Block.

Your MENTAL Block is now stored in your current drawing file for subsequent insertion.

INSERT Command _____

Now let's insert the Block.

1 Enter the **INSERT** command.   9.3

2 Insert the MENTAL Block using the following information.

— Insert near the lower left corner of your screen.
— Specify the scale of .75 on both the **X** and **Y** axes.
— Rotate the Block 45 degrees counterclockwise by simply typing 45.

Did it appear on your screen as you had expected? If not, try it again.

3 **ERASE** the circle from the Block.

What happened and why?

4 If you completed the ERASE command, enter **OOPS** to recover the object.

In the future, you may want to edit a Block by erasing portions from it. But, you cannot do it...or can you? Let's try!

1 Enter **INSERT** once again.

2 This time, when typing the Block name (**MENTAL**), place an asterisk (*)   9.3.7
before the name as shown below.

```
Command: INSERT   Block name (or ?): *MENTAL
```

3 Step through the entire INSERT command and enter whatever scale and
rotation factor you wish.

4 After it appears on the screen, try to **ERASE** the circle from the Block.

Did it work? What can you conclude about the * option?

After creating several Blocks, it's easy to forget their names. This is especially true when you edit the drawing file two or three weeks after you have created the Blocks. Is there a method for reviewing all named Blocks? Yes, let's do it.

1 Enter the **INSERT** command.

2 Type ? from the keyboard or select **listing** from the screen menu.   9.3.8

NOTE:

You can also obtain a listing of named Blocks by entering the BLOCK command and typing ? in response to "Block name (or ?)."

Drawing files from disk can also be inserted into your existing drawing using the INSERT command. Let's try it.

9.4

1 Enter the **INSERT** command.

2 Choose one of your *drawings* from disk and type the drawing file name. Omit the .DWG extension; it's assumed.

HINT:

Use the FILES utility command if you need to review your drawing file names.

3 Specify **0,0** for the Insertion base point.

4 If the drawing is large, scale it down. Be aware that it may overlap with what is already on your screen.

Did it work? If not, try it again with another drawing file.

WBLOCK Command

Now you understand that all drawing files are accessible for insertion in any drawing. But what about Blocks? Blocks are only accessible in the drawing file in which they reside. What if you'd like to use one of the Blocks in another drawing file? Is there a method of making the Block(s) available to other drawings? Yes, with the WBLOCK (short for Write Block) command.

Let's try it.

1 Enter **WBLOCK**.

9.5

2 Name the file **MENT**, and use the Block named **MENTAL**.

Note the light on your disk drive as you complete the command. The computer simply created a new file called MENT with the contents of MENTAL.

Let's take a look at the MENT.DWG file.

3 Enter the **FILES** command and list all drawing files.

Do you see MENT.DWG?

Now that the MENTAL Block is in a drawing file format, it can be inserted into any other drawing file. You'll never need to draw it again.

4 For practice, create another Block and store it as a drawing file using WBLOCK.

Questions

1. Briefly describe the purpose of Blocks.

   _____

   _____

2. Explain how the INSERT command is used.

   _____

   _____

3. In what submenu is INSERT located?

   _____

4. How can you list all defined Blocks contained within a drawing file?

   _____

   _____

5. A Block can be INSERTed with or without an asterisk preceding the name. Describe the difference between the two.

   _____

   _____

6. Explain how WBLOCK works.

   _____

   _____

7. In what submenu is WBLOCK located?

   _____

8. When would WBLOCK be useful?

   _____

   _____

Problem

In the following problem, draw the furniture representations and store each as a separate Block. Then draw the living room outline. Don't worry about exact sizes or locations, and omit the text. Insert each piece of furniture into the living room at any appropriate size and rotation angle. Feel free to create additional furniture and to use each piece of furniture more than once.

After creating the Blocks, write two of them (of your choice) to disk using WBLOCK.

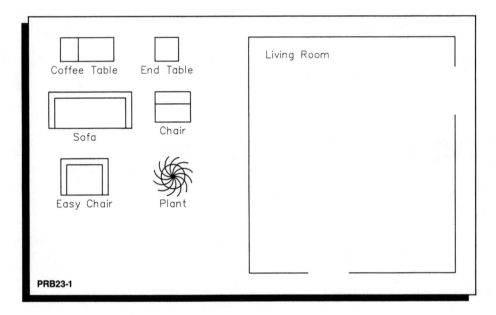

Unit 24 Symbol Library Creation

■ OBJECTIVE:

To create and use a library of symbols and details

The purpose of this unit is to create a group of symbols and details and to store them in a library. The library will then be used in a new drawing.

The following is a collection of electrical substation schematic symbols contained within an AutoCAD drawing file that was named LIBRARY1. Each of the symbols was stored as a single Block and given a Block name. (In this particular case, numbers were used for Block names rather than words.) The crosses, which show the Blocks' insertion base points, and the numbers were drawn on a separate layer and frozen when the Blocks were created. Therefore they are not contained within the Blocks; they are used for reference and retrieval purposes only.

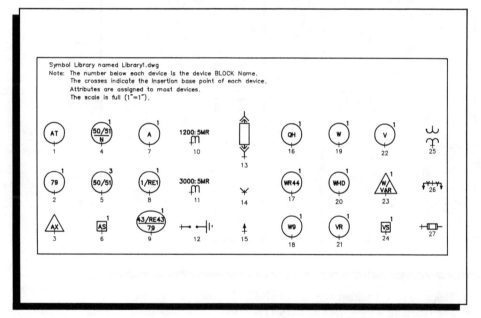

Courtesy of City of Fort Collins, Light & Power Utility

After the symbols were developed and stored in LIBRARY1, the LIBRARY1 file was INSERTed into a new drawing for creation of the electrical schematic shown on the following page.

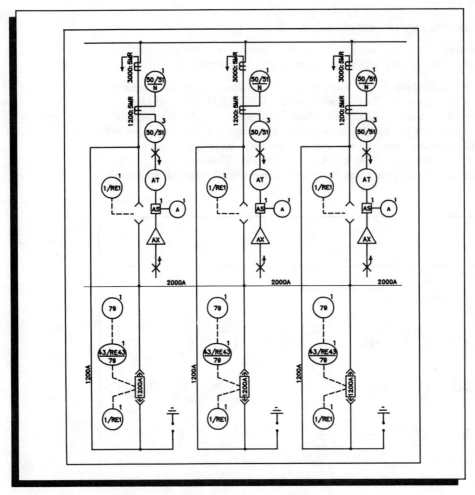

Since each of the Blocks was contained within LIBRARY1, they, too, were inserted into the new drawing along with LIBRARY1. Each Block was then retrieved and inserted into the proper location, and lines were used to connect each. Hence, 80 percent of the drawing was finished before it was started. This is the primary advantage of symbol libraries; they save time and effort.

Creating a Library

Now let's step through a simple version of the procedures just described.

1   Load AutoCAD and Begin a New Drawing. Name it **LIB1** (short for LIBRARY1).

NOTE:

Normally, you would use a specific prototype drawing when creating a new drawing. If using a prototype drawing, the new drawing name would look similar to this: LIB1=PROTO1. But for the purpose of this exercise, do not specify a prototype drawing since you have not created one specifically for this application.

② Create the following simplified representations of tools. Using Snap, Ortho, etc., make each relatively small on layer 0. Omit the text.

Table Saw   Drill Press   Jointer

Surface Planer

Work Bench

③ Create a New Layer called Text, and Set this layer.

④ On the layer called Text, create the reference information (*i.e.*, Block names and insertion base points) shown below. Do this now even though the Block names and insertion points technically do not yet exist.

HINT:

Create a cross (+) and store it as a Block. Use the cross at each of the components' insertion points as indicated below. Make the center of the cross its insertion base point.

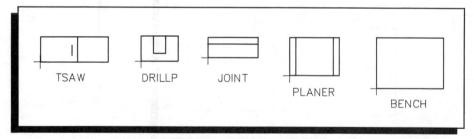

TSAW   DRILLP   JOINT

PLANER

BENCH

⑤ Next, Set layer 0 and Freeze layer Text.

The Block names and crosses (insertion points) should have disappeared.

⑥ Store each of the tool representations as a Block using the same Block names and insertion points you used above.

NOTE:

Blocks created on layer 0 can be inserted onto any other layer and will then reside on that new layer. This is why it was important to create the tool representations on layer 0.

⑦ Thaw the layer called Text.

The Block names and crosses (insertion points) should have reappeared.

8 To restore each of the tools, INSERT the Blocks into their exact locations according to their insertion base points.

9 Assign color number 1 to layer 0 and color number 2 to layer Text.

You are now finished with the symbol library creation.

10 Enter **END** to save your work and to exit to the Main Menu.

11 If you know how to plot drawings, plot LIB1. You could use a thick black pen for color 1 and a thin colored pen for color 2.

Using the Library

Now we're going to use the newly created symbol library called LIB1 for creation of a workshop drawing.

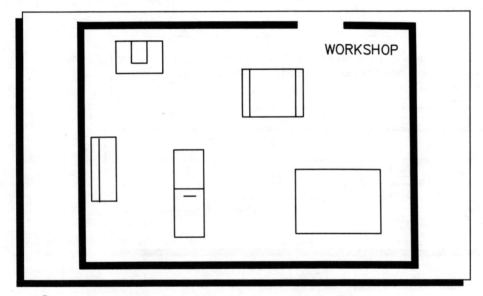

1 Begin a New Drawing and name it **WORKSHOP**.

2 Using PLINE, create the outline of the workshop as shown above. Make the starting and ending width .1 unit, and make the workshop outline large enough to fill most of your screen.

Now let's load and use the symbol library named LIB1.

3 Enter the **INSERT** command.

4 Type the drawing file name **LIB1**. Do not complete the rest of the steps in the command.

IMPORTANT: When AutoCAD asks for the insertion point, simply Cancel. Why? Well, let's continue and you'll see.

5 Select the **INSERT** command again and do a listing of all Blocks.

What Blocks are listed?

So now you see why we INSERTed LIB1 and why we Canceled the Insert before LIB1 was actually drawn on the screen. What we want from LIB1 is access to the Block definitions contained in LIB1, not the graphics themselves. Now that the Block definitions are present in our current drawing (WORKSHOP), we can insert each as we wish.

6 **INSERT** each of the symbols in a similar arrangement to the drawing shown on page 138. Rotate each as necessary.

Because you had access to a previously created symbol library, you have just created a drawing in a fraction of the time it would otherwise have taken. Now that you know how to do it, the next time will be even faster.

HINT:

A good practice is to continuously contribute to the library file (LIB1) by creating and storing new symbols, shapes, and details in the library. Eventually, you may want to create new libraries for other applications.

7 Enter **END** to save your work and exit the Drawing Editor.

AUTOCAD™ AT WORK

Building Wheelchairs with AutoCAD

Ralf Hotchkiss' occupation as a builder of wheelchairs came out of necessity. The first wheelchair he built was for himself after he was paralyzed from the waist down in a motorcycle accident nearly twenty years ago.

Recently Hotchkiss started using AutoCAD to help him design wheelchairs for Third World countries. Unpaved roads in underdeveloped countries place special demands on wheelchair riders, who must maneuver through mud and rocks and around chuckholes.

Using AutoCAD, Hotchkiss hopes to design a chair that is durable, compact, lightweight, and inexpensive. And AutoCAD's design features are helping him find ways to solve his biggest design challenge for the Third World: electric-powered wheelchairs for those people who are unable to push their own.

Hotchkiss contends that AutoCAD gives him the advantage he needs to accomplish his goals. "I do my design work much faster. I can modify and combine drawings, check the clearances of moving parts on the screen, and plot publication-quality drawings in a fraction of the time it took to do by hand. Tracing is a thing of the past — my drafting table and T-square are in mothballs."

AutoCAD allows Hotchkiss to sketch a design, see it in 3-D from different views, and make changes until he is satisfied that he can begin a working model. Another AutoCAD feature that Hotchkiss frequently uses is a "customized library," which allows him to create a file of wheelchair parts that can be easily incorporated in any drawing.

The library feature is especially helpful when Hotchkiss looks for ways to overcome the everyday obstacles faced by wheelchair riders. Says Hotchkiss, "Wheelchairs must be able to move close to a table, withstand collisions with curbs, and turn in a small radius with a minimum of effort. If a design fails, then I have to go back to the computer to make adjustments — and that's where drafting with AutoCAD really shines."

140

Questions

1. What is the primary purpose of creating a library of symbols and details?

   _____

   _____

2. When creating a library, on what layer should you create and store the Blocks? Why?

   _____

   _____

3. The Block names and insertion points are stored on another layer. Why is this information important, and why store it on a separate layer?

   _____

   _____

4. When inserting an entire library, at what point do you Cancel and why?

   _____

   _____

5. Identify one application for creating and using a library of symbols and details.

   _____

   _____

Problem

Based on steps described in this unit, create an entirely new symbol library specific to your area of interest and application. For example, if you practice architectural drawing, create a library of architectural symbols and details. Be sure to first create and/or specify a prototype drawing (such as the prototype drawing created in Unit 17, if it's appropriate). Remember, the library symbols will later be inserted into new drawings.

After you have completed and stored the library symbols and details, Begin a New Drawing and INSERT the new library file as you did before. Then, create a drawing using the symbols and details.

Unit 25 Remarkable Attributes

■ OBJECTIVE:

To create and display Attributes with the ATTDEF and ATTDISP commands

The purpose of this exercise is to experiment with AutoCAD's powerful Attribute feature.

Attributes are text information stored within Blocks. The information describes certain aspects of Blocks, such as sizes, materials, model numbers, cost, etc., depending upon the nature of the items. The Attribute information can be made visible, but in most cases, you do not need or want the information to appear on the drawing. Therefore it usually remains invisible, especially during plotting. Later, the Attribute information can be extracted to form a report such as a bill of materials. Let's take a look at an example.

11.1

The following electrical schematic contains Attribute information, even though you cannot see it. It's invisible.

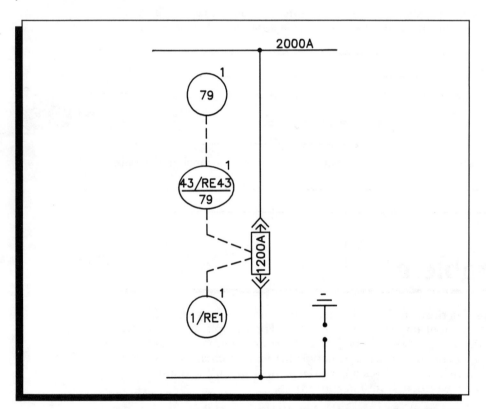

Courtesy of City of Fort Collins, Light & Power Utility

The following example shows a ZOOMed view of one of the schematic's components. Note that the Attribute information is on and is displayed near the top of the component.

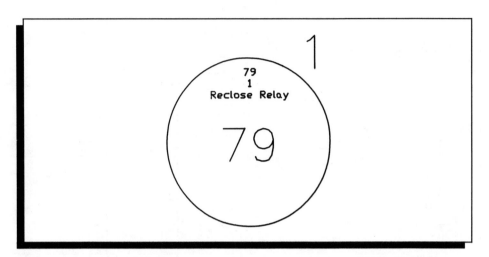

All of the Attributes were compiled into a file and placed into a program for report generation. The following report (or bill of materials) was generated from the electrical schematic drawing.

```
DESCRIPTION              DEVICE          QUANTITY/UNIT

Recloser Cut-out Switch  43/RE43/79      1
Reclose Relay            79              1
Lightning Arrestor       --              3
Breaker Control Switch   1/RE1           1
1200 Amp Circuit Breaker 52              1
```

Creating Attributes

Attributes can be used, and reports produced, from any type of drawing, not just electrical. Let's try it.

1 Load AutoCAD and bring up the drawing called **WORKSHOP**. It should look somewhat like the one on the next page.

NOTE:

If, for some reason, you do not have WORKSHOP on file, quickly create the following drawing and omit the text.

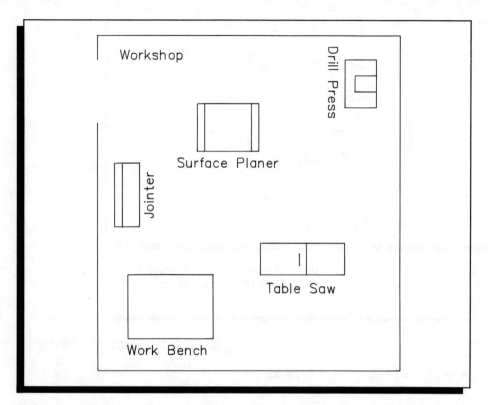

Let's assign Attribute information to each of the tools so that we can later generate a bill of materials. We'll design the Attributes so that the report will contain a brief description of the component, the model, and the cost.

2 **ZOOM** in on the first component (table saw). It should fill most of your screen.

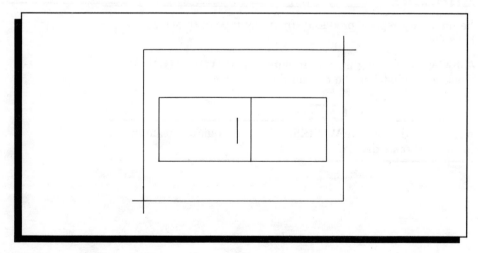

Now you're ready to assign Attributes to the table saw.

3   Enter the **ATTDEF** (Attribute Definition) command found in the Blocks Submenu.

4   Set the Attribute modes as follows, and then press **RETURN**.
Invisible: Y
Constant: Y
Verify: Y

HINT:
The modes can be changed from Yes to No or from No to Yes by simply typing the first letter of each mode. For example, if you want to change Invisible to Yes, type the letter I and press RETURN.

5   Type the word **DESCRIPTION** for the Attribute tag and press **RETURN**.

6   Type **Table Saw** for the Attribute value and press **RETURN**.

7   Place the information near the top and inside the tool. Be sure to make it small. When placing the information, use the same technique used with the TEXT command.

The word DESCRIPTION should appear. If it extends outside the table saw representation, that's OK.

8   Press the **space bar** to repeat the ATTDEF command.

9   The Attribute modes should remain the same, so press **RETURN**.

10   This time, type **MODEL** for the Attribute tag and **1A2B** for the Attribute value.

The word MODEL should now appear on the screen.

11   Repeat steps 8, 9, and 10, but enter **COST** for the tag and **$625.00** for the value.

You are now finished entering the table saw Attributes. That's all there is to it.

Storing Attributes

Now let's store the Attributes in the Block.

1   Using the **BLOCK** command, create a new Block of the table saw under a new name such as TSAW2. To select the Block, place a window around the entire table saw and Attribute information.

Your Attribute information should now be stored within the Block.

2   **INSERT** the Block in approximately the same location where the table saw was before. The Attribute tags should not appear.

145

Displaying Attributes _____

Let's display the Attribute values using the ATTDISP (Attribute Display) command.

1 Enter **ATTDISP** and specify **On**.

11.3

You should see the Attribute values, similar to the drawing below.

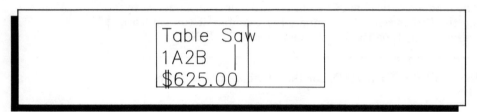

```
Table Saw
1A2B
$625.00
```

2 Enter **ATTDISP** again and specify **Off**.

The Attribute values should again be invisible.

Practicing What You've Learned _____

Now, let's assign Attributes to the rest of the power tools and components.

1 Using the **ATTDEF** command, assign Attributes to each of the other four components using the following information. Then create the new Blocks and INSERT them in the same locations as their predecessors.

Description	Model	Cost
Jointer	902-42A	$750.00
Drill Press	7C-234	$590.00
Surface Planer	789453	$2070.00
Work Bench	31-1982	$825.00

2 When you're finished assigning Attributes, recreating the Blocks, and INSERTing them, display the Attribute values to make sure they are complete.

3 Lastly, enter **END** to save your work and exit the Drawing Editor.

The following unit will involve the extraction of the Attributes and the generation of a bill of materials.

Questions

1. Explain the purpose of creating and storing Attributes.

_____

_____

2. Briefly define each of the following commands.

ATTDEF _____

ATTDISP _____

3. What are Attribute tags?

_____

_____

4. What are Attribute values?

_____

_____

5. Explain the Attribute modes Invisible, Constant, and Verify.

HINT: See 11.2 of the *User Guide*.

_____

_____

_____

Problem

Call up the drawing containing the furniture representations you created for Unit 11. If this file is not on disk, create a similar drawing. Outline a simple plan for assigning Attributes to each of the components contained in the drawing. Create the Attributes and redefine each of the Blocks so that the Attributes are stored within the Blocks.

Unit 26 — Bill of Materials Generation

■ OBJECTIVE:

To practice report generation using ATTEXT, BASIC, and ATTEXT.BAS

This exercise focuses on the Attribute extraction process using the ATTEXT command, as well as the bill of materials generation process using the BASIC program editor and AutoCAD's BASIC program called ATTEXT.BAS.

After finishing the Attribute assignment process (Unit 25), you are ready to create a report such as a bill of materials. The first step in this process involves extracting the Attribute information and storing it in a file that can be read by another computer program. This is actually a simple process. Let's do it.

Attribute Extraction _____

1 Load AutoCAD and bring up the drawing called **WORKSHOP**.

Each of the tools should contain Attributes as shown below. Note that ATTDISP must be on if you want to see the Attributes. You may need to ZOOM in order to read them.

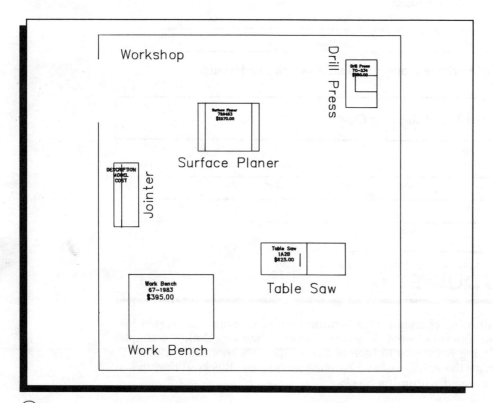

2 Enter the **ATTEXT** command.

11.5

148

NOTE:

ATTEXT stands for Attribute Extraction.

③ Specify a **DXF** output file.

NOTE:

This file type can be read by other computer programs.

④ Make the DXF (extract) file name the same as your current drawing file name (but without the .DWG extension) by simply pressing **RETURN**.

Your Attributes are now in a form that can be manipulated by other programs for report generation. That's all there is to it.

Attribute Reporting

Now let's load the new extract file into the BASIC program called ATTEXT.BAS. This will require exiting AutoCAD.

① Enter **END**.

② When you are in the Main Menu, select task **0**, "Exit AutoCAD."

You should now have the DOS prompt (such as A>) on the screen.

The next few steps will involve disk preparation. This preparation is necessary before you can proceed with the bill of materials generation.

① Locate your DOS diskette or directory containing the BASIC program Editor called BASIC.COM.

NOTE:

If you're operating a hard disk system, BASIC.COM is probably on it with the remaining DOS files.

② Then locate your AutoCAD Sample Drawings diskette or directory containing ATTEXT.BAS.

③ Place the ATTEXT.BAS file with the BASIC Program Editor called BASIC.COM so that they are both on the same disk (or hard disk directory). The extract file (WORKSHOP.DXX) should also be contained with these files. Although it does not have to be on the same disk or directory, your work will be simplified if it is.

Now you're ready to create a bill of materials.

① After the DOS prompt, type **BASIC** and press **RETURN**.

This will bring up the BASIC Program Editor.

2 Then type **LOAD"ATTEXT** and press **RETURN** to load the
ATTEXT program.

3 Type **RUN** and press **RETURN** to run the ATTEXT program.

4 When the program asks you for the extract file name, type **WORKSHOP.**

____ NOTE: ____

Be sure to indicate the drive or path (such as B:) if the extract file
WORKSHOP.DXX is located on another drive or directory.

At this time, the BASIC program will generate the bill of materials. Your report
should look very similar to the one below.

```
COST              DESCRIPTION       MODEL
--------          ---------------   -------

$750.00           Jointer           902-42A
$590.00           Drill Press       7C-234
$2070.00          Surface Planer    789453
$825.00           Work Bench        31-1982
$625.00           Table Saw         1A2B
```

If it does, congratulations!

5 To print the report, use your computer's keyboard print-screen feature.

6 To return to DOS (*e.g.,* A>), simply type **SYSTEM.**

Questions

1. Describe the purpose of AutoCAD's ATTEXT command.

   _____

   _____

2. What type of AutoCAD file can be read and manipulated by other computer programs?

   _____

3. Explain the process of bringing up the BASIC Program Editor.

   _____

   _____

4. Explain the process of loading and running AutoCAD's BASIC program called ATTEXT.BAS.

   _____

   _____

   _____

5. What command is used to exit BASIC and return to DOS?

   _____

Problem

Load the drawing that contains furniture representations. Using the steps outlined in this unit, create a simple bill of materials.

Unit 27 — Dressing Your Drawings

■ OBJECTIVE:

To apply the HATCH and SKETCH commands

This exercise covers the application of hatching using the numerous patterns made available by AutoCAD. Sketching is also practiced using the SKETCH command and subcommands.

Some drawings make use of special AutoCAD features to accurately and correctly communicate. Among these features are hatching and sketching, as illustrated in the drawing below.

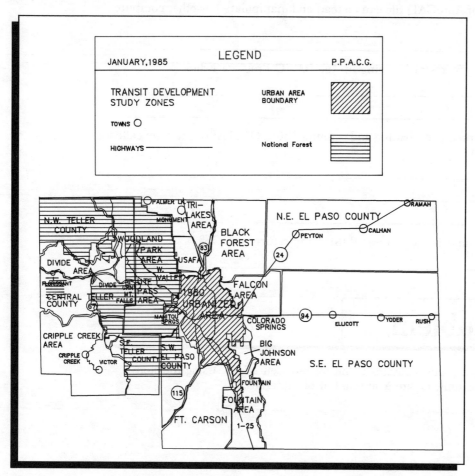

Courtesy of David Salamon, Pikes Peak Area Council of Governments

Both hatching and sketching can enhance the quality of drawings greatly, but both consume lots of memory. Therefore both hatching and sketching should be used only when necessary. Be aware of their memory requirements to avoid a system crash, particularly on a floppy diskette-based system.

HATCH Command _____

Let's see what AutoCAD's HATCH command can do.

1 Load AutoCAD and Begin a New Drawing. Name it **HATCH**.

2 Draw the following, but don't worry about exact sizes and locations. Include the text and outside rectangle as well.

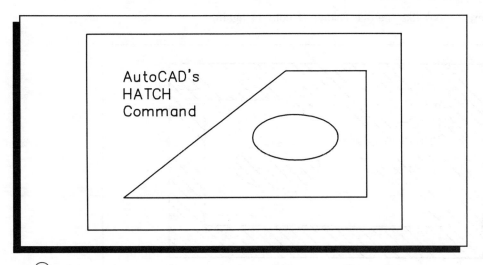

3 Select **HATCH** from the Root Menu.   10.2.3

The Hatch Submenu should now be on your screen.

4 Enter the **HATCH** command.

You should now have the following at the bottom of your screen.

```
Command: HATCH
Pattern (? or name/U,style):
```

5 Do a listing of all hatch patterns by selecting "listing" from the screen submenu or by typing ?.

As you can see, AutoCAD provides many hatch patterns—over forty, in fact. Let's use one of them on our drawing.

6 Bring up the **HATCH** command again, and this time type the hatch pattern **ANSI31** (the standard cross-hatching pattern).

7 Specify a scale of **1**.

NOTE:

> Like the DIMSCALE, the "Scale for pattern" should be set at the reciprocal of the plot scale so that the hatch pattern size corresponds with your drawing.

⑧ Specify an angle of **0**.

⑨ To define the hatch boundary, place a window around your entire drawing and press **RETURN**.

Does your drawing look like the one below? If not, try again.

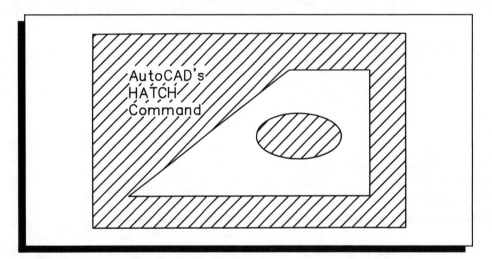

Note the areas which received hatching.

⑩ Construct other enclosed objects (polygons, circles, etc.) and experiment with several of the remaining hatch patterns.

⑪ Attempt filling the outermost areas only by using the O option. (When you enter the name of a pattern, follow it with a comma and O, as in CLAY,O.)

Did it work?

⑫ Use the I option (as in CLAY,I) to Ignore the internal structures.

Did the hatch pattern cover the internal areas?

SKETCH Command

Now let's try some freehand sketching.

① First, clear a small area of your screen so that you'll have room for the sketch.

② Enter the **SKETCH** command.

12.5

3 Specify **.0001** units for the Record increment.

You should now have the following at the bottom of your screen.

```
Sketch.  Pen eXit Quit Record Erase Connect .
```

The following is a brief description of each of the above subcommands.   12.5.3

Pen	Raise/lower pen (or toggle with pick button)
eXit	Record all temporary lines and exit
Quit	Discard all temporary lines and exit
Record	Record all temporary lines
Erase	Selectively erase temporary lines
Connect	Connect to a line endpoint
. (period)	Line to point

To begin sketching, simply pick a point where you'd like the sketch to begin.   12.5.1
The pick specifies (toggles) "pen down."

4 Move your pointing device to sketch a short line.

5 Pick again. This specifies (toggles) "pen up."

6 Move to a clear location on your screen and sketch the following lake.

NOTE:

If you make a mistake or need to back up, toggle "pen up" and enter **ERASE** from the Sketch Submenu (or type **E**). Then reverse the order of your crosshairs until you have erased that which needed to be removed.

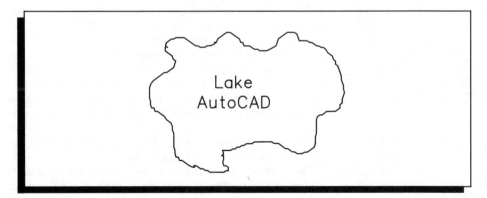

It's OK if your sketch doesn't look exactly like the one above.

7 When you're finished sketching the lake, select either **Record** or **eXit** to record and finalize your temporary lines.

⑧ Practice sketching by using the remaining SKETCH subcommands. Draw anything you'd like.

⑨ When you're finished, enter **END** to save and exit.

AUTOCAD™ AT WORK

Landscaping with AutoCAD

For 150 years, a typical landscape designer's work tools — a drafting table, pen and pencil, paper, and templates — remained virtually the same. But the introduction of AutoCAD changed the profession overnight; nowadays landscape architects who don't use AutoCAD are at a serious disadvantage. Layouts that traditionally took two days to prepare by hand can now be completed by AutoCAD in two hours.

Landscape architecture focuses on everything above the ground and outside a building, including vegetation, fountains, sculptures, and roads. In working with their clients, landscape architects must draw up detailed plans that can be adapted quickly and easily, and AutoCAD's special features complement the professional nicely.

By using the layering feature, the architect can plot buildings, roads, boundaries, irrigation systems, and recreation areas on separate layers. Or the architect can combine any of the layers to use for presentations to clients or for construction plans for engineers and work crews.

AutoCAD's library feature is especially useful. It can be utilized to store symbols, such as the drawing of a tree, or important project details, such as a style of lettering, standardized spellings, and data about materials and costs. Also, the architects can store symbols that can help them with future designs, such as different kinds of trees and plants and common building materials.

The Future. By using a telecommunications link, a landscape architect in one city and a client in another could view a proposed drawing and make immediate modifications. Also, the architect could exchange information with other professionals working on the project, and field personnel — such as surveyors — could make on-site suggestions about the project.

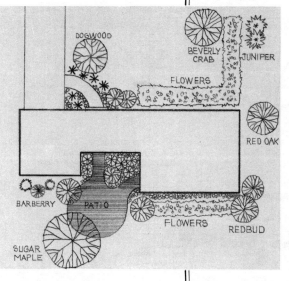

Questions

1. Explain how hatch patterns are useful.

   _____

   _____

2. How is the scale of a hatch pattern determined?

   _____

3. Briefly describe both of the following HATCH style options.

   O _____

   I _____

4. Briefly describe the purpose of each of the following SKETCH subcommands.

   Pen _____

   eXit _____

   Quit _____

   Record _____

   Erase _____

   Connect _____

   . (period) _____

5. You specify a number for the SKETCH Record increment. What does it determine?

   _____

   _____

Problems

Construct each of the following drawings. Use the HATCH and SKETCH commands where appropriate, and don't worry about specific sizes. The hatch patterns to be used are indicated below each of the drawings.

In PRB27-2 and PRB27-3, use the SKETCH and LINE commands to define temporary boundaries for the hatch patterns. Place the boundaries on a separate layer and freeze that layer after you are finished hatching.

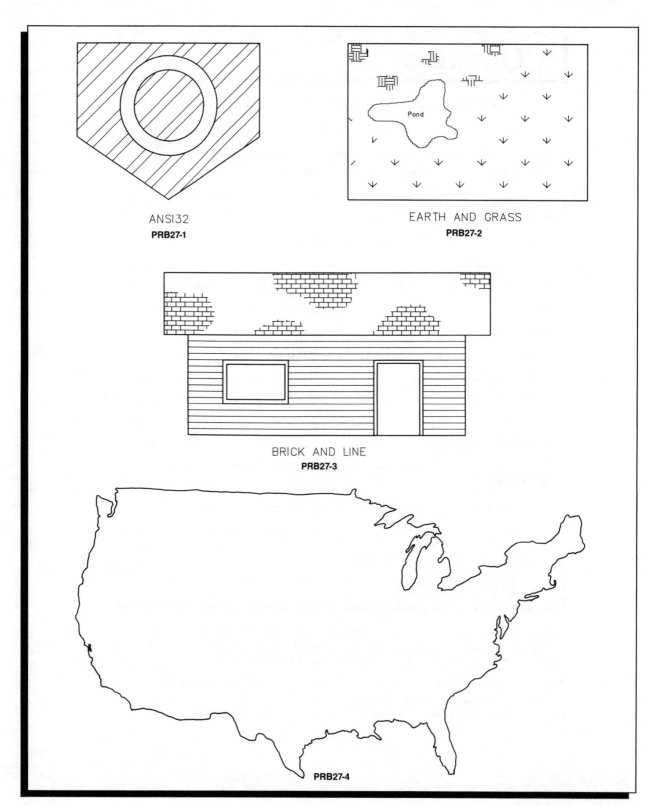

ANSI32
PRB27-1

EARTH AND GRASS
PRB27-2

BRICK AND LINE
PRB27-3

PRB27-4

AutoCAD Drawing Courtesy of Peter Barnett, Autodesk Inc.

Unit 28   From Display to Paper

■ **OBJECTIVE:**

AutoCAD™ User Guide Reference

Ch. 13

To practice the plotting procedure using the PLOT and PRPLOT commands

This exercise covers the steps necessary to properly send drawings to a pen plotter or matrix printer. Emphasis is given to setting and changing plot parameters for pen plotting since the use of pen plotters is the most popular for creating a hard copy of AutoCAD drawings.

Until plotting actually occurs, all AutoCAD drawing is done electronically via the computer display. It's easier to relate computer-aided drafting to traditional drafting when plotting because both methods involve placing lines on paper. Regardless of the method used, the goal is to end up with a drawing of proper scale, linetypes/thicknesses, and quality. Therefore AutoCAD has provided many options during the plot procedure which allow for a final plot exactly the way it was intended. Let's step through the process.

A Fast Plot

First, let's do it the quickest and easiest way even though it may not be exactly what you want.

Your computer may or may not be connected to a pen plotter. Regardless, let's plot the drawing named HATCH as though the computer were connected. If it's not, that's OK; the steps are the same either way.

1   Load AutoCAD and bring up the Main Menu.

2   Select Main Menu task 3, "Plot a drawing."

3   Specify that you want to plot the drawing called **HATCH**.

The following should now be on your screen:

```
Specify the part of the drawing to be plotted by entering:
Display, Extents, Limits, View, or Window <D>:
```

---

4   Specify **Display**.

Now you should have a screen similar to the following. Read over this information carefully.

```
Sizes are in Inches
Plot origin is at (0.00,0.00)
Plotting area is 15.00 wide by 10.00 high (MAX size)
Plot is NOT rotated 90 degrees
Pen width is 0.010
Area fill will be adjusted for pen width
Hidden lines will NOT be removed
Plot will be scaled to fit available area

Do you want to change anything? <N>
```

5 Respond to the question by specifying "No." (Since N is the default response, just press **RETURN**.)

NOTE:

If your computer is connected to a plotter, be sure all is set properly, including the paper size, plotter pens, and paper.

6 Lastly, press **RETURN** to activate the plotter.

Now, just sit back and enjoy.

NOTE:

Your drawing is not scaled, but remember, we plotted without making changes in the plot settings.

7 To stop the plotting at any time, press **CTRL C**. Then press **RETURN** to go back to the Main Menu. Do this now if your computer is not connected to a plotter.

A Customized Plot

The following plot procedure becomes much more involved. It utilizes the capabilities AutoCAD has provided for customizing the plot process according to your specific drawing requirements.

Let's plot a drawing that contains at least two layers, such as one of your dimensioning drawings from a previous exercise.

1 Load the drawing (*e.g.*, DIMEN) and do a layer listing.

2 If you have not yet created two layers, do so now. Call one layer OBJ and the other DIM.

Be sure that your object is contained on layer OBJ and your dimensions on layer DIM.

3 Assign color 1 to OBJ and color 2 to DIM. Do this regardless of your monitor type (color or monochrome).

This time, let's plot directly from the Drawing Editor.

1 Enter the **PLOT** command, and specify that you want to plot the Limits of the drawing.

By the way, do you remember the drawing limits? Unless you have changed them, they should be the default limits 0,0 and 12 units,9 units. This information is important when plotting the limits because the limits represent your scaled units.

Proceed as you did before by reading over the information now on your screen.

2 This time, reply with a **Yes** because we do want to make at least one change.

As a result, you should have something very similar to the following on your screen. (See next page.) Read over this information.

Layer Color	Pen No.	Line Type	Pen Speed	Layer Color	Pen No.	Line Type	Pen Speed
1 (red)	1	Ø	20	9	1	Ø	16
2 (yellow)	2	Ø	20	10	1	Ø	16
3(green)	3	Ø	20	11	1	Ø	16
4 (cyan)	4	Ø	20	12	1	Ø	16
5 (blue)	5	Ø	20	13	1	Ø	16
6 (magenta)	6	Ø	20	14	1	Ø	16
7 (white)	7	Ø	20	15	1	Ø	16
8	8	Ø	20				

```
Line types: Ø = continuous line          Pen speed codes:
            1 = ..................
            2 = .  .  .  .  .  .  .  .     Inches/Second:
            3 = -------------------         1, 2, 4, 8, 16
            4 = -  -  -  -  -  -  -  -
            5 = --  --  --  --  --  --  -   Cm/Second:
            6 = ---  ---  ---  ---  ---      3, 5, 10, 20, 40
            7 = --  -  --  -  --  -  --  -
            8 = __--__--__--__--__--_
```

```
Enter line types, pen numbers, pen speed codes
blank=go to next, Cn=go to Color n, S=Show current choices, X=Exit
Do you want to change any of the above parameters? <N>
```

③ Reply with a Yes—you do want to make changes to the above.

NOTE:

Ignore the Linetype category since it is recommended to specify all linetypes while in the Drawing Editor.

Now let's make changes so that your settings look identical to the following.

Layer Color	Pen No.	Line Type	Pen Speed	Layer Color	Pen No.	Line Type	Pen Speed
1 (red)	1	Ø	4	9	1	Ø	16
2 (yellow)	2	Ø	4	10	1	Ø	16
3 (green)	2	Ø	4	11	1	Ø	16
4 (cyan)	1	Ø	4	12	1	Ø	16
5 (blue)	1	Ø	4	13	1	Ø	16
6 (magenta)	6	Ø	20	14	1	Ø	16
7 (white)	7	Ø	20	15	1	Ø	16
8	8	Ø	20				

4 Assign pen 1 to color 1; hence, press **RETURN**.

5 Leave the linetype at 0; hence, press **RETURN**.

6 Enter **4** (4 inches per second) for the pen speed and press **RETURN**.

HINT:
If you make a mistake and need to return to color 1, simply type **C1** and press **RETURN**.

7 Assign pen 2 to color 2 and press **RETURN**.

8 Leave the linetype at 0 and press **RETURN**.

9 Enter **4** for the pen speed and press **RETURN**.

Since our drawing uses only colors 1 and 2, we're finished. However, if you'd like to practice, make the remaining changes as indicated in the above settings.

10 Check your new settings by entering **S** (for Show) and press **RETURN**.

Are the changes correct? If not, correct them now.

11 Enter **X** to exit and move on.

12 Step through each of the following and make each entry according to the settings listed here.

NOTE:
When you arrive at the "Plotting area is..." step, attempt to enter B size (17″ × 11″) paper. If your plotter does not accommodate B size paper, enter either A or C size.

Sizes are in Inches
Plot origin is at (0.00,0.00)
Plotting area is 15.00 wide by 10.00 high (MAX size)
Plot is NOT rotated 90 degrees
Pen width is 0.010
Area fill will be adjusted for pen width
Hidden lines will NOT be removed
Scale is 1=1

13 Ready your plotter and press **RETURN** to begin the plotting.

14 Lastly, return to the Drawing Editor and enter **END** to save your changes and to return to the Main Menu.

A Printer Plot _____

After completing the preceding steps, let's do a printer plot; that is, if you have a matrix printer supported by AutoCAD and connected to your computer. If not, you can step through the process just the same.

1 Select Main Menu task 4, "Printer Plot a drawing."

_____ NOTE: _____

"Printer Plot" can also be entered at the Drawing Editor with the PRPLOT command.

2 Choose any drawing you'd like.

The next steps are very much like the steps involved with pen plotting...

3 ....therefore step through the process on your own.

_____ NOTE: _____

Matrix printers contain only one printer head (*i.e.*, color). Therefore color/layer/pen assignments are omitted.

AutoCAD™ At Work

AutoCAD Artistry

When we think of an artist at work, we usually think of someone dabbing paint onto a canvas. But for some innovative artists who are experimenting with AutoCAD's creative potential, the easel is being replaced by the computer screen.

Ed Dadey, an artist in Nebraska, is using AutoCAD to design ceramics, commercial art, typography, graphics, and fine art. In addition, he collaborates with his wife to design handmade quilts and wall hangings.

Dadey became interested in setting up a CAD workstation in the fall of 1983, but he had trouble finding software that offered the accuracy and detail that his drawings required—until he tested AutoCAD: "The minute I saw the system's zoom feature, I was convinced this was the drafting program for me," Dadey says. "With AutoCAD's floating point format, I knew that I would get accuracy to the five or more decimal places I needed."

At present Dadey uses his drafting package most often for designing commercial art, such as logos for businesses and products. When designing logos, Dadey can zoom in to make sure that intersecting lines meet precisely, and he can try different colors, shapes, and scales by entering a few simple commands.

To create full-color designs, Dadey loads his plotter with an assortment of technical pens filled with airbrush paint. On some occasions he uses crayons to add texture to his drawings.

When Dadey isn't using AutoCAD for commercial work, he and his wife experiment with different quilt designs. Dadey matches airbrush paints to the fabrics his wife has selected, and he prepares a full-color design on paper. By using the library feature to store shapes, patterns, and colors, Dadey can experiment with an infinite number of combinations until he and his wife find the quilt design they are looking for.

Questions

1. Briefly describe each of the components in the following plot prompt:

   What to plot—Display, Extents, Limits, View, or Window <D>:

   Display _____

   Extents _____

   Limits _____

   View _____

   Window _____

2. Explain the relationship between the layer color and the pen number.

   _____

   _____

3. In regard to plotting, explain why it is important to draw certain components of your drawing on certain layers.

   _____

   _____

4. If a drawing plot scale is set at 1=4″, what exactly does this mean? In other words, what does the 1 represent, and what does the 4″ represent?

   _____

   _____

5. What AutoCAD command allows you to perform a printer plot?

   _____

Problems

In problems 1 and 2, prepare to plot a drawing using the given plot settings. Make up any name; it doesn't matter since you will not actually be plotting the drawing.

1. Specify the part of the drawing to be plotted by entering: Display, Extents, Limits, View, or Window <D>:L

   Sizes are in Inches
   Plot origin is at (0.00,0.00)
   Plotting area is 10.50 wide by 8.00 high (A size)
   2D Plots are rotated 90 degrees clockwise
   Pen width is 0.015
   Area fill will be adjusted for pen width
   Hidden lines will be removed
   Scale is 1=48

Layer Color	Pen No.	Line Type	Pen Speed	Layer Color	Pen No.	Line Type	Pen Speed
1 (red)	1	0	10	9	1	0	16
2 (yellow)	1	0	10	10	1	0	16
3 (green)	1	0	10	11	1	0	16
4 (cyan)	1	0	10	12	1	0	16
5 (blue)	1	0	10	13	1	0	16
6 (magenta)	1	0	10	14	1	0	16
7 (white)	1	0	10	15	1	0	16
8	1	0	10				

2. Specify the part of the drawing to be plotted by entering: Display, Extents, Limits, View, or Window <D>:L

Sizes are in Millimeters
Plot origin is at (0.00,0.00)
Plotting area is 381.00 wide by 254.00 high (MAX size)
Plot is NOT rotated 90 degrees
Pen width is 0.38
Area fill will be adjusted for pen width
Hidden lines will NOT be removed
Scale is 1=10

Layer Color	Pen No.	Line Type	Pen Speed	Layer Color	Pen No.	Line Type	Pen Speed
1 (red)	1	0	16	9	1	0	16
2 (yellow)	2	0	16	10	1	0	16
3 (green)	3	0	16	11	1	0	16
4 (cyan)	1	0	20	12	1	0	16
5 (blue)	1	0	20	13	1	0	16
6 (magenta)	1	0	20	14	1	0	16
7 (white)	1	0	20	15	1	0	16
8	1	0	20				

3. Choose at least two of your previously created drawings for which you provided a scale, paper size, UNITS, LIMITS, LTSCALE, DIMSCALE, new LAYERs, Color, and Linetype assignments. Plot each. Set each of the plot options so that the drawings properly plot to the scale you intended.

Unit 29 Isometrics: Creating Objects from a New Angle

AutoCAD™ User
Guide Reference

■ OBJECTIVE:

To apply AutoCAD's isometric drawing capabilities using the SNAP and ISOPLANE commands

The purpose of this exercise is to practice the construction of simple isometric drawings.

Isometric drawing is one of two ways to obtain a pictorial representation of an object using AutoCAD. Below is an example of an isometric drawing created on AutoCAD.

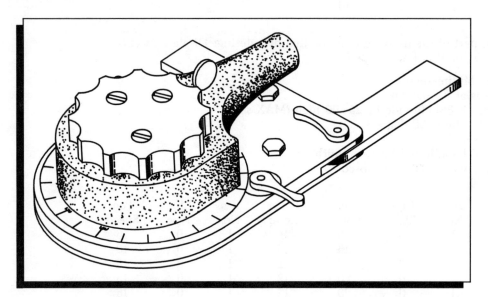

AutoCAD Drawing Courtesy of CAD Northwest, Inc.

Isometric Drawing

Let's do some simple isometric drawing.

1 Load AutoCAD and Begin a New Drawing. Name it **ISO**.

2 Set the grid at **1** unit and the snap resolution at **.5** units.

Setup for AutoCAD isometric drawing is accomplished by changing the SNAP style to isometric using the SNAP command...

3 ....therefore enter the **SNAP** command, select the Style option, and press **RETURN**.

8.1

4 Select the Isometric option by entering **I**, and set the vertical spacing at **.5** units (the default).

You should now be in the isometric drawing mode, with the crosshairs set for one of the three (Left, Top, or Right) isometric planes.

NOTE:

You are able to use all AutoCAD commands while constructing isometric drawings.

5 Select the **ISOPLANE** command from the Modes Submenu.

8.5

The crosshairs can be changed from one plane to another by picking the left, right, top, or next option from the screen menu, or by typing L, R, or T and pressing RETURN after each.

Another method of changing the crosshairs is to simply toggle them by pressing RETURN while the ISOPLANE command is entered.

Lastly, the crosshairs can be toggled by pressing CTRL E.

6 Experiment with each of the methods of changing the crosshairs.

7 Enter the **LINE** command and draw the following box. Don't worry about specific sizes.

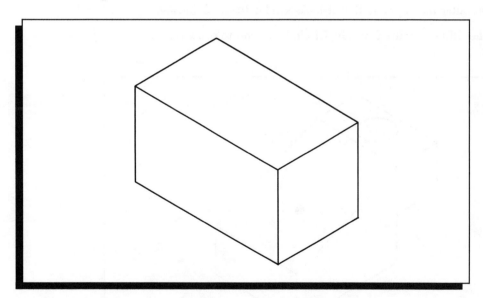

8 Now alter the box so that it looks similar to the one on the next page, using the **LINE**, **BREAK**, and **ERASE** commands.

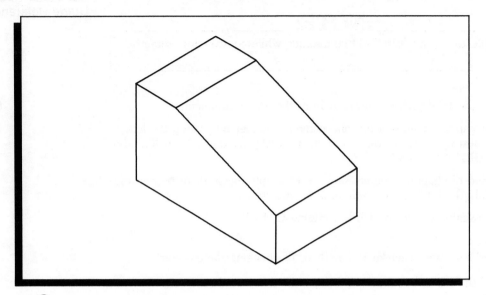

9 Further alter the object so that it looks similar to the following.

10 Use the Ellipse feature from the Circle Submenu to draw the isometric circle.

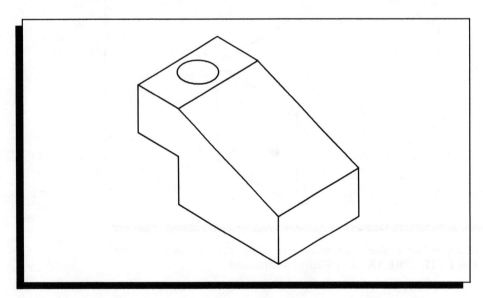

11 Experiment with isometric drawing by constructing other isometric objects.

12 Enter **END** to save your work and exit the Drawing Editor.

Questions

1. Explain how to change from conventional AutoCAD drawing to isometric drawing.

   _____

   _____

2. Describe the purpose of the ISOPLANE command.

   _____

3. Describe two methods of changing the isometric crosshairs from one plane to another.

   _____

   _____

   _____

4. Describe the limitation of AutoCAD's isometric drawing capability with regard to creation of circular and cylindrical objects.

   _____

   _____

Problems

Create each object in PRB29-1 through PRB29-4 using AutoCAD's isometric capability. Don't worry about their exact sizes.

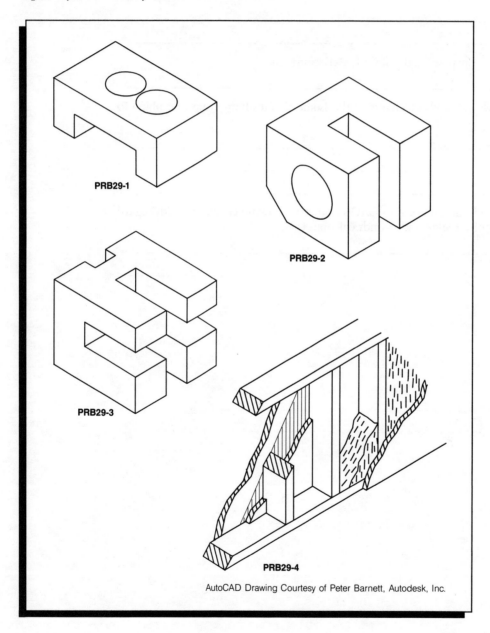

PRB29-1

PRB29-2

PRB29-3

PRB29-4

AutoCAD Drawing Courtesy of Peter Barnett, Autodesk, Inc.

In PRB29-5 accurately draw an isometric representation of the orthographic views. Draw the isometric according to the dimensions provided.

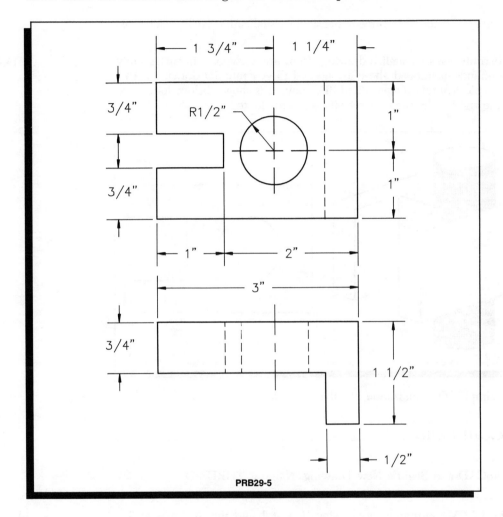

PRB29-5

Unit 30 A Look at the Third Dimension

■ OBJECTIVE:

To apply AutoCAD's 3D Level 1 using the ELEV, VPOINT, and HIDE commands

This unit focuses on AutoCAD's three-dimensional visualization facility called 3D Level 1.

3D Level 1 permits you to visualize drawings from any viewpoint in space. Only the three commands mentioned above are needed to generate 3D drawings. An example of a typical AutoCAD-generated 3D drawing is shown below, left. The drawing on the right is the same object viewed from the top.

14.1

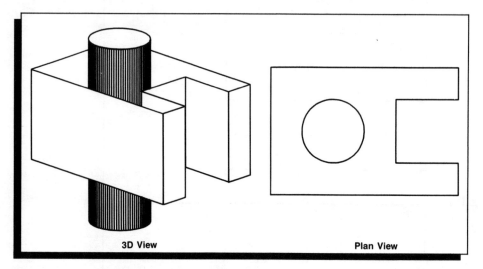

3D View   Plan View

Let's draw a simple 3D visualization like the one above.

■ *ELEV Command* _____

1 Load AutoCAD and Begin a New Drawing. Name it **THREE-D**.

2 Enter the **ELEV** command; set the elevation at **1** and the thickness at **3**.

14.2.1

_____ NOTE: _____

With these settings, all objects drawn will have an extrusion thickness (Z-axis) of 2.

3 Draw the "plan," or top, view of the object using the **LINE** command, and omit the circle (cylinder) at this time. Construct the object as shown above. Don't worry about exact sizes.

VPOINT and HIDE Commands _____

Now, let's view the object in 3D.

1 Enter the **VPOINT** command, and then select the **AXES** option from
the submenu.   14.2.2

2 Move your pointing device and watch what happens.

3 Place the small crosshairs in the globe representation as shown below and
pick that point.

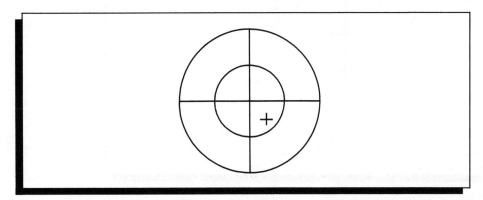

Study the globe representation on the next page carefully. The placement of
your crosshairs on the globe indicates the exact position of your viewpoint.
Placement of the crosshairs inside the inner ring (equator) will result in viewing
the object from above. Placing the crosshairs outside the inner ring will result in a
look underneath the object.

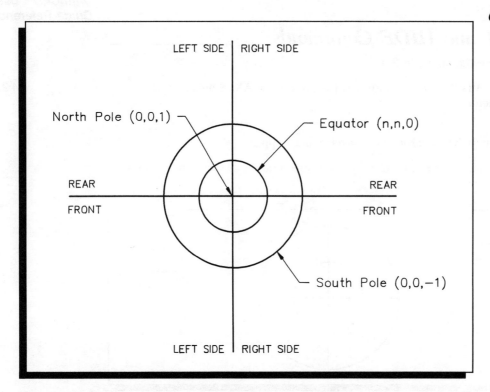

If your crosshairs are on the right side of the vertical line, your viewpoint will be on the right side of the object. Similarly, if your crosshairs are in front of the horizontal line, then your viewpoint will be in front of the object.

Your object should look somewhat like the one below.

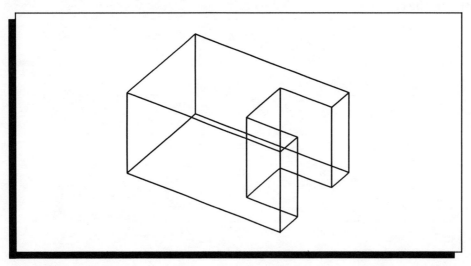

4 After viewing the object in 3D, enter the **HIDE** command to remove the hidden lines.

14.2.3

Your object should now look similar to the following.

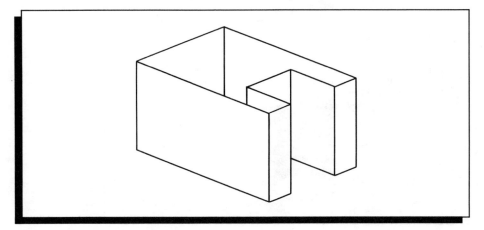

5 Return to your plan view (0,0,1) of the object by entering **VPOINT** and then selecting **PLAN**.

6 **ZOOM All** to obtain the original plan view.

Adding Objects of Different Elevation and Thickness

Now, let's add the cylinder to the object at a new elevation and thickness.

1 Enter the **ELEV** command; set the elevation at **-1** and the thickness at **6**.

Try to visualize how the cylinder will appear in relation to the existing object.

2 Draw a circle in the center of your object.

3 Enter **VPOINT** and **AXES**, and place the crosshairs in a similar location as before.

Does your object appear as you had visualized it?

4 Remove the hidden lines by entering the **HIDE** command.

14.5

Does your object now look similar to the object found near the beginning of this unit? It should.

5 Now, experiment with the viewpoint (VPOINT) to obtain a look from different points in space.

6 Attempt creating a 3D view of the object as shown on the following page.

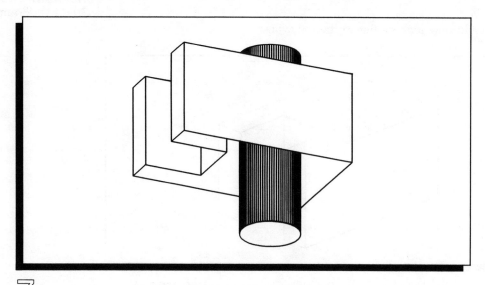

7 Enter **END** to save one of your 3D views and exit the Drawing Editor.

AUTOCAD™ AT WORK

CAD/CAM with AutoCAD

Cutting plastic parts is time-consuming and sometimes dangerous work. Working with a table saw and a hand-held router, a parts manufacturer could spend hours on a single job. And a slip of the hand could result in a serious cut or dismemberment.

A company which manufactures plastic parts for small household conveniences (such as paper towel holders) recently computerized its manufacturing division in order to increase production and reduce injuries. Using AutoCAD, the company's designers draw the path a router should follow. The drawing is then interfaced with an electronically operated router, a 5' × 10' table with a blade whose movements can be programmed. The router operator places the uncut plastic on the table and starts the programmed router, which cuts out a perfectly tooled part.

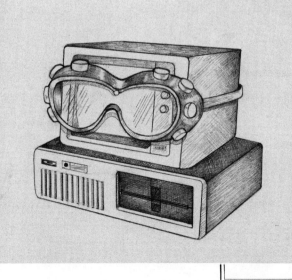

Not only have safety and product quality increased at the plant since the introduction of AutoCAD, but it has also simplified the designers' work. The company's president notes, "When I use AutoCAD to draw, I don't have to reach for a French curve—I have the choice of nine different ways to create an arc in AutoCAD. I pick whatever suits my needs and let the computer draw it for me."

AutoCAD's three-dimensional display feature offers another advantage for parts manufacturers. Having a three-dimensional drawing of the geometry of a tool path allows the designer to see what a shape will look like before it is created.

According to the president, CAD is responsible for dramatic increases in production in the last year: "Before acquiring AutoCAD, we were just cutting by hand. With one man operating a machine interfaced with AutoCAD, we can cut 1,000 paper towel holder blanks in a day. By hand there's no way to get that kind of output or product consistency."

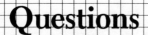 **Questions**

1. Describe the purpose of the ELEV command.

   _____

   _____

2. What is the viewpoint when viewing the plan view of a drawing?

   _____

3. The extrusion thickness of your object is specified with what command?

   _____

4. Briefly explain the process by which you create objects (within the same drawing) at different elevations and thicknesses.

   _____

   _____

   _____

   _____

5. When the small crosshairs are in the exact center of the globe, what is the location of the viewpoint in relation to the object?

   _____

6. Indicate on the globe below where the small crosshairs would be placed in order to view an object from the rear and underneath.

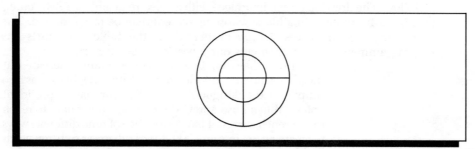

7. Match the following globe representations with the objects. The first one has been completed to give you a starting point.

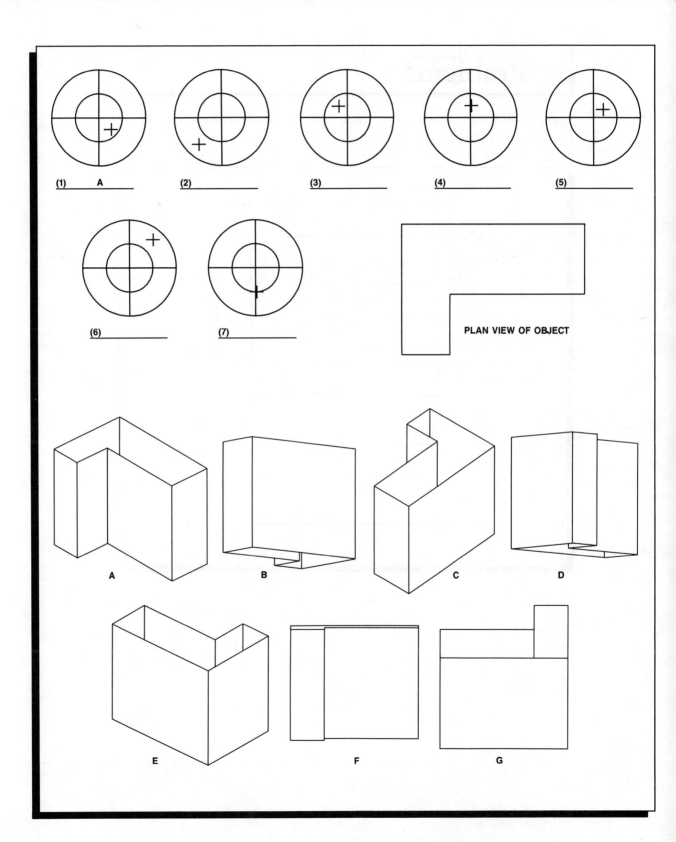

(1)　A

(2)

(3)

(4)

(5)

(6)

(7)

PLAN VIEW OF OBJECT

A

B

C

D

E

F

G

Problems

Draw the following objects and generate a 3D visualization of each.
In PRB30-1 set the elevation at 1 inch.

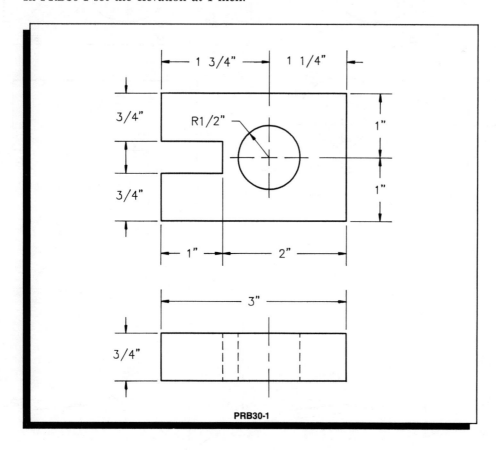

PRB30-1

In PRB30-2 set the elevation for the inner cylinder at 0.

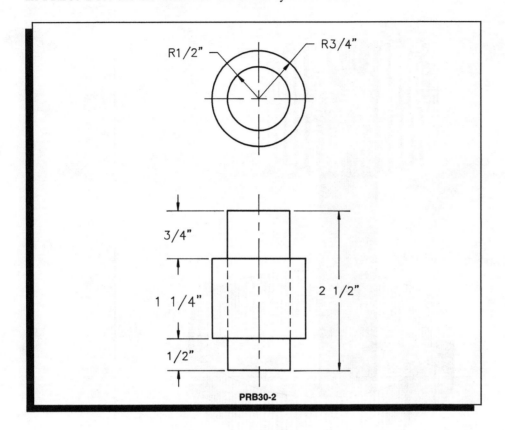

R1/2"   R3/4"

3/4"

1 1/4"   2 1/2"

1/2"

PRB30-2

183

In PRB30-3 try as best you can to draw a similar object.

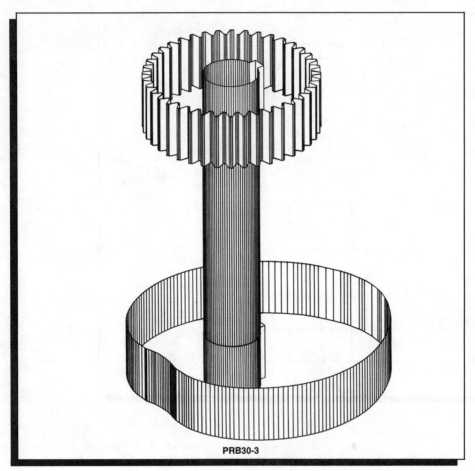

PRB30-3

AutoCAD Drawing Courtesy Gary Wells, Autodesk, Inc.

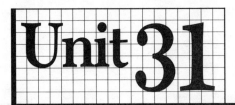

Unit 31 — A Look Inside AutoCAD's Screen Menu

■ OBJECTIVE:

To examine and understand the contents of AutoCAD's screen menu file ACAD.MNU

This unit concentrates on the components which make up the ACAD.MNU file. The unit involves reviewing the file in its raw form: the components you don't see when you're in the Drawing Editor. The main purpose of this unit is to allow you to later modify or create your own menu, a menu that can be as simple or as sophisticated as you'd like.

The following steps do not require a word processor, but it is desirable to have one. In a later exercise (when you actually create a custom menu), a word processor or text editor is highly recommended.

The Raw Menu

1 Boot your computer system and obtain your DOS prompt (*e.g.*, A> or E:).

2 Have the AutoCAD ACAD.MNU file resident on your disk drive.

NOTE:

If you are working on a floppy disk system, ACAD.MNU is normally found on your storage/data diskette (originally contained on the AutoCAD Support Files diskette).

3 Using the DOS "TYPE" command, list the contents of ACAD.MNU.

Example: A>**TYPE ACAD.MNU** (and press **RETURN**)

NOTE:

The file will scroll off the screen before you can read it. Quickly press **CTRL S** to stop the scrolling. To resume scrolling, press any key.

You may want to press CTRL C and start over so that you can see the first portion of the file.

4 Stop the scrolling so that you have the first portion of the file on your screen.

Your screen should have information almost identical to the following.

```
***BUTTONS                         [LASTMENU]$S=                    [HELP:]^C? ATTDEF
;                                  **E 1
^CREDRAW                           [ERASE:]^CERASE
^C                                 window
^B                                 [last:]last;;$S=
^O                                 add
^G                                 remove
^D                                 undo
^E                                                                  [CANCEL:]^C
^T                                 [OOPS:]^COOPS $S=                **ATTDISP 1
***SCREEN                                                          [ATTDISP:]^CATTDISP
**S                                [CANCEL:]$S= ^C                 [normal]NORMAL $S=
[ R O O T]                                                         [on]ON $S=
[ M E N U]                                                         [off]OFF $S=

[BLOCKS]$S=BL                                                      [HELP:]^C? ATTDISP
[DIM:]$S=DIM ^CDIM
[DISPLAY]$S=DS                                                     [CANCEL:]^C
[DRAW]$S=DR                        **BL                            **ATTEDIT 1
[EDIT]$S=ED                        [ATTRIB.]$S=ATT                 [ATTEDIT:]^CATTEDIT
[HATCH:]^CHATCH $S=HATCH           [BASE:]^CBASE $S=BASE           yes
[INQUIRY]$S=INQ                    [BLOCK:]^CBLOCK $S=BLOCK        no
[LAYERS]$S=LY                      [INSERT:]^CINSERT $S=INSERT     [window]W;
[MODES]$S=MD                       [WBLOCK:]^CWBLOCK $S=WBLOCK     [last]L;
[PLOT]$S=PLOT                                                      value
[UTILITY]$S=UT                                                     position
                                                                   height
                                                                   angle
                                                                   style
                                                                   layer
                                   [DISPLAY]$S=DS                  next
**O                                [DRAW]$S=DR                     [change]C;
[quick,]quick,^Z                   [EDIT]$S=ED                     [replace]R;
                                   [LAYERS]$S=LY
center                             [MODES]$S=MD                    [HELP:]^C? ATTEDIT
endpoint                                                           [OSNAP]$S=O
insert                                                             [CANCEL:]^C
intersec                           [LASTMENU]$S=                   **BASE 1
midpoint                           [ROOTMENU]$S=S                  [BASE:]^CBASE
nearest                            **ATT 1
node                               [ATTDEF:]^CATTDEF $S=ATTDEF     [HELP:]^C? BASE
perpend                            [ATTDISP:]^CATTDISP $S=ATTDISP
quadrant                           [ATTEDIT:]^CATTEDIT $S=ATTEDIT  [OSNAP]$S=O
tangent                            [ATTEXT:]^CATTEXT

none                               **ATTDEF 1                      [CANCEL:]^C
                                   [ATTDEF:]^CATTDEF               **BLOCK 1
                                   [invis]I;                       [BLOCK:]^CBLOCK
                                   [constant]C;                    [window]W;
                                   [verify]V;                      [last]L;
                                   [aligned]A;                     add
                                   [centered]C;                    remove
                                   [right]R;                       undo
                                   [style]S;                       [yes]Y;
```

5 Find each of the following components in ACAD.MNU. They should all be contained within the first portion (three screens of information) of the menu.

***BUTTONS —specifies a buttons menu for the buttons on a mouse or digitizer cursor control

***SCREEN —specifies a screen menu

**XY —specifies a submenu; XY can be any two characters, such as BL

$S=BL —means to go to submenu **BL

$S= —means to go to the last menu

[BLOCKS] —the text enclosed by brackets will appear in the screen menu; in this particular case, the word BLOCKS will appear in the screen menu

; —this character will tell the computer to automatically press RETURN

\ —the backslash will stop the computer, and the computer will expect keyboard input from the user

(a space) —an empty space is the same as pressing the space bar

^ —this character will automatically press the CTRL key

^C —this will cancel a command sequence the same as CTRL C

^O —this will activate the CTRL and O keys the same as if you were to press CTRL O to toggle the Ortho mode; ^O is used in the BUTTONS menu to assign button #6 to this function

Now let's take a look at the following menu items. Find them in ACAD.MNU.

[ERASE:]^CERASE —will display ERASE: in the screen menu and will cancel and enter the ERASE command.

[BLOCK:]^CBLOCK $S=BLOCK —will display BLOCK: in the screen menu and will cancel and enter the BLOCK command and take you to the Block Submenu.

[last]L; —will display last in the screen menu and will automatically enter L and press RETURN.

[LAYERS]$S=LY —will display LAYERS and will take you to the LY (Layers) Submenu.

AUTOCAD™ AT WORK

Powerful Connections: Linking AutoCAD to Other Programs

AutoCAD by itself is a powerful program; but by linking it with other programs, users can make their systems even more powerful and versatile. Over 150 products which complement AutoCAD are now available. Some of these are described below. You'll also find these, and many others, listed in the *AutoCAD Applications Catalog*, available from Autodesk Inc.

Architectural Design

For serious architectural design applications, AutoCAD can be used with a program called AE/CADD. The AutoCAD program was designed as a general-purpose drafting and design tool; the user community saw a need to build on the program for specific building and construction applications. Hence, AE/CADD was developed. AutoCAD and AE/CADD provide an extensive library of symbols and details, a capability for producing door and window schedules, and helpful drawing aids such as double lines for wall construction.

Bill of Materials Generation

AutoCAD users are discovering applications for linking AutoCAD with programs such as Lotus 1-2-3 and dBASE II. After making attribute assignments while in AutoCAD, users have the option to create an extract file (in DIF format) using a third-party program called LADS. After the AutoCAD drawing file is translated into a DIF format, it can be read into other programs, including Lotus and dBASE. Hence, users can perform calculations and display the attribute information in any form allowed by these two programs.

Large CAD Systems

Companies can now have the best of both worlds: the sophisticated engineering and modeling capabilities of large, expensive CAD systems and the low cost and functionality of AutoCAD. With third-party programs such as AutoLINK, companies can link conventional CAD systems such as Intergraph, CADAM, and Computervision with AutoCAD. The drawing files can be passed in both directions, thereby enabling users to take advantage of the benefits of both systems.

Numerical Control

Machinists and NC (Numerical Control) programmers are utilizing AutoCAD for creating their part design and tool path information. With a third-party program

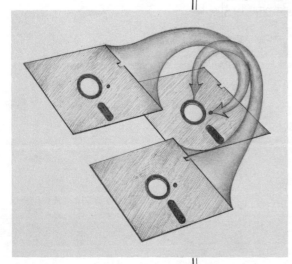

called NC Programmer, users are applying the entire computer-aided design/computer-aided manufacturing process using low-cost microcomputers.

Structural Engineering

Civil and structural engineers are discovering applications for performing both static and dynamic analyses for the design of structures. Finite element analysis programs such as AutoFRAME and SAP86 operate with AutoCAD to provide a more functional system for calculating stresses, heat transfer, and other types of structural engineering functions.

Word Processing

The text editing capability of word processors can be linked with the graphics capability of AutoCAD. If a drawing contains large amounts of notes and specifications, this text can first be prepared using a word processor. The text file is then converted into an AutoCAD drawing file using a third-party program called AutoWord. As a drawing file, the text can then be inserted into any AutoCAD drawing. Since AutoCAD is not a word processor, this process saves hours of time and produces a better end product.

Questions

Briefly describe what each of the following ACAD.MNU items will do.

[DIM:]$S=DIM^CDIM

_____

_____

[style]S;

_____

[HELP:]^C? BLOCK

_____

_____

**LINE

_____

[3-point:]^CARC \\DRAG

_____

_____

window

_____

[*]*

_____

[INSERT:]^CINSERT

_____

[ELLIPSE:]^CINSERT ELLIPSE \DRAG \DRAG

_____

_____

Problems

1. Print the ACAD.MNU file and then load AutoCAD. Get into the Drawing Editor and experiment with different command and submenu sequences. Locate the sequences on the ACAD.MNU printout.

2. Locate items in the ACAD.MNU printout that you cannot fully visualize. Then find the corresponding item in the screen menu and execute it.

Unit 32   Creating Screen Menus

■ OBJECTIVE:

AutoCAD™ User Guide Reference

B.2

To create a simple AutoCAD screen menu

This exercise involves the development of an AutoCAD screen menu which incorporates several commonly used AutoCAD commands. The exercise uses a very simple approach in creating the menu items; it does not require a word processor or text editor.

AutoCAD users can create any type of screen menu to include any AutoCAD commands and functions. Furthermore, users can develop "macros," which automatically execute any series of inputs from the keyboard. For example, a simple two-item macro can be created to enter ZOOM Window in one step, thereby minimizing input from the user. ZOOM W could then be included on, and activated from, a screen menu. Sophisticated macros can be created to activate several AutoCAD commands and functions in a single step.

Everything that can be entered using the keyboard can be entered automatically via macros. Thus, you can develop a menu at any level of sophistication with lots of flexibility and power.

Developing a Screen Menu with Macros _____

Let's develop a simple screen menu.

1 Boot your computer system and obtain your DOS prompt.

2 If you're working on a floppy disk system, place your storage/data diskette into the computer at this point. You will store the following file on this diskette.

_____ NOTE: _____

If you have a word processor or text editor, feel free to use it for the following. Create a new file and name it SIMPLE.MNU. Store the contents shown in Step 4.

3 If you don't have a word processor or text editor, type the following after the DOS prompt: **COPY CON:SIMPLE.MNU** and press **RETURN**.

You have just begun a new file named SIMPLE.MNU.

Your cursor should now be at the beginning of the next line.

4 Begin typing the contents of the following menu. Type exactly as shown. Use either upper- or lowercase letters for the macros (the information after the second bracket).

_____ NOTE: _____

Your only editing capability is your backspace key, so be very careful. If you make a mistake you cannot correct, you must start over.

```
***SCREEN (press RETURN)
[   A] (press RETURN)
[SIMPLE] (press RETURN)
[ MENU] (press RETURN)
(press RETURN)
(press RETURN)
[LINE]line (press RETURN)
[ERAS L]^CERASE L (press RETURN)
[ZOOM W]^Czoom W (press RETURN)
[TEXT]text (press RETURN)
[*Cancel*]^C (press RETURN)
press the F6 function key and press RETURN
```

5 When you're finished, make a backup copy of this file.

6 Load AutoCAD and bring up the Drawing Editor.

You should now have the standard ACAD.MNU items on your screen.

MENU Command

1 Enter the MENU command.

3.9

2 For the menu name, type SIMPLE.

Did your new SIMPLE menu appear? It should have.

3 Select each of the commands to see whether they work.

NOTE:

You also have full access to all other AutoCAD commands. Just type them.

AUTOCAD™ AT WORK

Young Disabled Designer Uses AutoCAD

Ron Grooms, a computer science researcher at Iowa State University in Ames, Iowa, is the director of the university's vocational training project for seriously disabled students. The purpose of the project is to teach students with disabilities to use computerized word processing, data bases, and spread sheets.

When Autodesk Inc. heard about the project, the company donated an AutoCAD program. For one of Grooms' star pupils, 15-year-old Jeff Hanson, AutoCAD opened the door to his talents as a graphic artist.

Although Jeff was born without hands or lower forearms, he has always been a talented artist. Jeff could draw and paint pictures by grasping a pen or brush between his forearms. The results were professional looking, but the process was slow and difficult. Grooms began to look for ways to make drawing easier for Jeff.

Grooms, who has backgrounds in electrical engineering, mathematics, and computer science, solved the problem by pairing AutoCAD with a Texas Instruments Professional computer that has voice recognition capability. Now Jeff can speak commands into the computer instead of having to type them on a keyboard, and his physical limitations no longer inhibit his ability to draw.

First Jeff learned the spoken commands he needed to operate AutoCAD. Then he and Grooms added voice commands that allowed Jeff to draw basic shapes, such as rectangles and ellipses. Next Jeff programmed the computer to respond to his voice by storing his voiceprints in the computer.

When Jeff speaks a command into the specially adapted mouthpiece, the computer scans its memory for the correct voiceprint. Once the computer finds the voiceprint, it translates the command to AutoCAD. Thus, when Jeff speaks the word *circle*, a circle appears on the computer screen. By using voice recognition and AutoCAD, Jeff hopes to eventually fulfill his dream of becoming a graphic artist or a designer in the aerospace industry.

The Future. Grooms thinks AutoCAD with voice recognition is not limited to disabled designers, and he sees a time when every computer will respond to voice commands. According to Grooms, "Voice recognition is so much faster and efficient than keying, and technological developments are coming so fast that it's just a matter of time before computer keyboards are obsolete."

Questions

1. Briefly define an AutoCAD macro.

   _____

   _____

2. Why are custom macros, contained in a screen menu, useful?

   _____

   _____

3. The INSERT command can be included in a macro like any other command. In conjunction with a drawing name, how could this macro be useful?

   _____

   _____

4. State one useful application for developing a new AutoCAD macro, and write this macro below.

   _____

   _____

   _____

5. What AutoCAD command allows you to bring up a new screen menu?

   _____

6. What is the file extension for a menu file?

   _____

7. What menu item specification must precede all screen menu contents?

   _____

Problems

1. Create the following screen menu and name it SECOND.MNU. Upon completion, load AutoCAD and Begin a New Drawing. Name it PRB32-1. Load the SECOND menu and execute each of its commands to see whether and how they work.

```
[LINE]line
[ERAS W]erase w
[ERASE]erase
[ZOOM W]zoom w
[ZOOM P]zoom p
[COMP S]style comp complex;;;;;;
[His Name]text 6,2 .2 0 John Doe;;Associate Professor;
[My Name]text s comp 6,3 .2 0;
[FLIPSNAP]^B
[ARCH U]units 4;;;;graphser
```

```
[FLIP T]textser;
[*Cancel*]^C
```

2. Modify the menu called SECOND.MNU so that it looks exactly like the one below. You'll need to use a word processor or a text editor such as EDLIN.

```
**SA
[LINE]line $S=ZZ
[ERAS W]erase w
[ERASE]erase
[ZOOM W]zoom w
[ZOOM P]zoom p
[COMP S]style comp complex;;;;;;
[His Name]text 6,2 .2 0 John Deer;;Associate Professor;
[My Name]text s comp 6,3 .2 0;
[FLIPSNAP]^B
[ARCH U]units 4;;;;graphser
[FLIP T]textser;
[*Cancel*]^C
[LASTMENU]$S=
[ROOTMENU]$S=S
```

```
**ZZ
[End Pt]end
[Mid Pt]mid
[Tang]tangent
[More]$S=O
```

Make a copy of the AutoCAD standard menu called ACAD.MNU and REName it to ACAD2.MNU. Then add the contents of SECOND.MNU to ACAD2.MNU as shown by the following printout. Be sure to add the item called SAMPLE to the Root Menu as indicated.

HINT:
Use a word processor such as Volkswriter® or Wordstar® to perform this operation. Use the word processor's "text merge" or "file read" capability.

```
***BUTTONS
;
^CREDRAW
^C
^B
^O
^G
^D
^E
^T
***SCREEN
**S
[ R O O T]
[ M E N U]

[BLOCKS]$S=BL
[DIM:]$S=DIM ^CDIM
[DISPLAY]$S=DS
[DRAW]$S=DR
[EDIT]$S=ED
[HATCH:]^CHATCH $S=HATCH
[INQUIRY]$S=INQ
[LAYERS]$S=LY
[MODES]$S=MD
[PLOT]$S=PLOT
[UTILITY]$S=UT
[SAMPLE]$S=SA




**SA
[LINE]line  $S=ZZ
[ERAS W]erase w
[ERASE]erase
[ZOOM W]zoom w
[ZOOM P]zoom p
[COMP S]style comp complex;;;;;;
[His Name]text 6,2 .2 0 John Deer;;Associate Professor
[My Name]text s comp 6,3 .2 0;
[FLIPSNAP]^B
[ARCH U]units 4;;;;graphscr
[FLIP T]textscr;
[*Cancel*]^C
```

[LASTMENU]$S =
[ROOTMENU]$S = S

**ZZ
[End Pt]end
[Mid Pt]mid
[Tang]tangent
[More]$S = O

**O
[quick,]quick,^Z

center
endpoint
insert
intersec
midpoint
nearest
node
perpend
quadrant
t a n g e n t

[LASTMENU]$S =
**E 1
[ERASE:]^CERASE
window
[last:]last;;$S =
add
remove
undo

[OOPS:]^COOPS $S =

[CANCEL:]$S = ^C

After completing the above, load AutoCAD and bring up ACAD2.MNU into the AutoCAD Drawing Editor to see whether each menu item works properly. Be sure to select the new item called SAMPLE from the Root Menu.

Also, be sure to experiment with selecting the LINE command from the Sample Submenu, and then pick each of its submenu items, including "more."

3. Develop a new custom screen menu (and buttons menu, too, if you'd like). Make the menu as sophisticated and powerful as you'd like.

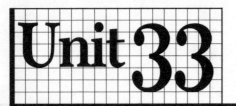

Unit 33 Creating Tablet Menus

■ OBJECTIVE:

AutoCAD™ User
Guide Reference

To apply the **TABLET** command, the tablet configuration steps, and the tablet menu development process

This unit focuses on configuring a digitizing tablet for use with a tablet menu and on creating tablet menus. You must, of course, have a digitizing tablet to complete this exercise.

As you know, part of your digitizing tablet allows for *screen menu* pointing. This enables you to select screen menu items with your pointing device instead of typing them in. Other areas of the digitizing tablet can be designated for *tablet menus*, enabling you to enter a wide variety of AutoCAD commands and functions quickly and conveniently.

12.1

The first step in designing a tablet menu is to sketch the entire tablet menu overlay on paper so that you have some sense of the placement of each menu component. The sketch is then used in developing the actual menu file. In this unit, a sample tablet menu overlay has been provided. Later, after you've learned the procedures, you'll be able to design your own.

■ *Developing a Tablet Menu* _____

The sample on the next page is a relatively simple but functional tablet menu overlay. Let's use it as the model for the following steps.

1 Make an enlarged photocopy of the tablet menu overlay. If your copier doesn't have enlargement capability, you may need to sketch the overlay by hand.

_____ NOTE: _____

The overlay must not extend outside the active area on your digitizer. For instance, if your active area is 1′ x 1′, then the overlay must not be larger than 1′ x 1′.

Now let's create the menu file that holds the menu items (macros). Notice how these menu items correspond to the items on the tablet menu overlay, starting with Tablet Menu 1.

2 Using COPY CON: or better yet, a word processor, enter the following. Name the file **FIRSTTAB.MNU**. Be sure to enter the following exactly as it is. Press **RETURN** after each entry.

_____ NOTE: _____

The Buttons Menu is for a three-button cursor control.

12.2

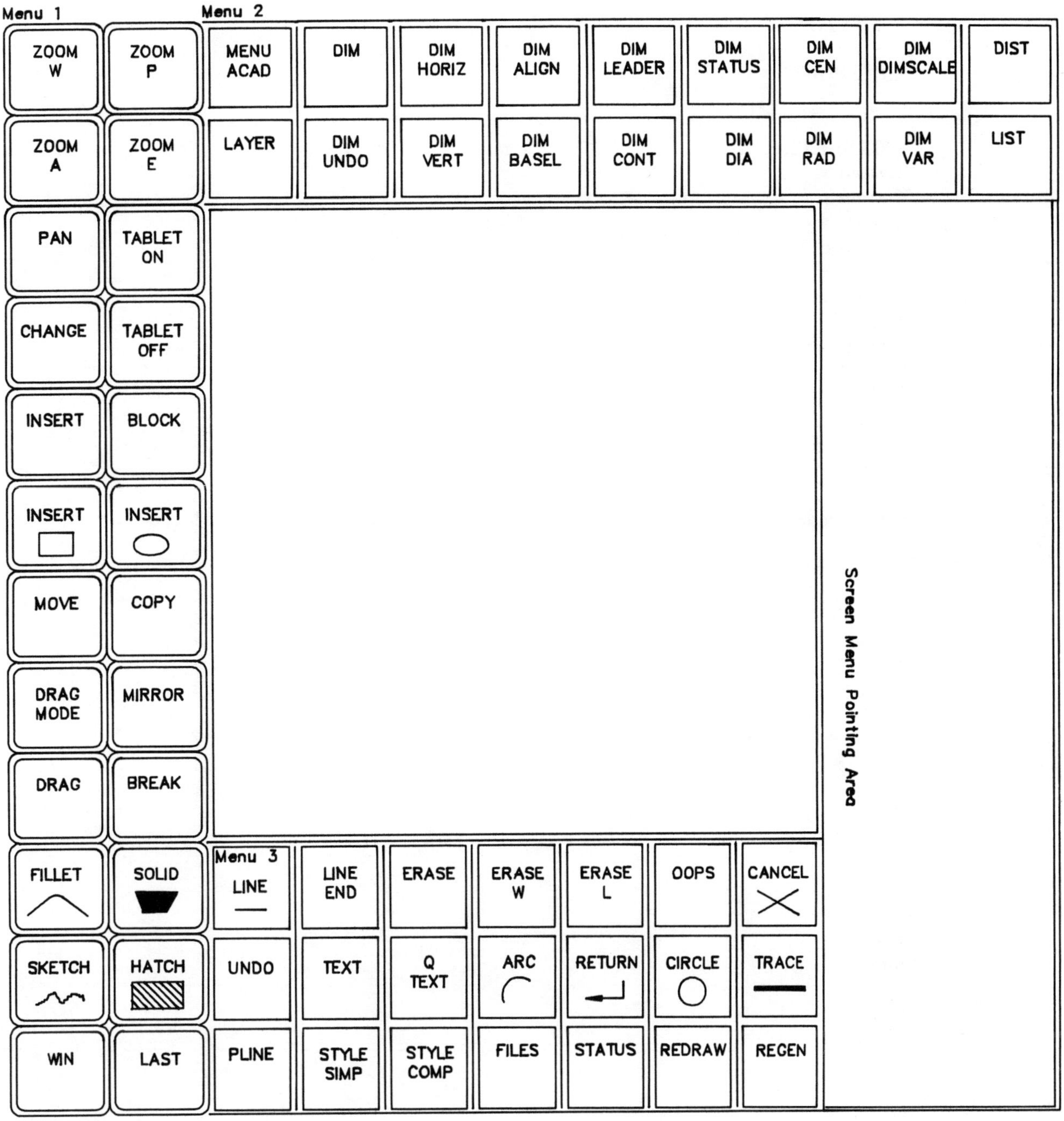

| ZOOM W | ZOOM P | MENU ACAD | DIM | DIM HORIZ | DIM ALIGN | DIM LEADER | DIM STATUS | DIM CEN | DIM DIMSCALE | DIST |
| ZOOM A | ZOOM E | LAYER | DIM UNDO | DIM VERT | DIM BASEL | DIM CONT | DIM DIA | DIM RAD | DIM VAR | LIST |

PAN	TABLET ON
CHANGE	TABLET OFF
INSERT	BLOCK
INSERT ▭	INSERT ⬭
MOVE	COPY
DRAG MODE	MIRROR
DRAG	BREAK
FILLET ⌒	SOLID ▼

Screen Menu Pointing Area

| SKETCH | HATCH |

Menu 3

FILLET ⌒	SOLID ▼	LINE —	LINE END	ERASE	ERASE W	ERASE L	OOPS	CANCEL ✕
SKETCH ⌇	HATCH ▨	UNDO	TEXT	Q TEXT	ARC ⌒	RETURN ↵	CIRCLE ○	TRACE ▬
WIN	LAST	PLINE	STYLE SIMP	STYLE COMP	FILES	STATUS	REDRAW	REGEN

199

```
***BUTTONS
;
^CREDRAW


***TABLET1
^Czoom  w
^Czoom  p
^Czoom  a
^Czoom  e
^Cpan
^Ctablet  on
^Cchange
^Ctablet  off
^Cinsert
^Cblock
^Cinsert  rectang
^Cinsert  ellipse
^Cmove
^Ccopy
^Cdragmode
^Cmirror
drag
^Cbreak
^Cfillet
^Csolid
^Csketch
^Chatch
window


last
***TABLET2
^Cmenu  acad
^Cdim
horizontal
aligned
leader
status
center
dimscale
^Cdist
^Clayer
undo
vertical
baseline
continue
diameter
radius
variables
^Clist
```

```
***TABLET3
^Cline
^Cline end
^Cerase
^Cerase w
^Cerase l
^Coops
^C
undo
^Ctext
^Cqtext
^Carc
;
^Ccircle
^Ctrace
^Cpline
^Cstyle simp simplex;;;;;;
^Cstyle comp complex;;;;;;
^Cfiles
^Cstatus
^Credraw
^Cregen
```

③ Be sure to store the menu contents, and then place the file on a drive accessible by AutoCAD if it is not already.

④ Make a backup copy of the file.

TABLET Command _____

① Secure the menu overlay to your digitizer tablet with tape.

_____ NOTE: _____

Be sure that all of the overlay is inside the active pointing area of your digitizer. If it is not, the tablet configuration process will not work.

② Load AutoCAD and bring up the Drawing Editor.

③ Enter the **TABLET** command, and then enter the Configuration (**CFG**) option.

You should get the following on your screen.

12.4

12.4.4

```
Enter number of tablet menus desired (0-4):
```

④ Enter 3.

You should now have the following.

```
Do you want to realign tablet menu areas? <N>
```

5 Enter **Y** for yes because we need to tell AutoCAD where we want the menus on our tablet.

You should now have the following on your screen.

```
Digitize upper left corner of menu area 1:
```

6 Locate the upper left corner of menu 1 and pick that point.

NOTE:

In this particular overlay, menu 1 is comprised of the first two columns.

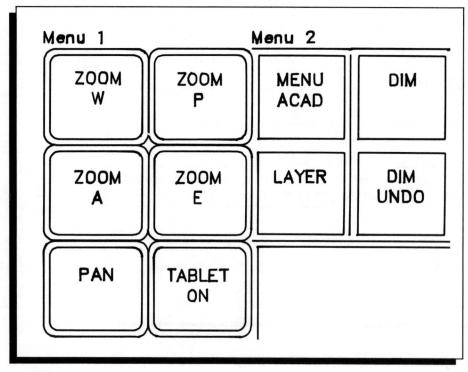

7 Pick the lower left corner of menu 1.

8 .... and the lower right corner of menu 1.

You have just defined the boundaries of menu 1.

9 Enter **2** for the number of columns in menu 1.

10 .... and **12** for the number of rows in menu 1.

AutoCAD should now be prompting you for the upper left corner of menu 2.

11 Locate menu 2 and its upper left corner, and pick that point.

——————— NOTE: ———————

Menu 2 is comprised of the upper two rows, beginning with the cell called MENU ACAD. Menu 2 consists of 9 columns and 2 rows.

12 Proceed exactly as you did with menu 1 until you are finished with menu 2, and then proceed with menu 3.

After you are finished with all three menus, you should get the following on your screen.

```
Do you want to respecify the screen pointing area? <N>
```

13 Reply with a Yes because we do.

14 Digitize the lower left and the upper right corners of the screen pointing area: the square area bounded by the three menus.

You are now finished with the tablet configuration.

Note that the right portion of the overlay is left open for selecting screen menu items.

MENU Command ——————————————

Now let's bring up the tablet menu called FIRSTTAB.MNU.

1 Enter the **MENU** command and type **FIRSTTAB**.

If you correctly completed the above steps, you should now have full access to your tablet menu.

2 Experiment with the tablet menu by picking each of the cells on the overlay.

Do they work?

Neat, huh?

③ To get the original ACAD.MNU back, pick the tablet menu item called **MENU ACAD** (near the upper left corner) or enter the **MENU** command and type **ACAD.**

Combining Menus

Now let's combine FIRSTTAB.MNU with AutoCAD's screen menu. This will provide us with the best of both worlds: availability of a full-function screen menu and availability of a full-function tablet menu.

NOTE:

This process will require a word processor.

To avoid changing (or accidentally corrupting) AutoCAD's ACAD.MNU, let's work with the file we previously created called ACAD2.MNU. If that file does not exist, simply copy ACAD.MNU onto another disk and directory and REName it ACAD2.MNU so that you won't disturb the original ACAD.MNU.

① Bring up the contents of ACAD2.MNU with a word processor.

② Using the capabilities of the word processor, insert (or read in) the entire contents of FIRSTTAB.MNU. Place it at the beginning of ACAD2.MNU.

③ Eliminate one of the Buttons Menus (***BUTTONS) by deleting the small one contained in FIRSTTAB.MNU.

④ Store all in the file called ACAD2.MNU.

Now let's try it out.

① Load AutoCAD and bring up the Drawing Editor.

NOTE:

Make sure the ACAD2.MNU file is accessible by AutoCAD.

② Enter the **MENU** command and type **ACAD2.MNU.**

You should now have access to all AutoCAD screen commands and submenus as well as all tablet menu commands and functions.

The power and functionality of your AutoCAD system have increased substantially, making it a more productive and valuable design/drafting tool.

AUTOCAD™ AT WORK

Designing Interiors Using AutoCAD

The job of an interior designer is to transform empty space into homes and offices. AutoCAD helps designers put together attractive, functional rooms. By reducing the labor involved in making and changing drawings, AutoCAD gives designers more time to be creative.

The interior designer using AutoCAD begins by viewing the architect's drawings on the computer screen. The next step is to fill the empty space, starting with interior walls and ending with small details, such as the color of the telephones. Then the finished plan is printed for the customer's review. AutoCAD's editing capabilities make alterations easy.

AutoCAD frees the designer from many routine tasks. For example, it can help furnish a room. Using AutoCAD, the designer first draws desks, chairs, and other items and stores them in a library file. Many designers store a variety of furniture styles, such as Victorian, Scandinavian, and so on. When the time comes to furnish a room, the designer simply calls up the desired items from the library — no need to draw them from scratch.

AutoCAD's layering capability is another useful aid. The designer can begin with a base layer consisting of walls, doors, and windows. The next layer might include the electrical layout, and still another layer, the furniture. Each layer can be printed in a different color to make it stand out, and the layers can be viewed individually or in any combination.

As an added advantage, AutoCAD can be used for nondrafting tasks. With a few simple commands, AutoCAD can be programmed to count chairs, lights, outlets, doors, etc., and to assemble a bill of materials for a project as it's being developed. This gives a designer the advantage of accurately estimating the cost of building and furnishing an entire office, and it can be done in minutes.

Finally, AutoCAD saves calculating time. It can compute the area of any shape, whether its sides are straight or curved—an indispensable feature for a profession that charges by the square foot!

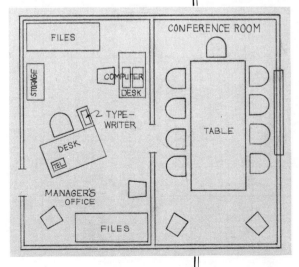

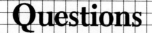

Questions

1. What AutoCAD command and command option are used to configure a digitizing tablet?

   _____

2. Explain the purpose of tablet configuration.

   _____

   _____

   _____

   _____

3. What is the minimum and maximum number of tablet menus that can be included on a digitizing tablet?

   _____

4. Briefly describe the process of combining a tablet menu with AutoCAD's original menu called ACAD.MNU.

   _____

   _____

   _____

   _____

Problems

1. Develop a new tablet menu and incorporate a symbol library into one section of the menu. Use the previously created library called LIB1.DWG or create a new one. The following is a sample which should help you get started.

   ***TABLET1
   ^Cinsert LIB1;^C
   ^Cinsert TSAW;drag \drag \drag
   ^Cinsert DRILLP;drag \drag \drag
   ^Cinsert JOINT;drag \drag \drag

   ***TABLET2
   ^Cline
   ^Cerase
   ^Czoom w

2. Develop a new tablet menu using the steps outlined in this unit. Make the menu as sophisticated and powerful as possible. Utilize, as much as possible, AutoCAD's macro development capability.

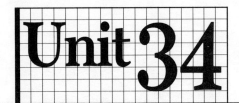

Unit 34   Digitizing Hardcopy Drawings

■ OBJECTIVE:

To practice inputting a hardcopy drawing into AutoCAD using the TABLET command

The intent of this unit is to step through the process of digitizing. Note that you must have a digitizing tablet connected to your CAD system before attempting this.

12.3

There will be times, especially in a business environment, when you'll wish that hand-completed drawings were stored in an AutoCAD format. For example, suppose your firm has recently implemented CAD and that all previous drawings were completed the traditional way. What if you need to revise the drawings? It's very time-consuming to redraw them by hand. Fortunately, most CAD systems, including AutoCAD, offer a method of getting those drawings onto disk. In some cases, it may not be practical to digitize a drawing; but in many cases, it is faster than starting the drawing from scratch. Let's try it.

■ *Setting Up* ⎯⎯⎯⎯⎯⎯⎯⎯⎯⎯⎯⎯

Ideally, you should digitize a drawing that is not yet in an AutoCAD format. Since you may not have fast access to a simple drawing not yet in AutoCAD, let's digitize the previously created drawing DIMEN. This drawing was completed during the dimensioning exercise (Unit 19) and is shown below.

⎯⎯⎯⎯⎯⎯⎯⎯ **NOTE:** ⎯⎯⎯⎯⎯⎯⎯⎯

If you do not have a hard copy of DIMEN, use the one printed here.

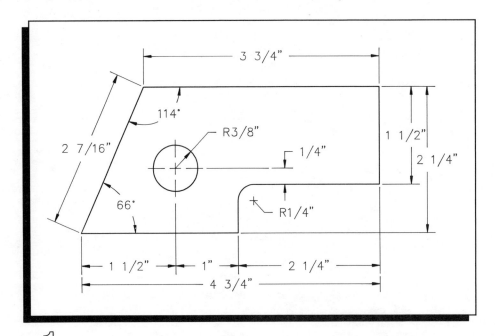

1   Load AutoCAD and select task **1**, "Begin a New Drawing."

To save time in establishing all of the drawing settings, you can use DIMEN as the prototype drawing.

2 Enter the name of the drawing as **DIGIT=DIMEN.**

3 When the drawing comes up, ERASE it.

If you choose not to use DIMEN as the prototype drawing, you will need to set each of the drawing parameters, such as the units, limits, etc.

NOTE:

Be sure the snap resolution is set at .25″ and is turned on. Also be sure your limits are ZOOMed All.

4 Set the layer called OBJ, if it is not already set.

5 Using drafting tape, fasten the drawing called DIMEN onto the center of your digitizing tablet.

NOTE:

If you are using the drawing in this book, make a photocopy to fasten to the tablet.

Calibrating the Drawing _____

Now, let's calibrate your drawing using the TABLET command.

1 Enter the **TABLET** command and select the **CAL**ibrate option.   12.4.1

We need to now identify two known (absolute) points on the drawing. Let's say the lower left corner of the object is absolute point 2,2.

2 In response to "Digitize first known point:" pick this point (be accurate) and enter the coordinates 2″,2″.

NOTE:

You will not have crosshairs on your screen.

Now we need to pick a second known point. Let's choose the corner located 2½″ to the right of the first point.

3 Pick this point and enter 4.5″,2″ for the coordinates.

You have just calibrated your drawing.

Digitizing the Drawing _____

Now let's begin to trace (digitize) the drawing by doing the object outline. Start at the lower left corner of the object, point 2,2.

1   Enter the **LINE** command.

2   Turn on the Tablet mode with the function key and digitize (pick) point 2,2.

HINT:
Whenever you digitize (pick) points from your drawing, the Tablet mode must be *on*. This mode can usually be toggled on and off with a function key. Whenever you select commands from the screen menu, the Tablet mode must be turned *off*.

13.3

3   With the Tablet mode on, digitize the next point (4.5,2), working counterclockwise. This should complete the first line segment.

HINT:
When drawing the first five line segments, have the Ortho mode turned on.

NOTE: _____

When digitizing the next point, ignore the fillet and pick the approximate location of the corner. The fillet will be inserted later. With Snap on, your selection of the corner will be accurate.

4   Continue on around the object until you Close the polygon.

...and that's all there is to it.

5   Using the **FILLET** command, place the fillet. Remember to turn Tablet off if you want to use the screen menu.

6   Reset the snap resolution at **.125"** (1/8").

7   Using the **CIRCLE** command, place the circle.

HINT:
When picking the circle's center and radius, be sure Tablet is on and digitize the center and radius from the hardcopy drawing.

⑧ Set the layer called DIM.

⑨ Using AutoCAD's dimensioning commands, fully dimension the object with Tablet mode off.

You're finished.

⑩ Enter **END** to save your work and to exit the Drawing Editor.

AUTOCAD™ AT WORK

Using AutoCAD's "Photographic Memory"

Computer-aided design became even more "user friendly" recently with the advent of CAD/camera™, a software program that transfers photographs of hand-completed drawings into the AutoCAD system.

Before CAD/camera, if designers using AutoCAD wanted to change a hand-completed drawing, they first had to record the existing drawing on disk by using AutoCAD to hand digitize it or redraw it. Sometimes the process took several days, and projects were often delayed weeks or months while operators translated detailed or multiple drawings.

But it takes CAD/camera only an hour or two to convert a paper drawing into a digitized drawing stored in AutoCAD. Once the drawing is in the AutoCAD system, the designer can edit or change the drawing at will.

The Future. The obvious advantage of CAD/camera is the time it saves designers by eliminating the tedious task of translating paper drawings into AutoCAD by hand. But as CAD/camera becomes more sophisticated, it won't be limited to translating line drawings.

Doctors could use CAD/camera to help in reconstructive surgery by transferring photographs and X rays to AutoCAD. Police detectives could translate photographs of crime scenes, suspects, victims, and murder weapons into AutoCAD for an in-depth computer analysis. Archaeologists and art historians could use AutoCAD-translated photographs to analyze and reconstruct important cultural and artistic achievements. CAD/camera's potential is nearly unlimited.

Questions

1. What command and command options are used to calibrate a drawing to be digitized?

_____

2. Why is the calibration process necessary?

_____

3. Briefly explain the process of calibrating a drawing to be digitized.

_____

_____

_____

_____

4. Why is the snap resolution important when digitizing?

_____

_____

5. Describe when the Tablet mode should be turned on and when it should be turned off.

_____

_____

6. If you have a mouse, explain whether you could digitize a drawing using only the mouse.

_____

_____

Problems

Select two or three hand-completed drawings you have access to and digitize each.

_____ NOTE: _____

It is possible to digitize drawings that are larger than your digitizing tablet. Simply move the drawing into the active area on your tablet and recalibrate.

 **Unit 35** Producing a Slide Show

■ OBJECTIVE:

AutoCAD™ User Guide Reference

To apply MSLIDE, VSLIDE, SCRIPT, RSCRIPT, DELAY, and RESUME in developing a slide show in a script file

The purpose of this exercise is to develop a slide show by making slides and including them in a script file. Though it may sound complicated, it is really very simple. A word processor is recommended for creation of sophisticated script files.

The following is a simple example of a script file. It's nothing more than a text file stored with an .SCR file extension. It can be executed when you begin a new drawing or after you are in the Drawing Editor.

10.3

UNITS 4 4 1 0
LIMITS 15',10'
ZOOM A
GRID 1
SNAP ON

With earlier versions of AutoCAD, users often used script files to store drawing parameters and settings, expediting the setup process. However, the use of prototype drawings has largely replaced this practice.

Script files can be used for other purposes. A common application is for showing a continuous sequence of drawings, a sort of electronic flipchart. AutoCAD calls this a slide show.

10.4

Before the script file can be created, we must first have slides to include in the script. Slides are created using existing drawings with the MSLIDE command (short for Make Slide). Let's call up a couple of drawings and create slides from them. Use the previously created drawings named THREE-D and DIMEN. Or, if you prefer, choose two others.

MSLIDE Command _____

① Load AutoCAD and Begin a New Drawing. Name it **SLIDE**.

② **INSERT** your drawing called THREE-D. Enter 0,0 for the insertion point. With VPOINT, create a 3D view.

9.4

③ Enter the **MSLIDE** command and give the slide file the same name as the drawing file (THREE-D).

10.4.1

_____ NOTE: _____

> The slide file will have a file extension of .SLD (THREE-D.SLD) and cannot be edited. The drawing file will remain untouched and can, of course, be edited.

④ **ERASE** the THREE-D drawing.

⑤ **INSERT** the second drawing (DIMEN) and create another slide.

VSLIDE Command

It's now appropriate and convenient to practice the VSLIDE command (short for View Slide), so let's do it.

1 Enter **VSLIDE** and type **THREE-D** (the .SLD extension is assumed). 10.4.2

Did it work?

2 To restore your original screen, enter **REGEN**.

If you'd like to create additional slides from other drawings, now is the time. 10.4.3

3 When you're finished making at least two slides, return to the Main Menu by entering **QUIT**.

4 Exit AutoCAD.

Creating the Script File

Now let's create the script file (slide show). It's going to be a short one!

1 If you have not done so yet, obtain your DOS prompt (*e.g.*, A>).

2 Begin a new file using the COPY CON method as shown below. Name the file SHOW.SCR, and be sure to specify the appropriate drive if necessary.

    A> COPY CON:SHOW.SCR (press **RETURN**)

3 Now simply type the following. Again, be sure to specify the appropriate drive if the slides reside on a drive or directory other than the default drive or directory. If you make a mistake, backspace or start over.

    VSLIDE THREE-D (RETURN)
    DELAY 1000 (RETURN)
    VSLIDE DIMEN (RETURN)
    DELAY 500 (RETURN)
    REDRAW (RETURN)
    (press **F6** function key and **RETURN**)

NOTE:

If you've chosen different drawings for slides, you must of course enter their names instead of "THREE-D" and "DIMEN."

You have just created a simple slide show stored in a script file.

NOTE:

The DELAY command tells AutoCAD to hold the slide on the screen for X number of milliseconds. Some computers run faster than others; nevertheless, 1000 milliseconds is approximately a one-second delay. 10.3.3

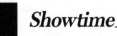

*Showtime*_____

Now let's try it out.

1 Load AutoCAD and bring up the Drawing Editor. It doesn't matter how you get there.

2 Enter the **SCRIPT** command, and type **SHOW**.   10.3.2

What happened?

3 To repeat the slide show, enter the **RSCRIPT** command.   10.3.6

This command could be included at the end of a script file to automatically repeat the slide show.

_____ NOTE: _____

> Pressing CTRL C or the back space key interrupts a running script. This allows   10.3.4
> you to issue other AutoCAD commands. If you wish to return to the script,
> simply enter **RESUME**.

4 Enter **QUIT** to exit the Drawing Editor.

AUTOCAD™ AT WORK

Artificial Intelligence and AutoCAD

Imagine this. You're designing an apartment building. At the beginning, the microcomputer asks for the style of the building, the approximate square footage, and the number of rental units. You enter the information. The computer then asks you for types and sizes of windows, doors, and rooms. Information about city codes and building regulations (such as maximum building height) is already in the system, thereby providing a knowledge base upon which to make design-related decisions. Additionally, good architectural design practices such as plumbing (bathrooms back-to-back) and traffic flow considerations have been previously programmed into the system.

The computer evaluates and synthesizes the information; and before your eyes, it draws an optimized floor plan of the building according to your specifications. The system also suggests efficient uses of floor space and building materials and calculates the approximate cost per square foot. At this point, the computer asks whether or not you like the preliminary floor plan and provides you an opportunity for making changes. Upon completion of the preliminary design, you are able to embellish the drawing with details.

We can expect to see this level of sophistication on a microCAD system in the near future. The "AI/AutoCAD" system of the future will offer power and intelligence well beyond our present-day microcomputer and CAD technology. Initial building designs will be expedited and optimized through AI programming techniques very similar to those described above, adding a totally new dimension to the design process.

Questions

1. Briefly describe the purpose of each of the following commands.

   MSLIDE _____

   VSLIDE _____

   SCRIPT _____

   RSCRIPT _____

   DELAY _____

   RESUME _____

2. Describe the purpose of an AutoCAD script file.

   _____

   _____

3. What is the file extension of a script file?

   _____

4. What does the number following the DELAY command indicate?

   _____

   _____

5. Is it more practical to store a drawing setup in a script file or in a prototype drawing? Explain why.

   _____

   _____

   _____

   _____

Problems

1. Create a dozen or so slides of previously created drawings. Include them in a slide show stored in a script file. Run the show.

2. Develop a script file using AutoCAD commands. Make it as sophisticated as possible by incorporating several different AutoCAD commands. When you're finished, print the file so that you can work out bugs as you run it.

Optional Problems

INTRODUCTION

The following problems are provided to give you additional practice with AutoCAD. These problems will help you to expand your knowledge and ability, and they will offer you new and exciting experiences with the system.

The problems range from simple to advanced, and they encompass a variety of disciplines. They have been correlated to the units of this book, but these correlations are simply suggestions. Your instructor may ask you to complete the problems in a different order.

Regardless of the type of problem, the key to successful completion is: **plan before beginning!** Review previously learned commands and techniques and ask yourself how they can best be applied to your problem. For example, when laying out rectangular objects, plan to utilize the Grid, Snap, and Ortho features. When drawing lines of specific lengths and angles, consider using relative and polar methods of specifying endpoints. Plan how to use COPY, MIRROR, and ARRAY to simplify and speed up your work.

As you discover new and easier methods of creating drawings, apply these methods while solving the problems. Since there is usually more than one way to complete a drawing, experiment with alternative methods. Discuss these alternatives with other users and create strategies for efficient completion of the problems.

Remember, there is no substitute for practice. The expertise you gain will be in direct proportion to the time you spend on the system. Set aside blocks of time to work with AutoCAD, think through your approach, and have fun!

Optional Problems for Units 6-11

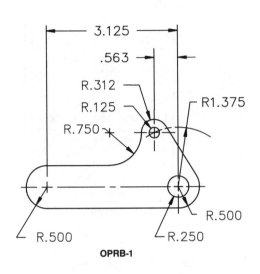

OPRB-1

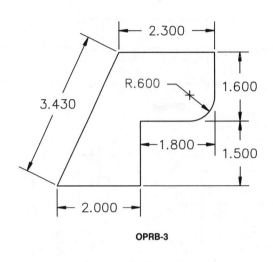

OPRB-3

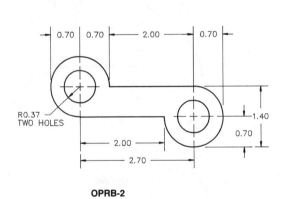

OPRB-2

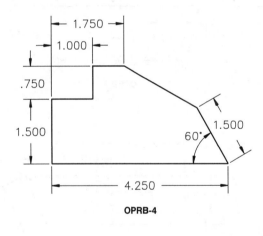

OPRB-4

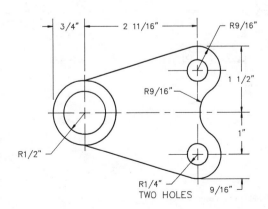

OPRB-5

Optional Problems for Units 12-22

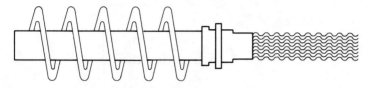

RUBY CRYSTAL LASER

OPRB-6

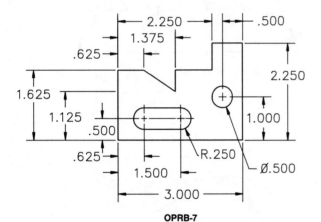

OPRB-7

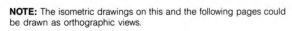

OPRB-8

OPRB-9*

COVER PLATE

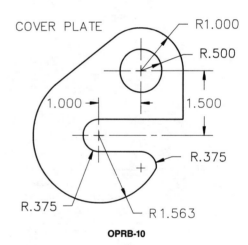

OPRB-10

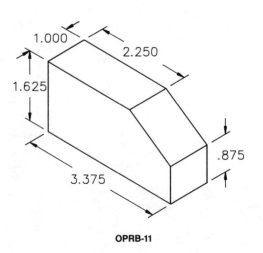

OPRB-11

NOTE: The isometric drawings on this and the following pages could be drawn as orthographic views.

*Courtesy of Paul Driscoll

220

Optional Problems for Units 12-22 (continued)

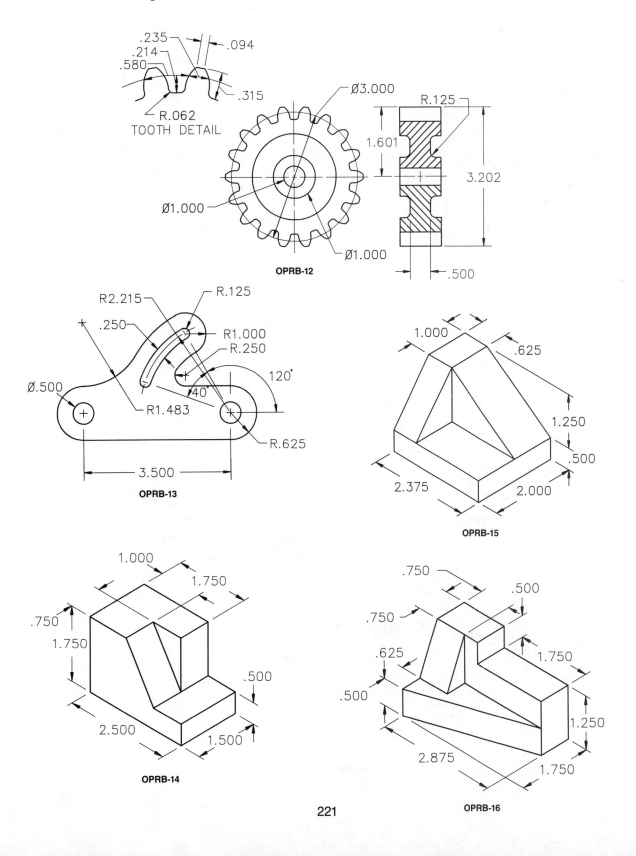

.235 .214 .580 .094 .315 R.062 TOOTH DETAIL

Ø3.000 R.125 1.601 3.202 Ø1.000 Ø1.000 .500

OPRB-12

R2.215 R.125 .250 R1.000 R.250 120° Ø.500 40° R1.483 R.625 3.500

OPRB-13

1.000 .625 1.250 .500 2.375 2.000

OPRB-15

1.000 1.750 .750 1.750 .500 2.500 1.500

OPRB-14

.750 .500 .750 1.750 .625 .500 1.250 2.875 1.750

OPRB-16

Optional Problems for Units 12-22 (continued)

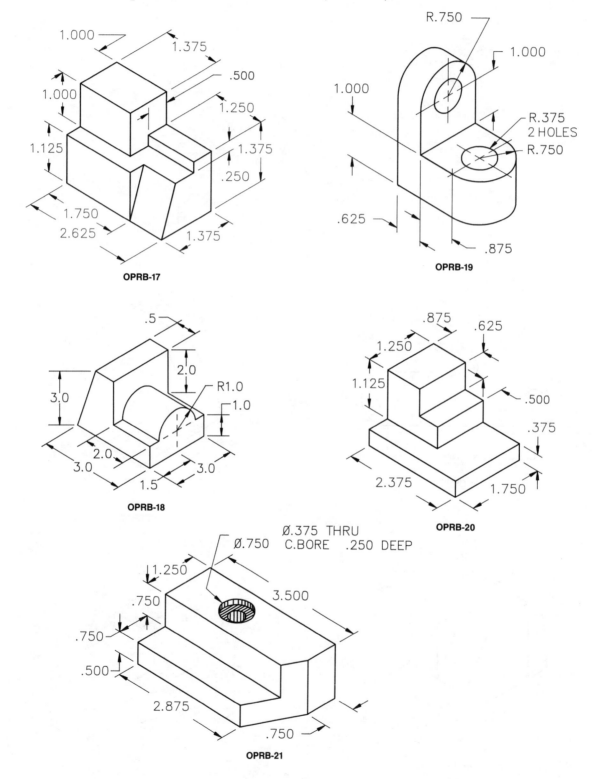

1.000
1.375
.500
1.000
1.250
1.125
1.375
.250
1.750
2.625
1.375

OPRB-17

R.750
1.000
1.000
R.375
2 HOLES
R.750
.625
.875

OPRB-19

.5
2.0
R1.0
3.0
1.0
2.0
3.0
3.0
1.5

OPRB-18

.875
.625
1.250
1.125
.500
.375
2.375
1.750

OPRB-20

Ø.375 THRU
Ø.750 C.BORE .250 DEEP
1.250
.750
3.500
.750
.500
2.875
.750

OPRB-21

Optional Problems for Units 12-22 (continued)

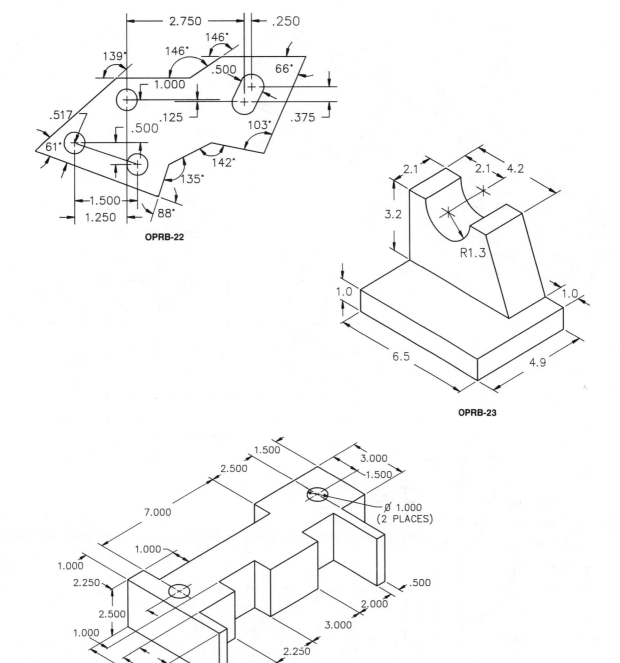

OPRB-22

OPRB-23

OPRB-24

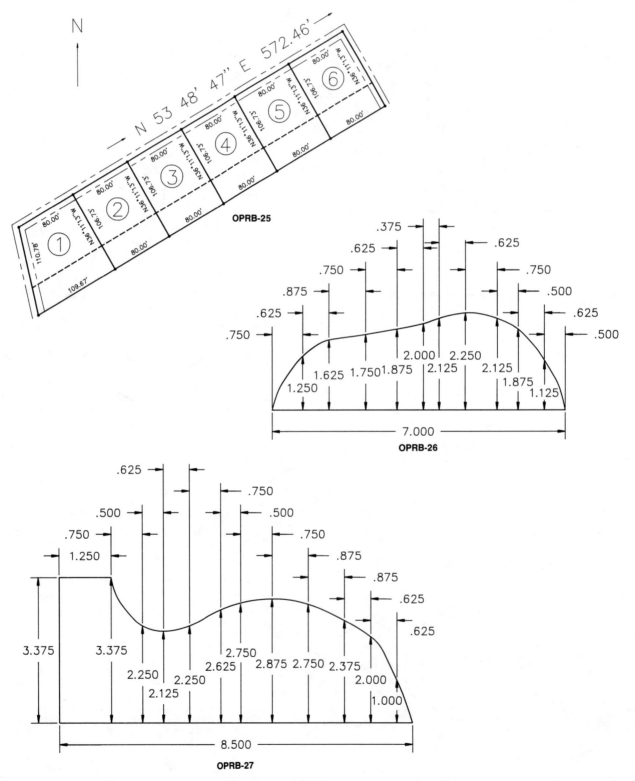

OPRB-25

OPRB-26

OPRB-27

Optional Problems for Units 12-22 (continued)

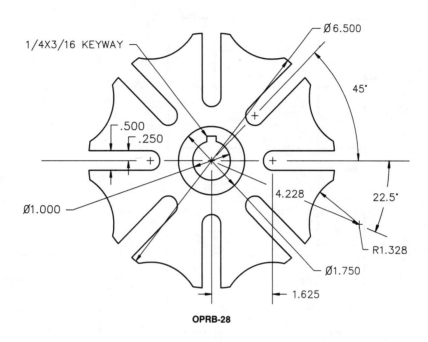

OPRB-28

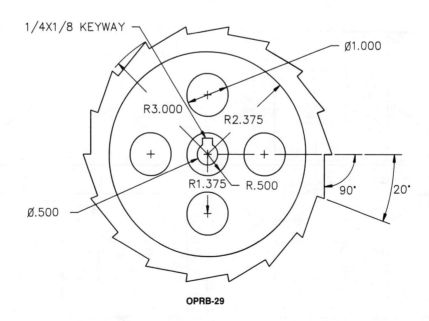

OPRB-29

Optional Problems for Units 23-29

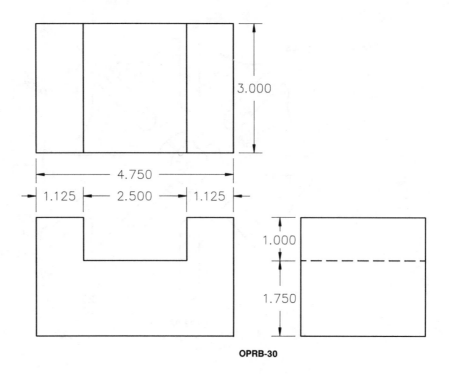

OPRB-30

NOTE: These objects could be drawn in isometric.

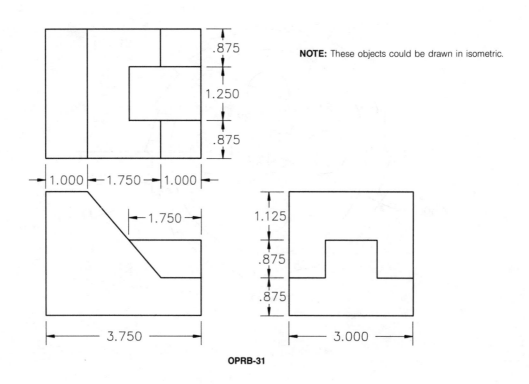

OPRB-31

226

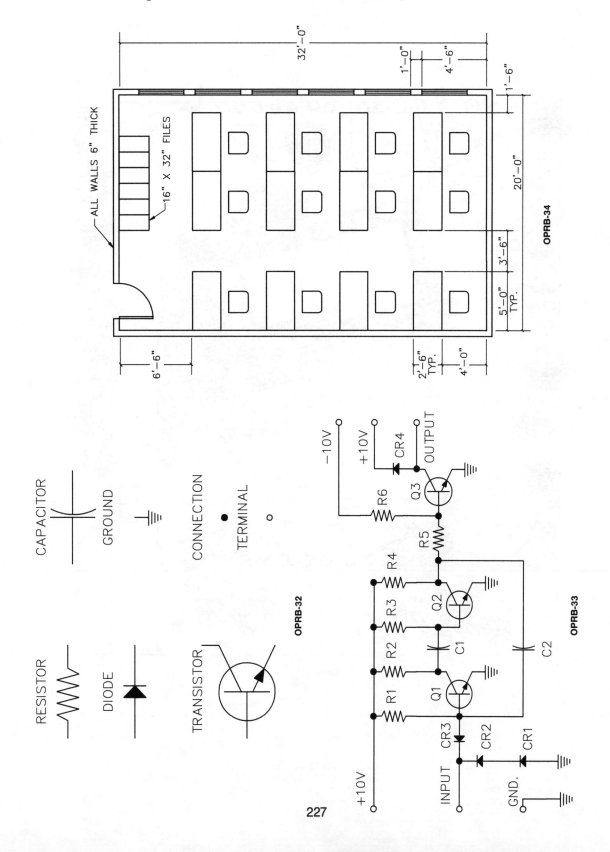

OPRB-34

OPRB-32

OPRB-33

227

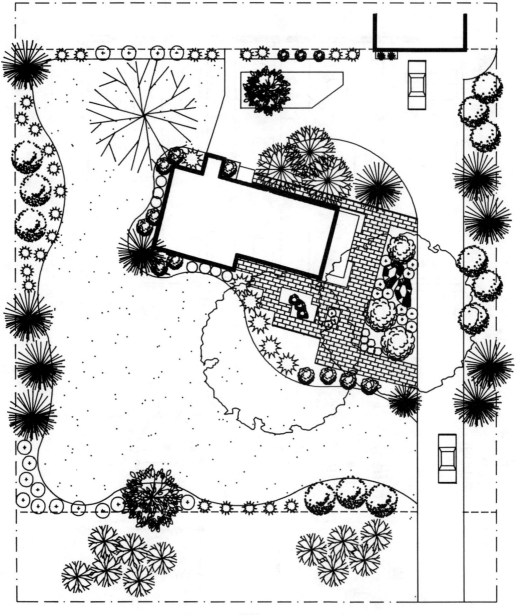

OPRB-35*

*Courtesy of Mill Brothers Landscape and Nursery, Inc.

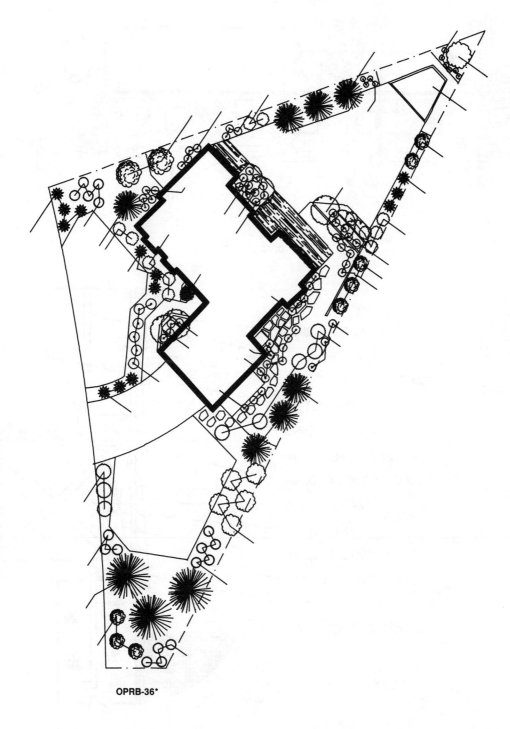

OPRB-36*

*Courtesy of Mill Brothers Landscape and Nursery, Inc.

Optional Problems for Units 23-29 (continued)

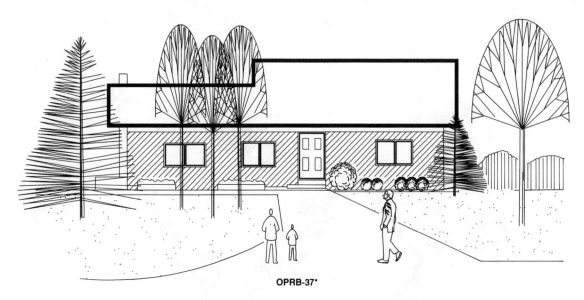

OPRB-37*

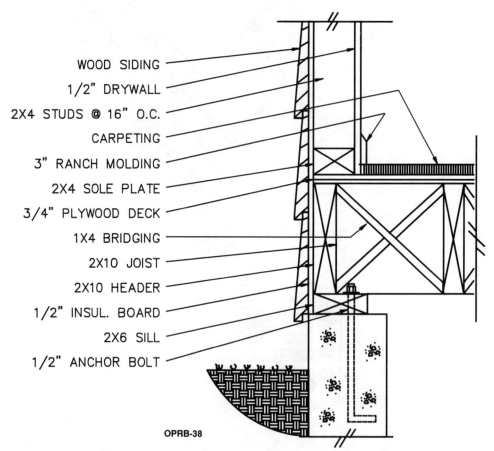

WOOD SIDING

1/2" DRYWALL

2X4 STUDS @ 16" O.C.

CARPETING

3" RANCH MOLDING

2X4 SOLE PLATE

3/4" PLYWOOD DECK

1X4 BRIDGING

2X10 JOIST

2X10 HEADER

1/2" INSUL. BOARD

2X6 SILL

1/2" ANCHOR BOLT

OPRB-38

*Courtesy of Mill Brothers Landscape and Nursery, Inc.

230

Optional Problems for Units 23-29 (continued)

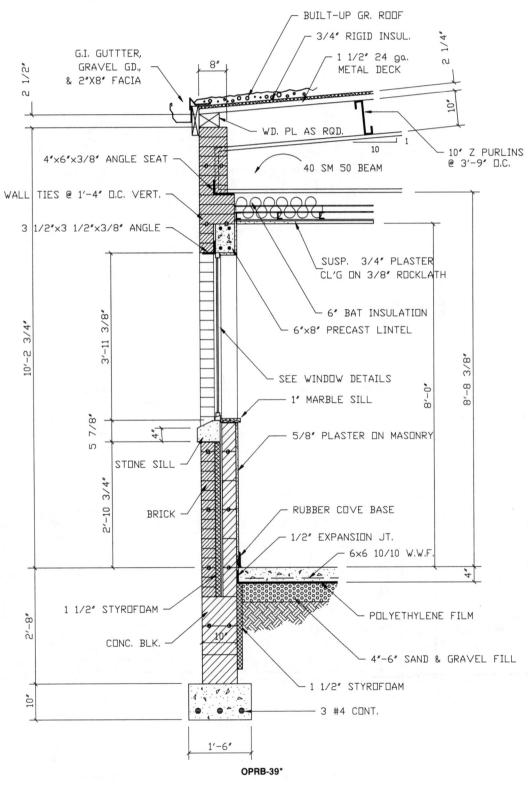

BUILT-UP GR. ROOF
3/4" RIGID INSUL.
1 1/2" 24 ga. METAL DECK
2 1/4"

G.I. GUTTTER, GRAVEL GD., & 2"X8" FACIA
2 1/2"
8"
10"
WD. PL AS RQD.
1
10
10" Z PURLINS @ 3'-9" O.C.
4"x6"x3/8" ANGLE SEAT
40 SM 50 BEAM
WALL TIES @ 1'-4" O.C. VERT.
3 1/2"x3 1/2"x3/8" ANGLE
SUSP. 3/4" PLASTER CL'G ON 3/8" ROCKLATH
6" BAT INSULATION
6"x8" PRECAST LINTEL
10'-2 3/4"
3'-11 3/8"
8'-0"
8'-8 3/8"
SEE WINDOW DETAILS
1" MARBLE SILL
5 7/8"
4"
5/8" PLASTER ON MASONRY
STONE SILL
BRICK
RUBBER COVE BASE
2'-10 3/4"
1/2" EXPANSION JT.
6x6 10/10 W.W.F.
4"
1 1/2" STYROFOAM
CONC. BLK.
10"
POLYETHYLENE FILM
2'-8"
4"-6" SAND & GRAVEL FILL
1 1/2" STYROFOAM
10"
3 #4 CONT.
1'-6"

OPRB-39*

*Courtesy of Paul Driscoll

231

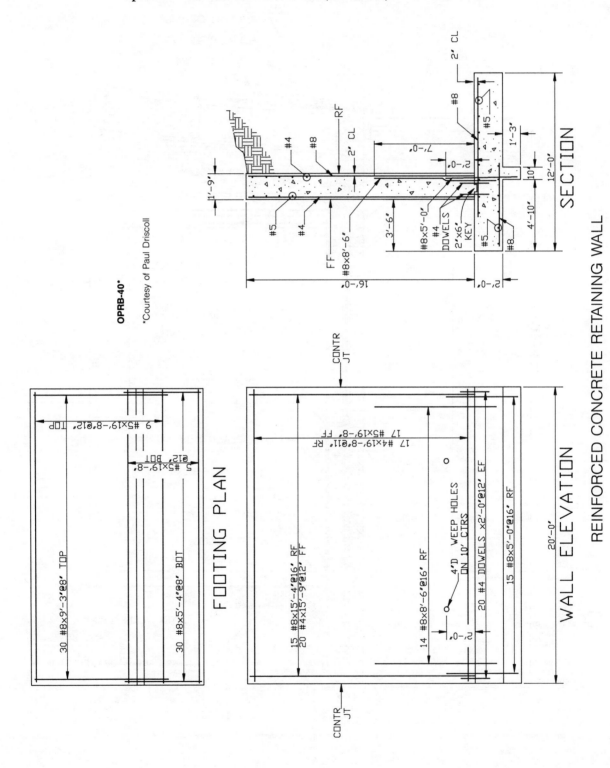

OPRB-40"

*Courtesy of Paul Driscoll

FOOTING PLAN

SECTION

WALL ELEVATION

REINFORCED CONCRETE RETAINING WALL

Appendix A

Odds 'n' Ends

This appendix describes commands and/or command options that were not covered in this book's units or that were only briefly mentioned. Some of these commands are seldom used and therefore did not warrant application in a unit. However, it is useful to be aware of them and their functions. Hence, the following list was developed.

AutoCAD™ User
Guide **Reference**

ATTEDIT	Permits editing of Attribute Tags and Values.	11.4
BASE	Allows you to specify a base origin of your current drawing. This origin becomes the drawing's insertion base for subsequent insertion into other drawings.	9.4.1
CHANGE	Alters properties of selected objects. Examples include changing the endpoints of lines; the radii of circles; Text style, height, rotation angle, and text string; text properties of Attribute Definitions; Block origins; placement of objects on Layers; and Elevation and Extrusion thicknesses of 3D objects.	5.2.6
DXBIN	Inserts specially-coded binary files into a drawing. DXBIN is a special-purpose command for programs such as CAD/camera.	C.5.1
DXFIN and DXFOUT	The DXFIN command loads a drawing interchange file (.DXF file), and the DXFOUT command writes a drawing interchange file.	C.2, C.1
GRAPHSCR	Flips to the graphics display from the text display on single-screen systems. GRAPHSCR is typically used only in menu and script files.	10.3.5
LOAD and SHAPE	The LOAD command loads a file of user-defined Shapes to be used with the SHAPE command. The SHAPE command draws predefined shapes. Because of the Block feature, most AutoCAD users will never need to use either of these commands.	4.10.1, 4.10.2
POINT	Draws a single point, which is treated as a single entity.	4.2
PURGE	Removes unused Blocks, Text Styles, Layers, or Linetypes from the drawing. Immediately after entering the Drawing Editor, you can use the PURGE command. As a safeguard, PURGE will not work at any other time.	3.10.2
REGENAUTO	Allows control of automatic drawing regeneration caused by certain commands.	6.10
RENAME	Allows you to change the names of Text Styles, Named Views, Layers, Linetypes, and Blocks.	3.10.1
REPEAT and ENDREP	Provide an alternate method of creating rectangular patterns. These commands are seldom used since the ARRAY command is preferable for creating rectangular arrays.	5.2.11
TEXTSCR	Flips to the text display from the graphics display on single-screen systems. Like GRAPHSCR, TEXTSCR is used in menu and script files.	10.3.5

Appendix B

Contents of Prototype Drawing ACAD.DWG

This appendix lists the general contents of the standard AutoCAD prototype drawing named ACAD.DWG. This information is important because it contains the default modes and settings of all new drawings, unless you choose to use a prototype drawing of your own.

```
STATUS of ACAD.DWG


        0 entities in ACAD
Limits are          X:      0.0000      12.0000      (Off)
                    Y:      0.0000       9.0000
Drawing uses        X:      0.0000       0.0000
                    Y:      0.0000       0.0000
Display shows       X:      0.0000      14.2373
                    Y:      0.0000       9.0000
Insertion base is   X:      0.0000   Y:    0.0000     Z:     0.0000
Snap resolution is  X:      1.0000   Y:    1.0000
Grid spacing is     X:      0.0000   Y:    0.0000

Current layer: 0
        Color: 7 (white)    Linetype: CONTINUOUS
Current elevation:    0.0000      thickness:    0.0000
Axis off Fill on Grid off Ortho off Qtext off Snap off Tablet off
Object snap modes: None
Free RAM: 27467 bytes    Free disk:  84992 bytes
I/O page space: 124K bytes
```

```
LAYER Listing of ACAD.DWG

    Layer name(s) for listing <*>:

        Layer name        State        Color          Linetype
    -------------------   --------   -------------   -------------
        0                 On          7 (white)      CONTINUOUS

        Current layer: 0
```

234

TEXT STYLES in ACAD.DWG

Text styles:

Style name: STANDARD   Font file: TXT
    Height: 0.0000   Width factor: 1.00   Obliquing angle: 0
    Generation: Normal

DIM STATUS of ACAD.DWG

Dim: status

DIMSCALE 1.0000   Overall scale factor
DIMASZ   0.1800   Arrow size
DIMCEN   0.0900   Center mark size
DIMEXO   0.0625   Extension line origin offset
DIMDLI   0.3800   Dimension line increment for continuation
DIMEXE   0.1800   Extension above dimension line
DIMTP   0.0000   Plus tolerance
DIMTM   0.0000   Minus tolerance
DIMTXT   0.1800   Text height
DIMTSZ   0.0000   Tick size
DIMTOL   Off   Generate dimension tolerances
DIMLIM   Off   Generate dimension limits
DIMTIH   On   Text inside extensions is horizontal
DIMTOH   On   Text outside extensions is horizontal
DIMSE1   Off   Suppress the first extension line
DIMSE2   Off   Suppress the second extension line
DIMTAD   Off   Place text above the dimension line

Other Modes and Settings Contained in ACAD.DWG

```
        APERTURE            10 pixels
        ATTDISP             Normal (controlled individually)
        AXIS                Off, spacing (0.0,0.0)
        BASE                Insertion base point (0.0,0.0)
        BLIPMODE            On
        CHAMFER             Distance 0.0
        DRAGMODE            On
        ELEV                Elevation 0.0, thickness 0.0
        FILLET radius       0.0
        FILL                On
        GRID                Off, spacing (0.0,0.0)
        ISOPLANE            Left
        LAYER               Current/only layer is "0", On, with color
                            7 (white) and linetype "CONTINUOUS"
        LIMITS              Off, drawing limits (0.0,0.0) to (12.0,9.0)
        LINETYPE            Only loaded linetype is "CONTINUOUS
        LTSCALE             1.0
        MENU                ACAD
        ORTHO               Off
        OSNAP               None
        PLINE               Line-width 0.0
        QTEXT               Off
        REGENAUTO           On
        SKETCH              Record increment 0.0
        SNAP                Off, spacing (1.0, 1.0)
        SNAP/GRID           Standard style, base point (0.0,0.0),
                            rotation 0.0 degrees
        STYLE               Only defined text style is "STANDARD", using
                            font file "TXT", with variable height, width
                            factor 1.0, and no special modes
        TABLET              Off
        TEXT                Style "STANDARD", height 0.20, rotation
                            0.0 degrees
        TRACE               Width 0.05
        UNITS (linear)      Decimal, 4 decimal places
        UNITS (angular)     Decimal degrees, 0 decimal places
        ZOOM                To drawing limits
```

Of course, you can modify the ACAD prototype drawing to achieve whatever initial conditions you like. To do this, simply edit the ACAD drawing, set the modes you prefer, and save your updated version via the END command.

ACAD is just the *default* prototype drawing. When reconfiguring AutoCAD (Appendix G), you can choose a different prototype drawing to be the default. As described in Units 17 and 18, you can also specify an explicit prototype when creating a new drawing via Main Menu task 1. To do this, type the name of your new drawing followed by the equal sign and the name of the prototype drawing.

Example:

Enter NAME of drawing: **STAIRD=PROTO1**

Appendix C

Formatting New Diskettes

Before the computer can accept a new diskette for any type of data storage, it must first be formatted. To format a new diskette, you must locate the DOS diskette (or DOS subdirectory) containing the format file called FORMAT.COM.

1 Insert the DOS diskette into your computer.

NOTE:

If you are working on a hard drive system, the DOS files (including FORMAT.COM) are probably contained on a subdirectory. Therefore change to that directory using the **CD** (Change Directory) command.

CAUTION:

If your computer contains a hard disk drive, BE CAREFUL THAT YOU DO NOT ACCIDENTALLY FORMAT YOUR HARD DISK INSTEAD OF THE FLOPPY DISKETTE. Formatting hard disks will permanently erase their entire contents.

2 To look at the contents of the DOS diskette or subdirectory, type **DIR** (short for Directory) and press **RETURN**.

NOTE:

To stop the scrolling, press **CTRL S**. To resume scrolling, press any key.

Your directory should look somewhat like the following, depending on your specific version of DOS. (See next page.)

```
Directory of IBM DOS 3.1

COMMAND     COM     22042     8-14-85     8:00a
ANSI        SYS      1641     8-14-85     8:00a
SORT        EXE      1632     8-14-85     8:00a
SHARE       EXE      8544     8-14-85     8:00a
FIND        EXE      6363     8-14-85     8:00a
ATTRIB      EXE     15123     8-14-85     8:00a
MORE        COM       320     8-14-85     8:00a
ASSIGN      COM       988     8-14-85     8:00a
PRINT       COM      7811     8-14-85     8:00a
SYS         COM      3629     8-14-85     8:00a
CHKDSK      COM      9275     8-14-85     8:00a
FORMAT      COM      9015     8-14-85     8:00a
VDISK       SYS      3080     8-14-85     8:00a
BASIC       COM     17024     8-14-85     8:00a
BASICA      COM     26880     8-14-85     8:00a
FDISK       COM      8076     8-14-85     8:00a
COMP        COM      3471     8-14-85     8:00a
TREE        COM      2473     8-14-85     8:00a
BACKUP      COM      5440     8-14-85     8:00a
RESTORE     COM      5413     8-14-85     8:00a
LABEL       COM      1260     8-14-85     8:00a
DISKCOPY    COM      4165     8-14-85     8:00a
DISKCOMP    COM      3752     8-14-85     8:00a
KEYBSP      COM      2073     8-14-85     8:00a
KEYBIT      COM      1854     8-14-85     8:00a
KEYBGR      COM      2111     8-14-85     8:00a
KEYBUK      COM      1760     8-14-85     8:00a
KEYBFR      COM      2235     8-14-85     8:00a
MODE        COM      5194     8-14-85     8:00a
SELECT      COM      2079     8-14-85     8:00a
GRAPHICS    COM      3111     8-14-85     8:00a
RECOVER     COM      4066     8-14-85     8:00a
EDLIN       COM      7183     8-14-85     8:00a
GRAFTABL    COM      1169     8-14-85     8:00a
           33 File(s)
```

Do you see the FORMAT.COM file?

Since FORMAT.COM is resident in your computer, you can now format a new diskette.

3 Place a new diskette in an open drive in your computer.

4 After the DOS prompt (*e.g.,* A>), type FORMAT in either upper- or lowercase letters. Note the example below.

A> FORMAT B: (press RETURN)

The preceding would format the diskette contained in drive B. If necessary, replace "B:" with the appropriate drive specification.

5 Follow the instructions given by your computer until the format process is complete.

When the format process is complete, the new diskette is ready to accept data.

6 Remove the new diskette from your computer and place it back into its sleeve.

7 Print your name, the date, and any other pertinent information on a self-stick label. Place the label on the newly formatted diskette.

The diskette is now ready for storing data such as AutoCAD drawing files.

Let's format another diskette, but this time let's place the DOS System on the diskette. This will allow us to use the diskette for booting (bringing up) the computer system.

1 Locate another new diskette and place it into your computer.

NOTE:

As before, the FORMAT.COM file must be in your computer before you can format new diskettes.

2 This time enter the FORMAT command followed by a /S. Note the example below:

A> FORMAT B:/S (press **RETURN**)

The above will format the diskette contained in drive B and will also place the DOS System on the diskette.

NOTE:

The DOS System is comprised of three files: COMMAND.COM and two hidden files. These three files allow you to boot the computer system, to use DOS commands such as DIR, COPY, DEL, and REN and to run other programs such as AutoCAD.

3 Follow the instructions given by your computer until the format process is complete.

4 Enter **DIR** to look at the contents of your newly formatted diskette. Note the example below:

A>DIR B: (press **RETURN**)

The above entry would generate a display of the contents of drive B.

Is the COMMAND.COM file contained on your newly formatted diskette? It should be.

This newly formatted diskette containing the DOS System files can now be used for booting the computer system. In addition, this diskette could contain the AutoCAD EXEcute files and could be used both to boot the computer system and to activate AutoCAD. This would eliminate the need to load the DOS diskette to boot the computer prior to loading AutoCAD (if working on a dual floppy diskette-based system).

Appendix D

Commonly Used DOS Commands

The DOS commands most often used are DIRectory, COPY, DELete (or ERASE), REName, DISKCOPY, and CHKDSK (Checkdisk). The intent of this appendix is to briefly work with each so that you can effectively manage all AutoCAD-related files.

DIR

First, let's work a bit with the DIR command. The purpose of DIR is to view the "table of contents" of your disk. DIR also gives you the size of each file and the date and time each was created.

There are three different ways of using the DIR command. The simplest is to enter DIR. A second method is to type /P after the DIR, like this: DIR/P. The third way is to type /W after the DIR, like this: DIR/W. Let's try the DIR command.

1 Bring up (boot) your computer system.

2 After the DOS prompt (*e.g.*, A>), type **DIR** and press **RETURN**.
2 Press **CTRL S** to stop the scrolling; press any key to resume scrolling.

That's all there is to it.

Note each column in the directory and the information each provides. Also note the file names and their file extensions. The file extension indicates the type of file. A list of commonly used file extensions and their meanings is provided here.

File extension	Meaning
.BAK	AutoCAD backup file*
.CFG	AutoCAD configuration file
.DWG	AutoCAD drawing file
.EXE	AutoCAD execution file
.HLP	AutoCAD help file
.LIN	AutoCAD linetype library file
.MNU	AutoCAD menu file
.OVL	AutoCAD overlays file
.PAT	AutoCAD hatch file
.SCR	AutoCAD script file
.SHX	AutoCAD compiled shape or font file
.SLD	AutoCAD slide file
.$RF	AutoCAD vector file
.BAS	DOS BASIC file (file written in the BASIC language)
.BAT	DOS batch file
.COM	DOS command file

* This file type does *not* serve as a true backup file. AutoCAD automatically creates the .BAK file each time you edit a drawing file. The .BAK file stores the drawing as it was prior to editing. Thus the .BAK file does not contain the latest version of the drawing but rather the one prior to it. Only the .DWG file contains the latest version.

3 Next, select a diskette or directory that contains more than one screen full of directory information.

4 Enter **DIR/P** (P is for Page) and press **RETURN**.

How was DIR/P different from DIR by itself?

5 Enter **DIR/W** (W is for Wide) and press **RETURN**.

How is this different from DIR/P?

COPY

The COPY command allows you to copy files (produce backup copies) from one diskette (or directory) to another. A common use of the COPY command is to make backups of existing files such as drawing files. Let's work with it.

1 With the COPY command, copy a file (of your choice) from one disk (or directory) to another as shown in the example below.

A> COPY HOUSE.DWG B: (press **RETURN**)

The above entry would copy the file named HOUSE.DWG from drive A to drive B. When using the COPY command, be sure to specify the correct drives depending upon where the files reside and where the files are being copied.

2 Perform a **DIR**ectory to make sure the file was copied.

3 This time, COPY all *drawing* files from one drive to another. Note the example below.

A >COPY *.DWG B: (press **RETURN**)

This entry would copy all drawing files from drive A and place them on drive B. When you do this, be sure to give the correct file specification.

4 COPY *all* files from one diskette (or directory) to another. Note the example below.

A>**COPY *.* B:** (press **RETURN**)

This entry would copy all files from drive A and place them on drive B.

REN

Now let's focus on the REName command. The REN command allows you to change the name of any of your files. Let's try it.

1 Rename one of the files you copied onto your diskette by using the REN command. Note the example below.

A>**REN B:HOUSE.DWG HUT.DWG** (press **RETURN**)

The entry above would find the file on drive B named HOUSE.DWG and rename it HUT.DWG.

2 Perform a **DIR**ectory to make sure the file name was changed.

That's all there is to the REN command.

DEL (ERASE)

The DEL (ERASE) command allows you to do exactly that: delete or erase a file. Before using one of these commands, be sure you don't want the file. Once you've erased a file, it's almost impossible to get it back.

1 DELete the file you renamed. Note the example below.

A>**DEL B:HUT.DWG** (press **RETURN**)

The above entry would delete the file located on drive B named HUT.DWG.

2 Do a **DIR**ectory to see whether the file really was deleted.

DISKCOPY

Now let's take a look at the DISKCOPY command. DISKCOPY allows you to produce a "carbon copy" of an entire diskette. Let's do it.

NOTE:

> The DOS file called DISKCOPY.COM must first be in your computer before entering the DISKCOPY command, just as you need the FORMAT.COM file before you can format a new diskette.

1 On a fresh diskette (FORMATted or unFORMATted), enter the **DISKCOPY** command to make a copy of another diskette, such as your storage/data diskette. Note the example below.

A>**DISKCOPY A: B:** (press **RETURN**)

The above example would copy everything from drive A onto drive B. Drive B would then be identical to drive A.

CAUTION:

The DISKCOPY command will erase everything presently on the target diskette as it copies new information onto it. Therefore be sure the target diskette does not contain important files.

CHKDSK

The CHKDSK command allows you to check for bad sectors or damaged disks.

NOTE:

The CHKDSK.COM file must be in your computer before the CHKDSK command will work.

1 Enter the **CHKDSK** command. Note the example below.

A>**CHKDSK B:** (press **RETURN**)

This entry would provide information on drive B. You would receive information similar to the following:

```
362496 bytes total disk space
 22528 bytes in 2 hidden files
 90112 bytes in 28 user files
249856 bytes available on disk

524288 bytes total memory
499712 bytes free
```

If your disk does not pass inspection, the computer will tell you what's wrong with it.

In summary, the DIR, COPY, DEL, and REN commands are available at any time when the DOS prompt is on your screen. The FORMAT, DISKCOPY, and CHKDSK commands, however, require specific files resident in the computer before these commands can be used. Those file names are FORMAT.COM, DISKCOPY.COM, and CHKDSK.COM, and they are contained on the DOS diskette or directory.

Appendix E

Preparing a Data/Storage Diskette (for Use with AutoCAD Version 2.1)

This appendix will step through the process of creating a data/storage diskette to be used with AutoCAD version 2.1.

When using a dual floppy diskette-based computer system and AutoCAD version 2.1, users must create data diskettes to store AutoCAD drawing files. Data diskettes must include what AutoCAD calls the AutoCAD "Support Files." If these files are not present on the data diskette, many functions of AutoCAD will not work. Therefore users must first copy these files onto their data diskette before using it with AutoCAD.

The following shows the files from the AutoCAD Support Files diskette. Note that the diskette contains the AutoCAD menu file ACAD.MNU and the help file ACAD.HLP.

```
ACAD       HLP     52835     5-13-85     10:55a
ACAD       HDX      1322     7-11-85     10:45a
ACAD       MNU     13809     4-20-85      2:21p
COMPLEX    SHX      5248     8-01-84      7:36p
ES         SHX       256     7-05-84     11:27p
PC         SHX       512     7-05-84     10:24p
SIMPLEX    SHX      3200     8-01-84      7:42p
TXT        SHX      1792     8-01-84      7:44p
VERTICAL   SHX      2176     8-01-84      7:45p
ITALIC     SHX      6784     8-01-84      7:40p
ACAD       PAT      5120    11-01-83     10:47p
ACAD       PGP       103     4-10-85      6:04p
ELLIPSE    DWG       896     7-13-84      5:05p
RECTANG    DWG      1024     7-13-84      5:05p
ACAD       LIN       600     2-26-85     10:45p
ACAD       DWG      1095     4-18-85      3:55p
SUPT       MID       131     9-16-85     11:49a
       17 File(s)      256000 bytes free
```

1 Boot (bring up) your computer system so that you have your DOS prompt (*e.g.*, **A>**) on your screen.

2 Obtain the AutoCAD Support Files diskette and place it into your computer (in either drive, but preferably in drive A).

3 Next, place a newly FORMATted diskette into the remaining disk drive (preferably drive B).

4 Using the wild-card method of copying files, COPY all files from the Support Files diskette onto the newly FORMATted diskette. Note the example below.

A>COPY *.* B: (press **RETURN**)

The above would copy all files from drive A to drive B.

5 Perform a **DIR**ectory of the new diskette to see if all files were copied. Note the amount of free space for storing AutoCAD drawing files.

HINT:

See Appendix D for instructions on using the DIR command.

The directory should look similar to the one shown at the beginning of this appendix.

Your new data/storage diskette is now ready for use with AutoCAD 2.1.

Appendix F

Loading AutoCAD

AutoCAD has grown to the point where loading the program from floppy diskettes can be somewhat of a challenge (at first, anyway). The purpose of this appendix is to step you through the process.

When working with AutoCAD on a floppy diskette-based computer system, the diskettes used are of two different types: the AutoCAD *system diskettes* and the AutoCAD *data/storage diskette(s)*.

Usually there are two AutoCAD system diskettes:

• Execution diskette (often called the EXE disk)

• Overlays diskette (also called the OVL disk)

The AutoCAD data/storage diskette is used mainly for storing drawing files. In addition, this diskette contains the AutoCAD Support Files (see illustration on next page). Appendix E describes fully how to create a data/storage diskette for use with AutoCAD version 2.1.

The following graphically illustrates all three AutoCAD diskettes necessary for running AutoCAD on a floppy diskette-based system.

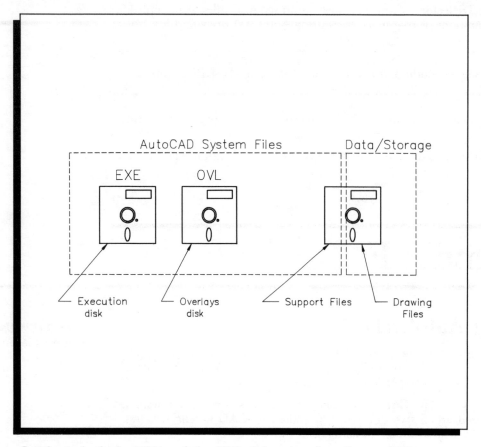

AutoCAD System Files   Data/Storage

EXE   OVL

Execution disk   Overlays disk   Support Files   Drawing Files

1. Obtain both the EXE and the OVL diskettes and perform a **DIR**ectory of each.

HINT:

See Appendix D for instructions on doing a DIRectory.

The directory from your EXE diskette should look similar to the directory below.

```
COMMAND    COM    17664    3-08-83    12:00p
ACAD       EXE   250784   12-03-85     1:14p
ACADL      OVL    68160   11-07-85     8:33a
ACAD1      MID      129   12-03-85     1:25p
AUTOEXEC   BAT       18    1-01-80    12:01a
           5 File(s)              0 bytes free
```

How much free space is left on this diskette? How much free space is left on yours?

The directory from your OVL diskette should look similar to the directory below.

```
ACAD      OVL    196234    3-13-86    11:40a
ACAD1     OVL     78154   11-01-85    10:40a
ACAD2     OVL     15162   11-01-85    10:40a
ACAD3     OVL     35866   11-01-85    10:40a
ACAD2     MID       129   12-03-85     1:30p
ACADDS    OVL      7874    4-03-86     5:15p
ACADDG    OVL      1762    4-03-86     5:18p
ACADPL    OVL      6898    4-03-86     5:19p
ACADPP    OVL      2754    4-03-86     5:21p
RCIRC     DWG      1024    2-18-85     5:02p
ACAD      CFG      1278    1-01-80     2:54a
LCIRC     DWG      1024    2-18-85     5:03p
TCIRC     DWG      1024    2-18-85     5:02p
        13 File(s)       8192 bytes free
```

Note the different file types and sizes and the amount of free space on this diskette.

As you know, "booting" the system is starting up the computer system from the beginning. To do a "cold boot" means to start the system when it is cold by simply turning it on with a boot (system) diskette in the computer. A boot diskette is any diskette containing the COMMAND.COM file and the remaining two hidden files (see Appendix C).

2 Obtain a diskette that was FORMATted with the /S option (described in Appendix C). Use the EXE diskette if it contains the COMMAND.COM file.

NOTE:

Normally diskettes containing the COMMAND.COM file were formatted with the /S option and therefore are considered bootable diskettes.

3 Place this diskette in your computer.

4 Next, turn on the computer using the computer's on/off switch.

After entering the date and time (or just pressing RETURN twice), you should receive your DOS prompt (*e.g.*, A>).

Is the DOS prompt the last item on your screen? If so, you have correctly booted your computer system.

NOTE:

If your computer contains an internal clock, the date and time are automatically entered for you.

You're now ready to load the AutoCAD system and data diskettes into your computer.

1 Locate the AutoCAD system diskettes (EXE and OVL) and a properly prepared data/storage diskette.

2 Insert the EXE diskette (preferably into drive A) and the OVL diskette (preferably into drive B).

3 Type **ACAD** and press **RETURN**.

At this point, AutoCAD will load everything from the EXE disk and then look for the OVL files in drive A.

4 Tell the computer where the OVL files are located (*e.g.*, type **B:** and press **RETURN**).

5 After you arrive at the AutoCAD Main Menu, remove the EXE diskette and replace it with your data/storage diskette.

You're now ready to bring up the Drawing Editor.

6 For practice, Begin a New Drawing. Remember, your drawing should be stored on the drive containing your data/storage diskette.

7 Enter **QUIT** to exit the Drawing Editor and to return to the Main Menu.

8 Practice the entire process of booting the computer system and loading AutoCAD by repeating the preceding steps.

NOTE:

The use of an AUTOEXEC.BAT file is highly recommended and should be placed on the EXE diskette. This will simplify and speed up the process of booting and loading AutoCAD. An example of creating an AUTOEXEC.BAT file is provided below.

> **A> COPY CON:AUTOEXEC.BAT** (press **RETURN**)
> *DATE* (press **RETURN**)
> *TIME* (press **RETURN**)
> **ACAD** (press **RETURN**, and press the **F6** function key)
> **^Z** (this comes up as a result of pressing F6)

Now, when you perform either a cold or a warm boot, the system will activate AutoCAD automatically.

Appendix G

Reconfiguring AutoCAD

This appendix covers the process by which users can change the AutoCAD software so that it will work with different types of hardware components. For example, if you want to change from using a mouse to using a digitizer, you must tell AutoCAD about the new device. Otherwise, it won't work. Also, when you first purchase the AutoCAD software, you must configure the software for the hardware on which it will run.

Let's step through the reconfiguration process.

1 Load AutoCAD and bring up the Main Menu.

2 Select menu task #5, "Configure AutoCAD."   D.1

Your screen should look similar to the following.

```
Current AutoCAD configuration


     Video display:        TI Color/Graphics

     Digitizer:            Kurta Series I

     Plotter:              Houston Instrument DMP Series DMP 52

     Printer plotter:      TI Omni 800


Press RETURN to continue:
```

---

3 Press **RETURN**.

You should receive the Configuration Menu as shown below.

```
     Configuration menu

        0.   Exit to Main Menu
        1.   Show current configuration
        2.   Allow I/O port configuration

        3.   Configure video display
        4.   Configure digitizer
        5.   Configure plotter
        6.   Configure printer plotter
        7.   Configure system console
        8.   Configure operating parameters
```

In order to make configuration changes, you must have the AutoCAD Device Drivers diskette. If you are working on a hard disk drive system, the drivers are probably contained on a separate directory. If they are not, they should be placed on a new subdirectory.

4 Obtain the AutoCAD Device Drivers diskette and place it into your computer.

NOTE:

If you're working on a floppy diskette-based system, the EXE should be removed and replaced with the Drivers diskette. The OVL diskette must remain in your system because the configuration file is stored on the OVL diskette.

If you are working on a hard drive system, tell AutoCAD the location of the configuration files by specifying the correct directory.

Let's proceed through the configuration process by first reconfiguring the digitizer.

5 Select menu task #4, "Configure digitizer."

6 Respond to the next step with a Yes—you do want a different one.

You should receive a list of all digitizer options similar to the following.

```
Available digitizers:

     1.   None
     2.   Calcomp 2000
     3.   Calcomp 2100
     4.   Calcomp 9000 Series
     5.   Calcomp 9100 Series
     6.   Disc Instruments Lynx Trackball
     7.   GTCO Digi-Pad (Types 5 & 5A)
     8.   GTCO Micro Digi-Pad (Type 7)
     9.   Geographics Drafting Board
    10.   Hitachi HICOMSCAN HDG Series
    11.   Hitachi Tiger Tablet
    12.   Houston Instrument HIPAD
    13.   Houston Instrument Series 7000
    14.   Joystick or Koala Pad
    15.   Kurta Series I
    16.   Kurta Series II and III
    17.   Logitech Logimouse R-5 Mouse
    18.   Microsoft Mouse
    19.   Mouse Systems Mouse
    20.   Mutoh CX3000
  -- More --
```

```
21.   Numonics 2200
22.   Pencept 320 Character Recognition Tablet
23.   SAC Grafbar
24.   Seiko DT-3103/4103 Series
25.   Summagraphics Bit Pad One
26.   Summagraphics MM Series
27.   Summagraphics MicroGrid
28.   Summagraphics SummaMouse
29.   Torrington Manager's Mouse (3 Button)
30.   USI Optomouse
```

7 Choose one by typing its number.

NOTE:

If you are on a floppy diskette-based system and you get an error message, you may not have enough free space on your OVL diskette. Therefore simply cancel with a CTRL C.

If you are serious about making configuration changes, then you will have to DELete the following files from your OVL diskette and REName ACAD.BAK to ACAD.CFG. Then you should be able to properly configure.

ACAD.CFG
ACADDS.OVL
ACADDG.OVL
ACADPL.OVL
ACADPP.OVL

8 Continue by answering each question until you are able to return to the Configuration Menu.

9 Now, on your own, experiment with each of the other configuration tasks.

10 Lastly, select menu task #1 to check your current configuration.

If the current configuration is not correct according to your hardware, make the appropriate change(s).

11 Select menu task #0, "Exit to Main Menu." Save your configuration changes ONLY if you had intended for them to be changed.

12 When you're finished (and if you are working on a floppy diskette-based system), remove the Device Drivers diskette. Then try the new configuration by bringing up the Drawing Editor and/or by plotting.

Appendix H

Standard Linetypes

A standard library of linetypes is supplied with AutoCAD, in a file named ACAD.LIN. The linetypes in it are illustrated below.

NAME	SAMPLE
Dashed	— — — — — — — — —
Hidden	--------------------------
Center	— — · — — · — — · —
Phantom	— — · · — — · · —
Dot	····························
Dashdot	— · — · — · — · — ·
Border	— — · — — · — — · —
Divide	— · · — · · — · · —

Courtesy of Autodesk Inc.

Appendix I

Standard Text Fonts

AutoCAD is supplied with several text fonts. You can use the STYLE command to apply expansion, compression, or obliquing to any of these fonts, thereby tailoring the characters to your needs. (See Unit 16.) You can draw characters of any desired height using any of the fonts.

The fonts supplied with AutoCAD are:

TXT	This is the standard AutoCAD text font. It is very simple and can be drawn very quickly.
SIMPLEX	This is a "simplex" Roman font drawn by means of many short line segments. It produces smoother-looking characters than those of the TXT font.
COMPLEX	This is a "complex" Roman font with short line segments and multiple strokes, forming smooth characters with varying thickness.
ITALIC	This is a true Italic font.

VERTICAL   This font contains the same characters as the simple TXT font, but each character has been "turned on its side" and adjusted so that, if drawn with a rotation angle of 270 degrees, the characters will appear in a vertical column, with each character centered below the previous character.

Samples of these fonts appear here. (The VERTICAL font is not shown; as noted above, its characters are the same as those in the TXT font.)

Each font resides in a separate disk file with the name <font>.SHX. This is the "compiled" form of the font, for direct use by AutoCAD. Another file named <font>.SHP is supplied as well; this file contains the symbolic description of the font's characters and is not normally needed by AutoCAD. The ".SHP" files are provided as examples for those users who might want to define their own text fonts. If you wish to do this, see Appendix B of the AutoCAD *User Guide*.

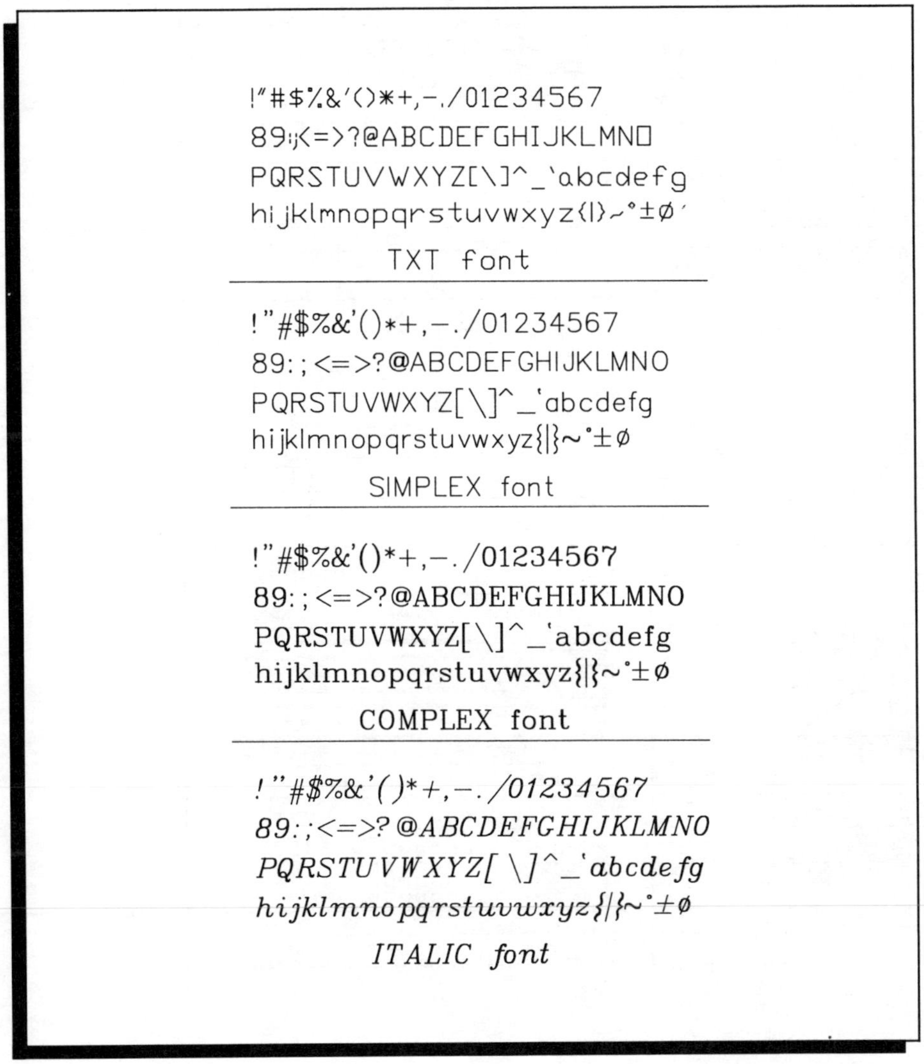

!"#$%&'()*+,-./01234567
89:;<=>?@ABCDEFGHIJKLMNO
PQRSTUVWXYZ[\]^_'abcdefg
hijklmnopqrstuvwxyz{|}~°±ø'

TXT font

!"#$%&'()*+,-./01234567
89:;<=>?@ABCDEFGHIJKLMNO
PQRSTUVWXYZ[\]^_'abcdefg
hijklmnopqrstuvwxyz{|}~°±ø

SIMPLEX font

!"#$%&'()*+,-./01234567
89:;<=>?@ABCDEFGHIJKLMNO
PQRSTUVWXYZ[\]^_'abcdefg
hijklmnopqrstuvwxyz{|}~°±ø

COMPLEX font

!"#$%&'()+,-./01234567*
89:;<=>?@ABCDEFGHIJKLMNO
PQRSTUVWXYZ[\]^_'abcdefg
hijklmnopqrstuvwxyz{|}~°±ø

ITALIC font

Appendix J

Standard Hatch Patterns

The following pages illustrate the standard hatch patterns supplied in file
ACAD.PAT for systems with the ADE-1 package.

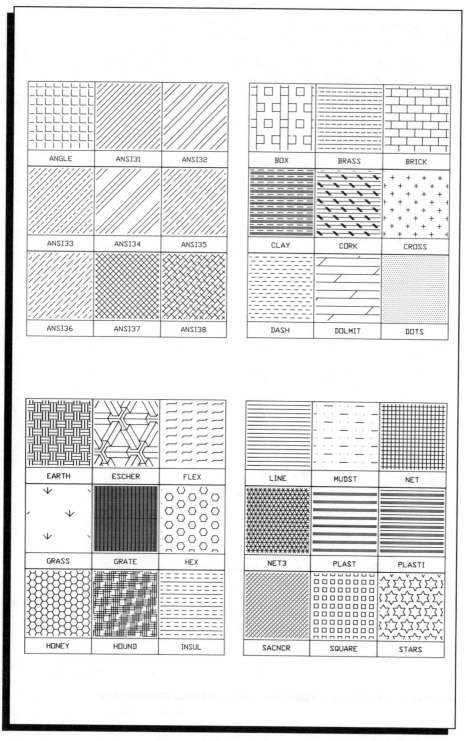

Courtesy of Autodesk Inc.

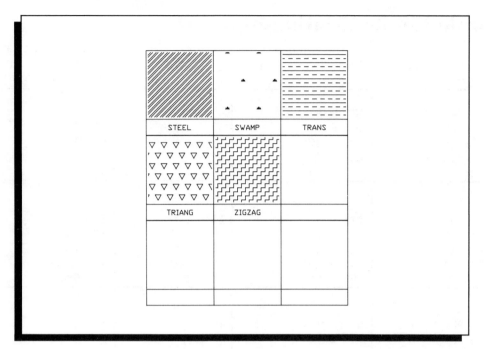

Courtesy of Autodesk Inc.

Appendix K

Paper-Scale-Limits Relationships

	SHEET (paper) SIZE (X x Y)	Approximate DRAWING AREA (X x Y)	SCALE	UPPER RIGHT LIMIT (X, Y) (LOWER LEFT LIMIT is 0,0)
ARCHITECT'S SCALE	A: 12″ × 9″	10″ × 8″	⅛″ = 1′	80′,64′
	B: 18″ × 12″	16″ × 11″	½″ = 1′	32′,22′
	C: 24″ × 18″	22″ × 16″	¼″ = 1′	88′,64′
	D: 36″ × 24″	34″ × 22″	3″ = 1′	11.3′,7.3′
	E: 48″ × 36″	46″ × 34″	1″ = 1′	46′,34′
CIVIL ENGINEER'S SCALE	A: 12″ × 9″	10″ × 8″	1″ = 200′	2000′,1600′
	B: 18″ × 12″	16″ × 11″	1″ = 50′	800′,550′
	C: 24″ × 18″	22″ × 16″	1″ = 10′	220′,160′
	D: 36″ × 24″	34″ × 22″	1″ = 300′	10,200′,6600′
	E: 48″ × 36″	46″ × 34″	1″ = 20′	920′,680′
MECHANICAL ENGINEER'S SCALE	A: 11″ × 8½″	9″ × 7″	1″ = 2″	18″,14″
	B: 17″ × 11″	15″ × 10″	2″ = 1″	7.5″,5″
	C: 22″ × 17″	20″ × 15″	1″ = 1″	20″,15″
	D: 34″ × 22″	32″ × 20″	1″ = 1.5″	48″,30″
	E: 44″ × 34″	42″ × 32″	3″ = 1″	14″,10.6″
METRIC SCALE	A: 279 mm × 216 mm (11″ × 8½″)	229 mm × 178 mm (9″ × 7″)	1 mm = 5 mm	1145 units,890 units
	B: 432 mm × 279 mm (17″ × 11″)	381 mm × 254 mm (15″ × 10″)	1 mm = 20 mm	7620 units,5080 units
	C: 55.9 cm × 43.2 cm (22″ × 17″)	50.8 cm × 38.1 cm (20″ × 15″)	1 cm = 10 cm	508 units,381 units
	D: 86.4 cm × 55.9 cm (34″ × 22″)	81.3 cm × 50.8 cm (32″ × 20″)	2 cm = 1 cm	40.5 units,25.5 units
	E: 111.8 cm × 86.4 cm (44″ × 34″)	106.7 cm × 81.3 cm (42″ × 32″)	1 cm = 2 cm	213 units,163 units

NOTE: 1″ = 25.4 mm

Appendix L

AutoCAD System Management

The use and maintenance of a CAD system entail considerations not found in traditional methods of drafting. For example, with CAD, disk files must be properly stored for subsequent revision and plotting, and backup files must be produced regularly. If considerations such as these are overlooked or not taken seriously, the CAD system may fail. Files will get lost, drawings will have to be redrawn, and users will become frustrated.

Whether you are an AutoCAD user or a system manager, the following information will help you fully tap the power and capability of the system while creating and managing AutoCAD drawings. If the system is properly managed, users should never have to draw the same component twice.

The implementation of the system is an evolving process and does not always occur quickly. Refer back to this appendix as you become more and more familiar with the capabilities and limitations of AutoCAD.

Key Management Considerations

- Disk directory and file management
- Drawing file development (storage, documentation, retrieval, and use)
  —Block creation
  —Layer creation
  —Text style creation
  —Use of time-saving facilities such as QTEXT and LAYER Freeze
- Prototype drawing development (storage, documentation, and use)
- Symbol library creation, development, and use
- Menu development (documentation and use)
- Procedural standards within the organization
- Hardware components, upgrades, and their maintenance

Fitting together these considerations for effective system use may at first seem somewhat overwhelming, particularly to new users. Let's take a look at the overall management considerations from a different angle: as though you were beginning a new drawing. What questions should you ask yourself prior to drawing start-up? The following five questions should help to put things into perspective.

1. What prototype drawing is on file that may work well for beginning my specific drawing?
2. Are there existing drawings on file that are similar to what I plan to create?
3. Are there predefined libraries of symbols or details that I can use while I develop my drawing?
4. Is there a screen or tablet menu that would lend itself better to my specific drawing application?
5. Where should my drawing be stored, what should it be named, and how can I make it available to myself and others in the future?

Good answers to these questions depend on how the system is implemented and managed. Hence, the following is provided to give AutoCAD users and managers tips on how to best use and manage an AutoCAD system. The following addresses the five questions as well as the key management considerations listed previously.

Generally, all of the following applies to all AutoCAD users and drawings. However, there are inevitable differences among users (backgrounds/interests), drawing applications, and the specific hardware and software which make up the system.

Effective System Management

One person (possibly two, but no more) in the organization should have the responsibility for managing the system and overseeing its use. This person should be the resident AutoCAD system authority and should answer questions and provide directions to the users of the system. The manager should oversee the main components of the system, including software, documentation, and hardware. The manager should also establish procedural standards for use of the system.

Software/Documentation

OVERALL FILE MANAGEMENT — Know where files are located and the purpose of each. Understand which ones are AutoCAD system files and which are not. Print (or document) directories, keep them for later reference, and make them available to others. Create a system for backup files, and back up regularly. Emphasize this to all users. Delete "junk" files.

PROTOTYPE DRAWINGS — Create a simple system for development, storage, and retrieval of AutoCAD prototype drawings. Allow for ongoing correction and development of each prototype drawing. Hard disk users: store the prototype drawings in the main AutoCAD directory so that they are more easily accessible by other users. **Important:** document the contents of each prototype drawing by printing the drawing status information, layer listing, text styles, and the status of the dimensioning variables. On the first page of this information, write the name of the prototype drawing and its plot scale. Keep this information in a three-ring binder or similar holder for future reference by other users.

USER DRAWING FILES — Store these on the appropriate floppy diskettes or hard disk directories. (See the hard disk structure found at the end of this appendix.) When creating a drawing, place drawing components on the proper layers to allow for colors, linetypes, and line thicknesses when plotting. Make a backup copy of the drawing and store in the appropriate location. Plot the drawings most likely to be used by others and store them in a three-ring binder or similar holder for future reference.

SYMBOL LIBRARIES — Develop a system for ongoing library development. (See Unit 24 for details on creating symbol libraries.) Make the libraries available to others by plotting the symbol library drawing file. Then place the drawing on the wall near the system or in a binder. Encourage users to contribute to the libraries.

MENU FILES — Develop, set up, and make available screen and/or tablet menu files and tablet overlays. (See Units 32 and 33 for details on creating screen and tablet menus.) Store so they are accessible to others.

AUTOCAD UPGRADES — Handle the acquisition and installation of AutoCAD software upgrades. Inform users of the new features and changes contained in the new software.

AUTOCAD THIRD-PARTY SOFTWARE — Handle the acquisition and installation of third-party software developed for specific application and utility purposes. Inform users of its availability and use.

Hardware

Oversee the proper use and maintenance of all hardware components which make up the system. Consider hardware upgrades as the user requirements and software requirements change.

Procedural Standards

Develop clear and simple standards within your organization to minimize inconsistency and confusion. For example, each prototype drawing should have a standard set of drawing layers, with a specific color and linetype dedicated to each layer. A layer called DIM could be reserved for all dimensions and could always be shown in the color 2 (yellow) with a continuous linetype. Then, when plotting, color 2 could be assigned to pen 2, which could be a .3 mm black pen. That way, whenever dimensions are on a drawing, they'll be yellow on the screen and will be plotted with a .3 mm black pen. Furthermore, assign a specific pen to each stall on your pen plotter and make this information available to others. This will avoid confusion and improve consistency in all plotting within your organization. Develop similar standards for other AutoCAD-related practices.

In summary, take seriously the management of your AutoCAD system. Set up subsystems so that users can contribute to the system's ongoing development. Encourage users to experiment and to be creative by making software and hardware available to them. Make a team effort out of learning, developing, and managing the AutoCAD system so that everyone learns and benefits from its tremendous power and capability.

Hard Disk Directory Structure _____

The following chart outlines a sample structure for hard disk users who are familiar with DOS hard disk tree structuring. Note the subdirectories and files contained in the AutoCAD subdirectory.

With AutoCAD's path specification capability, subdirectories can be contained in the main AutoCAD subdirectory. The DOS commands MD (Make Directory), CD (Change Directory), and RD (Remove Directory) are available to create a tree structure similar to the one shown here. The benefits of this are better file organization, categorization, and retrieval.

Keep the AutoCAD subdirectory clean of user files. This directory should contain only the ones indicated on the next page; otherwise it will grow too large and cumbersome.

All backup files should be stored on a separate hard disk, tape backup system, or on floppy diskettes. There is always a chance of a hard disk system crash and loss of all files.

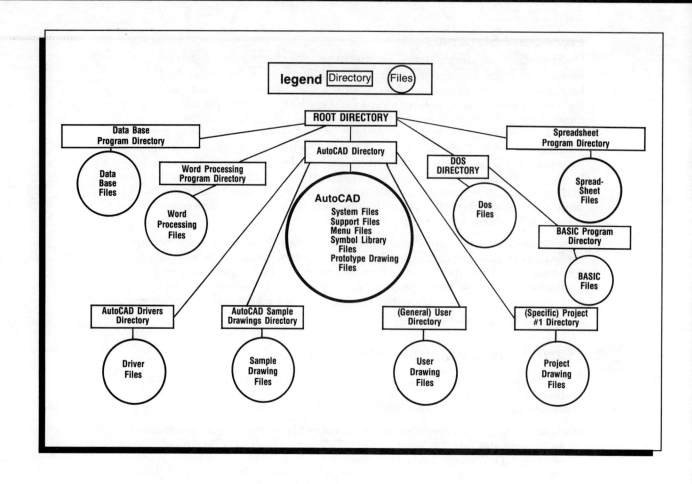

Index

Appendix N: Menu Tree

AUTOCAD 2.1 (PRIMARY MENU HIERARCHY)

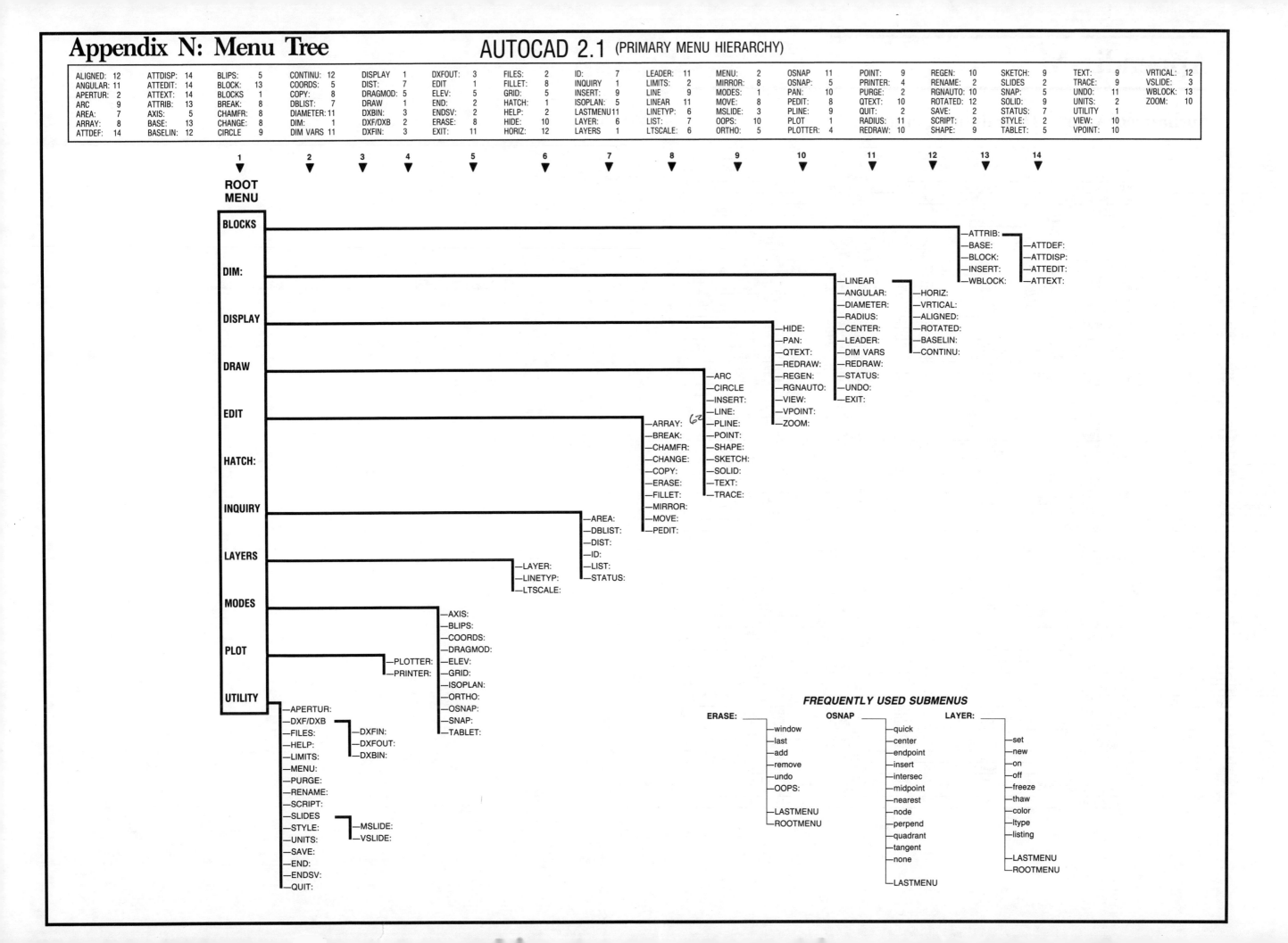

Appendix M

Authorized AutoCAD Training Centers

CENTER NAME	ADDRESS	CITY	ST	ZIP	PHONE	CONTACT
Southern Arkansas University Tech	SAU Tech Station	Camden	AR	71701	(501)574-4538	Larry G. Owen
C.A.D. Institute	2741 W. Southern Ave., Suite 24A	Tempe	AZ	85282	(602)438-0944	Don Brown
Bakersfield College	1801 Panorama Dr.	Bakersfield	CA	93305	(805)395-4224	Bob Funk
CAD Counsel	5032 Lankershim Blvd., Suite 4	N. Hollywood	CA	91601	(818)505-0952	Marsha Robison
MTI College	1091 Batavia Ave.	Orange	CA	92667	(714)532-4320	Barry Maleki/Ton Bui
Decision Vision, Inc.	325 W. Washington, Suite 2	San Diego	CA	92103	(619)295-5377	David Gmach
Systems Unlimited	100 N. Winchester, Suite 260	San Jose	CA	95128	(408)247-1142	Robert Pantangco
Corporate Computer Systems	500 Sheppard Ave., East #209	Willowdale, Ont	CN	M2N 6H7	(416)229-6477	Trevor Blair
Denver Institute of Technology	7350 N. Broadway	Denver	CO	80221	(303)466-0708	Karl Andrus
Colorado State University	Dept. of Industrial Sciences, ORDT	Fort Collins	CO	80523	(303)491-5278	Terry T. Wohlers
Porter and Chester Institute	2139 Silas Deane Highway	Rocky Hill	CT	06067	(203)529-2519	Joseph Doering
CAD Corporation	5005 West Laurel Street, Suite 215	Tampa	FL	33607	(813)875-1818	Forrest Hurst
Data Development Corporation	157 New England Avenue, Suite 365	Winter Park	FL	32789	(305)628-2088	Tom Wilkins/Sandra Schuster
Microsouth	1009 Sun Valley Drive	Roswell	GA	30076	(404)993-6245	Lola Price/Tom Santelle
Kapiolani Community College	4303 Diamond Head Road	Honolulu	HI	96816	(808)735-8211	Virginia Chock
Morrison Institute of Technology	P.O.Box 410	Morrison	IL	61270	(815)772-7218	Emma Schroeder
CAD Design Systems, Inc.	1305 Remington Road, Suite D	Schaumburg	IL	60195	(312)882-0114	Mehlinae Douglas
University of Evansville	Technical Assistance Center (VETAC)	Evansville	IN	47702	(812)479-2899	Ronald Devaisher
Wichita State University	Campus Box 146	Wichita	KS	67208-1595	(316)689-3525	Richard Graham
Western Kentucky University	Dept. of Industrial and Eng. Tech.	Bowling Green	KY	42101	(502)745-3251	Ken Mussnug
University of Louisville	209 J.B. Speed	Louisville	KY	40292	(502)588-7908	Richard Latimer
Wentworth Institute of Technology	550 Huntington Ave.	Boston	MA	02115	(617)442-9010 X371	Anthony DeRosa
A-CAD Company	13 New Salem Street	Wakefield	MA	01880	(617)245-4223	Andy Wood
CADTECH, Inc.	8611 Ramsey Avenue	Silver Spring	MD	20910	(301)495-7355	Teresa Kim/Jeffrey Frank
GMI Engineering & Management Inst.	1700 West Third Avenue	Flint	MI	48502-2276	(313)762-9866	Doug Beatenhead
INACOMP Computer Centers	1824 West Maple Road	Troy	MI	48084	(313)649-0910	Nabil Sater
Thief River Falls Tech Institute	Highway One, East	Thief River Falls	MN	56701	(218)681-5424 X11	Bob Bolleson
St. Louis Community College	5600 Oakland	St. Louis	MO	63110	(314)644-9291	Jerry Craig
NC/CADD	3326 Chapel Hill Blvd., Suite 100A	Durham	NC	27707	(919)489-9009	Nada Staddon
CADSource Training Center	190 Lincoln Highway	Edison	NJ	08820	(201)494-7722	Art Bianconi
Computer Graphics Learning Center	7710 Menaul Blvd NE, Suite F	Albuquerque	NM	87110	(505)884-0284	Carla Rachowski
New York University	Midtown Center, 11 W 42nd Street	New York	NY	10036	(212)790-1300	Arlyne Lesser
Rochester Institute of Technology	33 North Fitzhugh Street	Rochester	NY	14614-1269	(716)262-2721	Liz Paciorek/Charles Layne
Syracuse University Center for Computer Education and Training	610 E. Fayette Street	Syracuse	NY	13244-6020	(315)423-3273	Jack Manno
A/E Micro Systems, Inc.	11223 Cornell Park Drive	Cincinnati	OH	45246	(513)489-8070	David Holmstrom
University of Cincinnati, Microcomputer Applications Center	100 East Central Parkway	Cincinnati	OH	45210	(513)475-4243	Sharon A. Hinkle
Franklin University	201 S. Grant Avenue	Columbus	OH	43215	(614)224-6237	James D. McBrayer
Owens Technical College	300 Davis Street	Findlay	OH	45840	(419)666-0580	David Winters
Owens Technical College	Caller #10,000, Oregon Road	Toledo	OH	43699	(419)666-0580	David Winters
Oklahoma State University	Department of Drafing Technology	Okmulgee	OK	74447	(918)756-6211 X250	Bill Jones
CAD Northwest	722 S.W. 2nd Street	Portland	OR	97204	(503)224-5240	Mitch Landau
Spring Garden College	7500 Germantown Ave.	Philadelphia	PA	19119	(215)248-7900 X506	Donald E. Keyt
Computer Research, Inc.	Airport Off.Pk #2, 400 Rouser Road	Pittsburg	PA	15108	(412)262-4430	Francis Soen
Lancaster County Vo-Tech	1730 Nans Herr Drive, Box 527	Willow Street	PA	17584	(717)464-3359	Michael Curley
New England Institute of Technology	184 Early Street	Providence	RI	02907	(401)467-7744	Seth Kurn
Greenville Technical College	P.O.Box 5616, Station B	Greenville	SC	29606	(803)242-3170	Logan Gilstrap
University of Tennessee	310 Perkins Hall	Knoxville	TN	37996-2000	(615)974-2171 X6001	Steve Foster
Computer Park	12770 Merit Dr.	Dallas	TX	75251	(214)770-4000	Betty Walker
CAD CAM Centre	8552 Katy Freeway, Suite 123	Houston	TX	77024	(713)467-4994	Jose Torres
C & Z Systems	4201 Lake Shore Drive, Suite G	Waco	TX	76708	(817)776-7336	Betty Gregurek
Republic Research, Inc.	801 West Main Street	Charlottesville	VA	22901	(804)296-9747	Gregg Kendrick
Old Dominion University	School of Engineering	Norfolk	VA	23508	(804)440-3765	Moustafa R. Moustafa
Vermont Technical College	AutoCAD Training Center	Randolph Center	VT	05061	(802)728-3391	Harry Miller
CAD Northwest of Seattle	720 Olive Way, Suite 604	Seattle	WA	98201	(206)622-4412	Mitch Landau
ITT Technical Institute	N. 1050 Argonne Rd.	Spokane	WA	99212-2610	(509)926-2900	Michael J. Kelly
Putnam County Voc. Technical Center	P.O. Box 530 Route 62	Eleanor	WV	25070	(304)586-2127	Leo E. Arbaugh, Jr.